D0889344

生命意義的追尋

余元愷 著

一個華裔美國人的感受

A SEARCH FOR MEANING:

ESSAYS OF A CHINESE AMERICAN

Albert H. Yee

Li Sao*
Encountering Sorrow

*See footnote, next page.

節錄自離騷

離騷　原文：

何方圓之能周兮，　　夫孰異道而相安？
屈心而抑志兮，　　　忍尤而攘詬。

步余馬于蘭皋兮，　　馳椒丘且焉止息；
進不入以離尤兮，　　退將復修吾初服。

高余冠之岌岌兮，　　長余佩之陸離；
芳與澤其雜糅兮，　　唯昭質其猶未虧。

吾令羲和弭節兮，　　望崦嵫而勿迫；
路曼曼其修遠兮，　　吾將上下而求索。

Encountering Sorrow*

How can the square just fit the circle right?
With views opposed, who can unite in peace? . . .
I shall repress my heart and cool my zeal,
I'll bear the blame and wipe off all the shame. . . .

I pace my horse along the orchid bank
Rush up the pepper hill, and then take rest.
I advance, but enter not to face rebukes!
Retiring I shall mend my whilom dress. . . .

My hat's height I raise till it's like a hill;
My pendant's length and beauty I increase.
My dress and pendant various hues reflect,
But what is bright in me has ne'er grown less! . . .

I bid Hsi Ho restrain the fleeting time;
And hurry not when facing Yen-tzu's peak.
The road is tedious and extremely long;
And I shall search all regions high and low.

*Li Sao, a classical poem by Ch'u Yuan (338–278 B.C.), translated by Lim, Boon Keng. *The Li Sao: An Elegy Encountering Sorrows by Ch'u Yuan* (Shanghai: Commercial Press, 1929), pages 84–93. (Ancient classical script, opposite; modern version this page, top; English translation, below.)

Published by the Chinese Historical Society of America
A Search for Meaning: Essays of A Chinese American by Albert H.
Yee. © 1984 by Albert H. Yee. All rights reserved. Printed in the
United States of America. No part of this book may be used or
reproduced in any manner whatsoever without written permission,
except in the case of brief quotations embodied in critical articles
and reviews. For information, write to the Chinese Historical Society
of America, 17 Adler Place, San Francisco, California 94133.

First edition

ART AND PHOTO CREDITS: The photographs in the center of the book
were taken by the author. "Sunrise Over West Lake, Hangzhou,"
was taken in May 1981; "Sun Yat-sen" was taken in October 1981;
and "Entrance to Monticello, Home of Thomas Jefferson" was taken
in November 1980. The photograph of the author was taken by G.
Paul Bishop.

Grateful acknowledgment is given Dr. Wong Pui-yee for the cover
calligraphy.

Contents

Foreword

Chinese have been in America for almost two hundred years. Yet their history in this country was not well known, even to members of the Chinese-American community. In recent decades, as this community has matured, there has been a growing demand for a clearer definition of the Chinese-American role as a part of American history. This was one of the motivating forces leading to the founding of the Chinese Historical Society of America in 1963. Since that time the Society's activities have resulted in the development of a historical museum and the publishing of a monthly bulletin. The Society also published the first syllabus and convened the first seminar on Chinese-American history, as a result of which Society members developed and taught the first course on Chinese-American history in this country at San Francisco State College in 1969. All these efforts have helped to disseminate knowledge on the role played by the Chinese in America and have contributed toward sensitizing the general public to recognition of the important roles assumed by ethnic minorities in the building of American society.

One important aspect of the Society's activities has been to collect and to preserve historical documentary materials on the Chinese of America and to make such materials available to researchers in the field. To facilitate the latter effort, the Society has worked closely with the San Francisco Public Library and, more recently, with the Asian American Studies Collection of the University of California, Berkeley. Continuing our implementation of this objective, the Society now offers this book, *A Search for Meaning: Essays of a Chinese American.*

The author, Dr. Albert H. Yee, who grew up in the San Francisco Bay Area, is the son of a Chinese immigrant. His maternal grandmother was born in San Francisco's Chinatown in the last decade of the nineteenth century, and used to describe the earthquake and fire of 1906 to her grandchildren. In 1947, in response to the beckoning of the land of his ancestors, he crossed the Pacific to attend Lingnan University in Guangzhou (Canton). Returning the following year, he plunged into academic work (see biographical sketch at the end of the book).

Dr. Yee's rich experiences covering both sides of the Pacific constitute the core of his book, which is biographical in nature. The work goes into a range of related topics, providing many insights on the Chinese American as a product of East and West. These, however, are not merely one man's personal experiences and observation. They also form part of the body of Chinese-American experience and, as such, provide stimulating reading for pleasure or research.

The Society wishes to express its thanks to Dr. Yee, a life member of this Society, for the privilege of making this material available to the public.

Him Mark Lai
Chinese Historical Society of America
December, 1983

Preface

This book is an attempt to demonstrate that relations between the East and West have been more extensive and significant than common awareness exhibits. A broader appreciation—especially by educational, governmental, and business leaders—of the history of Chinese Americans and of Sino-American relations would help to enhance world understanding and peace. Another objective of this book is to stimulate reflection upon the blending of the East and the West, as can be found in the experiences of Chinese Americans. It is the author's belief that Chinese Americans have the opportunity along with other Asian Americans to bring about an even greater enrichment of East-West relations as they develop new ethnicities of great significance. The author makes no claim that his experiences are exemplary or widely representative. It is hoped that the experiences and reflections of one Chinese American will help others to examine and better understand their own lives.

The first essay, "A Search for Meaning," presents an inquiring theme which the reader might hold in mind while reading the other essays. Growing up as a Chinese American, as for other ethnic minorities having cultural attributes that contrast with the American mainstream, can be troublesome and bewildering for the individual. How does one answer questions such as: Where have I come from? Who am I? and Where am I going? The second essay, "The Twain Did Meet," makes a case for East-West relations by relating a history that is so provocative and extensive that we must wonder why so few

Americans are aware of its basic details. In the third
essay, "In War-Torn China, 1947–1948," the reader travels with the author to a China that has not recovered
from the effects of World War II and is suffering in the
throes of a soon-to-be-decided civil war. In this essay,
the author comes face-to-face with many harsh realities
in the land of his ancestors. Naive and unprepared, he
undergoes experiences that are alien and often objectionable, and returns to the United States with enough
memories for a lifetime of reflection. Ancient China is
confronted most vividly in the essay titled "Field Trip
into the Past," an unforgettable journey to a Buddhist
monastery. It portrays a China that no longer exists. The
essay "Medicine: A Cross-Cultural Study" examines
contrasting philosophies and practices of medicine,
health care, and life perspectives in the West and in old
and new China. This essay on medicine suggests the
possibility of taking the best from these seemingly contrasting patterns and forming a new synthesis. It illustrates how this synthesis of Eastern and Western approaches to solve common concerns can benefit all. "GI
American, 1952–1955," the sixth essay, illustrates both the
very individual nature as well as the universality of what
it can mean to be an American. The setting is the Korean
War where the author's experiences as a soldier helped
him to understand himself and those about him better.

The seventh essay, "Visits to the New China," covers
visits to the People's Republic of China in 1972 and the
1980s. In 1972, the author went to Tokyo to lecture at the
Tokyo University and Tamagawa University as a Senior
Fulbright Lecturer. While in Japan, he received permission to enter China and did so in December 1972 on a
mission for the American Psychological Association to
seek out and establish communication with Chinese
psychologists. Following the end of the Cultural Revolution, the author accepted the invitation of the Chinese
Academy of Sciences to be the first American psychologist to lecture in the People's Republic of China. In

1981, the author made two follow-up visits to Chinese universities. The visits to China caused the author to realize that although his heritage is largely Chinese, China does not provide easy handles for identity. As wonderful as the visits were, he learned more fully that the search for meaning must be pursued through his own self-integration rather than through assimilation with other persons and places. The final essay, "Race Versus Ethnicity," elaborates on ethnic identity and hindrances to its attainment.

A Search for Meaning

The Master said:
Life leads the thoughtful man
on a path of many windings.
                                    I Ching

We must each find our separate meaning
In the persuasion of our days
Until we meet in the meaning of the world.
CHRISTOPHER FRY, *The Firstborn (1946)*

This book relates experiences, lessons, and reflections that have been important to the author. Though an autobiographical line runs through this volume, each essay is more or less self-contained. I dedicate this book to all of those who mean so very much to me and hope that its pages reveal the source from which my love and hopes for them stem. Very special appreciations go to the Chinese Historical Society of America for helping to make this book possible. I thank Him Mark Lai and Judy Yung for their favorable reviews, as well as Society President Pauline K. Lee for her kind help. Thomas W. Chinn, who not only helped to found the society and fulfill so many of its activities over the years, gave unselfishly of his time and printing skills to produce this work. Thanks go to Rebecca Pepper for her helpful editing of the manuscript. Any shortcomings in this book are the author's own alone, while its merits, if any, stem from the love and patience of others.

Today, at fifty-four, I remember my childhood and

youth as being somewhat schizoid. A fourth generation Chinese on my mother's side and second generation on my father's, I grew up as a Chinese-American, with a hyphen (as used at chop suey cafes) that meant "versus" more than "and." It seemed that the attitude of all fixed my family as aliens in America. When I was in kindergarten in Merced, California, I recall how terrified I was when the teacher punished me by putting soap and water in my mouth and keeping me after school. My misdeed was saying the word "shit" to a tattle-telling classmate when I tried to warn her not to step on some dog droppings. I learned from that incident that the class and the teacher expected a "Chinaboy" to be foulmouthed and treated me as such. Sympathizing, but offering no protest to the school for such treatment, my mother told me, "You must learn to take abuses from the whites. Try to understand and swallow your pride. Go to school and learn no matter what."

When I was in second grade, the principal brought a small Chinese child to my class who appeared quite shy and frightened. The principal took the two of us into the closet where the coats and sweaters hung in the heavy, lunchbox atmosphere. The well-intentioned lady asked me to translate for her and the little girl. Frightened myself and barely comprehending the child, I wondered why I had been chosen to speak to the little girl. I realized that we had nothing in common besides our Chinese ancestry. As it turned out, the girl knew much more English than Chinese. However, the principal had mistaken her shyness as a language problem. Everyone in the school expected us, as two Chinese, to be the same, not realizing that the girl and I could be from entirely different backgrounds.

When the Depression hit hard a year or so after my birth in 1929, my father was forced to give up his college work and travel with the family up and down the San Joaquin Valley looking for work. He found odd jobs wherever he could, and was often employed by Chinese gambling halls. I recall the poverty of the 1930s and the prejudices we encountered, as well as the occasional kindness of people. Yet interaction rarely failed to involve our being Asians, not Americans or even Chinese Americans. I remember with considerable distaste how I used to get chewing gum by scraping it off of Merced sidewalks. Some of the pieces of gum seemed to have more grit than others and I became more discriminating about the color and age of the pieces, especially after tasting fresh gum. All of this I recall because my mother spanked me for using a table knife to do the scraping and because a man, observing what I was doing, became so mortified that he gave me a coin and said something like, "You pitiful Chinaboy. Go get some real gum or go back to China!"

I recall what happiness there was when my father found a five-dollar bill in a Watsonville park. He had been unemployed for some time and we literally had nothing to eat. As my parents told me years later, there was talk of food riots and shortages (in that agricultural area!), and so my parents used most of the money "from Heaven" to buy many loaves of bread. I suppose most people even today would have expected us to stock up on rice. Nevertheless, we ate lots of toast and jam, as we sang a popular song of the day which went, "Lookee lookee, here comes cookie coming around the bend." The pungent memories I have of my youth in California help to illustrate the situation of Chinese Americans then and the degree to which we regarded this land as our own as much as did other Americans, though the common attitude reminded us regularly that we were perceived as Asians in America.

In 1937, we moved to a town in northern California and within a year the fourth son was born. There my parents opened a cafe in the local Chinatown after relatives gave them some quick lessons in cooking chop suey and chow mein. Stretching for nearly one long block, Chinatown was composed of about twenty weather-worn buildings in which fewer than thirty Chinese—mostly elderly men—lived. As I recall, few of these men were fully employed or had much income. The old gents would sun and talk during the day, and at night they would try their luck by marking tickets for one or two games of White Pigeon Lottery in the local gambling hall. At about 9 P.M. the gamblers would begin to sing a chanting song, punctuated by the stamping noise of the random punch that cut the winning numbers. These men had come from China to labor at every form of agricultural and city work that required strong backs and dependability. They were a quickly fading lot when I knew them. The old men passed their last years with dignity and quiet, bothering no one and asking for no help, except for having my brothers and me rap their backs with their canes as a form of massage to ease their pains.

Wee Ghong had to be the most memorable of the old men. He had a large, ruddy nose that we always found amusing, for he used to rub it as he gave us a toothless greeting. His home was quite simple and he slept on a hard table-like bed with a curved wooden headrest for a pillow. Inviting us into his home one moment, he would chase us away the next. He was ambivalent about letting people enter into his private world. Wee Ghong had sunned himself in the same spot by the sidewalk for some years; to the side of his rocking chair was a sizable mound of chewing tobacco he had created with countless spits. We used to mimic the way he would rub his nose and spit at the same time, which we marveled at as an art of coordination. He used to tease us for being so Americanized and for wanting to think of the United States as our home. Winning a White Pigeon Lottery ticket, Wee would take us into the cafe and order a round of milk for us, proclaiming to all present what good boys we were for massaging his tired and worn back and how we brought him good luck.

When Wee grew so old that he became an invalid, my father took him to the old folks' home where he passed away within a few months. We visited him several times before he died, and he was extremely uneasy there. He felt unwanted by the staff and other patients and believed that people were stealing his few valuables. I had the feeling that Wee was as alien there as if he had just been transported from China. He probably felt lost not just because he was surrounded by whites in a totally strange, American setting, but also because he was helpless and unable to manage for himself as he had always done. Wee Ghong had given good service to many people by working in cafes, mines, and at many kinds of farm work for whatever wage he could get. His work was, however, anonymous and unrecognized—he worked at the same jobs as many other early Chinese immigrants, and to white Americans, Wee and others like him looked the same and were indistinguishable as individuals. Maybe due to his gambling, he never amassed sufficient cash to return to China, but I wonder if he really intended to return as he said. Given some education and better treatment, rather than being seen simply as Asians in America, Chinese such as Wee could have had happier and fuller lives.

Like the old men, the Chinatown in which I was growing up was also fading away into the past. The tidy but worn buildings looked a bit like the remnants of a frontier town. The city fathers wanted to clear the wooden buildings out, which they did, replacing the buildings with parking lots. Gone are the people, the buildings, and a way of life by which the early Chinese accommodated themselves to America. Some of these early immigrants were sojourners at heart like my great-grandfather, who returned to China after making a fair fortune in California, but most were schizoid like my family. Because the way of life in Chinatown was superficial and temporary in terms of both American and Chinese cultural patterns, it could not last beyond the life and needs of the China-born generation. Because of World War II, the Chinatowns I knew as a youngster passed away and the American-born generation came increasingly into social contact with other Americans. Their greater educational exposure in the public schools and their military service during World War II ensured the acculturation process.

Once a week, probably on Saturday nights, the local Salvation Army band consisting of about ten to fifteen people would march down the middle of the street into Chinatown and play hymns under a street lamp. From an upstairs window, I could hear the tinny sounds above the steady booming bass: "Brighten the corner where you are. . . ." As the band circled under the street lamp, I found it fascinating to watch the large moths and other insects spin wildly about the lamp's bulb, high above the preoccupied, uniformed circle of musicians. After a series of hymns and prayers, the band would break up and members would walk through the area holding out tambourines for donations and asking all to attend their worship services. I can still see how boldly the band marched into our street in order to save Chinese souls from hell. To the Chinese men, it probably seemed just the opposite as they tried to escape the racket and solicitation as quickly as they could. It was difficult for me, a child of seven to twelve, to fit pieces such as the Saturday night band into a cohesive identity.

Charles H. Cooley, in *Human Nature and the Social Order* succinctly expresses his theory of social psychology: "Each to each a looking-glass reflects the other that doth pass," meaning that a person's self arises from contact and social interaction with others.* The reactions of the people with whom we interact supposedly reflect our reactions to them, and thus people in turn

*New York: Scribner, 1902.

determine each other's behavior. Provocative though that viewpoint may be, I must assume that those who encountered the Chinese Americans perceived the wrong signals and that the wrong signals were perceived by Chinese Americans themselves. The ritual of the Saturday night band, for all of its altruism and good intentions, was so blinded by its members' preconceived notions of what Chinese were like that it met with poor success. From their point of view, the Chinese regarded the band as more evidence of white barbarism and disrespect of their privacy.

In the process of acculturation, the dominant culture will, in time, prevail. Despite conflicting cultural influences, an individual seeks logical resolution and a sense of being. So in high school, the American concept of a "melting pot" began to take hold of me. Science, math, and track seemed culture-free—the subject matter and endeavor helped me go beyond the self. Studies in English, history, and music gave me an appreciation of Western thought and culture which seemed to include me. Studying the piano and performing pieces such as Beethoven's "Pathetique" sonata gave me insight into Western aesthetics and discipline. Plato, Shakespeare, Keats, Wordsworth, Poe, Hemingway, and many other writers impressed me as universal thinkers. Thomas Jefferson's Declaration of Independence surely included all peoples. Did I thrill any less than others to the recitation of the Gettysburg Address and the Preamble to the Constitution?

Compared to the influence of the high school, Chinese language school was a dismal loser. Most weekdays after public school and on Saturday mornings, about ten or twelve of us from five Chinese-American families were sent to read and write Chinese characters we often did not comprehend. It seemed that the characters we wrote were all that mattered and their meaning counted for little. We were beginners in an ancient ritual of language, requiring an enormous amount of practice and memorization, to which we could not commit ourselves.

Model American

Instead of allowing me to enroll at the University of California, Berkeley, my family decided to send me to study at Lingnan University in Guangzhou, China. My elders thought the American-sponsored school in China would satisfy their educational and cultural expectations. From 1947 to 1948, China had not recovered from World War II, and its turmoil increased steadily as Mao Zedong's armies moved closer to victory. The abject poverty, corruption, and chaos of Nationalist China just prior to the victory of Mao made me think, "If this is China, thank God I'm an American!" What I saw in China seemed so alien and tragic that instead of identifying with what I found, I separated myself from it. I felt some compassion and sorrow, but only as a detached and uninvolved observer. I saw dead and starving people on the streets of Guangzhou and babies floating in the Pearl River, victims of famine. I remember the haunting shrieks of the female coolie who painfully hauled my baggage into the dormitory and my companions' callous assessment that she exaggerated her pain to get extra pay. After almost a year, during which Mao's armies burst out of Manchuria, my family allowed me to return to the United States.

Back "home," I plunged into university studies and resumed the intellectualism I had begun in high school. Living in Berkeley, away from my family, I began to regard myself as a model American, one who could exemplify the "melting pot" principle despite the bigotry of some. The biased news I read about events in China and the mounting of the Korean War sharpened my sense of allegiance to American values and sentiments. My closest friend took an army commission and was killed in Korea a month after he arrived on the front. Another close friend died after joining the marines. Shortly after graduation, I, too, was in uniform.

Army life does much to discourage patriotism, but, as in college, I felt compelled to prove myself and worked to become a model soldier. Working in the Signal Corps, above the 38th Parallel, I viewed the enemy as Communists, not as Chinese or Asians. My uniform and the life-or-death nature of my duties gave me a common bond with my American buddies. However, I suffered recurring nightmares, not of being captured by the enemy but by fellow GI's who would not believe that I too was a GI. For no matter what my actual identity was, Americans who did not know me well, at college and in the military, had always regarded me as an Asian in America, a foreigner in my own country. I did my best to disregard such perceptions and committed myself to whatever I was doing.

I had much the same experience throughout my graduate studies and teaching. Most of my elementary school pupils and some of the university students I have taught have interacted with me as simply another person, and my experiences with them have given me a deep sense of reward and achievement. I felt that prejudice reflected the problems of those who rendered it, not any shortcomings of my own, though my humor faded when people would say, "How long have you been over here?" "What part of Asia are you from?" "Your English is really quite good," (for an alien), or refer to another Chinese as "your fellow countryman."

Who Am I?

Asian Americans, or anyone who is out of the ordinary in appearance and background, have good reason to be reflective, for their inner identity is challenged by identities that others want to impose upon them. People see greater complexity in themselves than in others, especially when the others appear to fit into a pigeon-hole stereotype. During my youth, I could see that stereotype confronted stereotype between the Chinese and the mainstream Americans. I became extremely sensitive to and aware of the two-way myopia, but I chose to avoid my feelings rather than try to understand them. Re-solving my inner feelings was not easy or sudden, for my consciousness did not know what I needed until a cru-cial experience initiated an awakening.

One afternoon in 1966–1967 while I was a postdoc-toral fellow at the University of Oregon, I saw a film by Felix Greene about the People's Republic of China. The hour-long panorama of China filled me with great emo-tion and many questions, for it showed a rational and progressive China—one that was the complete opposite of the China I had seen from 1947 to 1948 and the China that had been portrayed by the media as a crazed ad-versary throughout the 1950s and 1960s. The film's con-tradiction of all that I had thought and been told since leaving China caused me much consternation and re-flection. I yearned for the day that I could see the People's Republic of China for myself, not in order to adopt a new national loyalty, but to support a growing sense of the relativity of information about China and to begin to identify with others, which I realized was overdue.

Other factors reinforced my need to answer questions that were becoming increasingly important, such as, "Who am I?" "Where am I going?" "What is the mean-ing of life?" and "How does one relate to others?" Being human, I grow older and, I hope, become more mature and knowledgeable through study and reflection. Ob-serving our three children, and giving them more of our time and a better education than our elders could give us, my wife and I seek to help them understand persis-tent myths of and prejudice against Asians, and to come to terms with their own identity. Another factor was my promotion in 1970 to full professor at the University of Wisconsin, Madison. I had done much empirical research, most of which I recognize today as having been too narrowly conceived and pedantic to be of much public service, but I was not intrinsically satisfied by the promotion. At that point, the inescapable question arose, "What have I done to make the world better for others as well as for myself?" Rites of passage for the mere sake of status seemed surprisingly superficial after gaining the most important promotion of my career. Perhaps I had anticipated that the promotion would have more meaning because I had taken little from my persistent research to consider my basic values and long-range purpose. The Vietnam War and social disorders in the country also helped me become aware of my blind adherence to social norms and my unconscious acceptance of the culture.

In 1972, a Fulbright lectureship to Tokyo University and Tamagawa University provided me with a timely opportunity to observe cultural patterns and to test my perceptions of myself and others. My family accompanied me, and our collective experiences and observations helped me to clarify some issues. A dramatic experience for meaning took place during an individual tour of the People's Republic of China in late 1972. It was wonderful to be the first Fulbright Scholar and representative of the American Psychological Association to visit the People's Republic and to talk with its psychologists. Seeing the progress the country had made and the self-reliant spirit of the people was inspiring. The transformation of China made me take pride in being Chinese, yes, but far more important was my elation at seeing how the people's life conditions had improved since my departure in 1948.

Following my 1972 mission to China, I continued my efforts to promote the welfare of Chinese psychologists and maintained communication with them throughout

China's devastating Cultural Revolution. After the anti-intellectualism began to subside in 1977, the Chinese psychologists invited me, under the auspices of the Chinese Academy of Sciences and the Chinese Psychological Society, to accept the honor of being the first American psychologist to tour the People's Republic of China as a distinguished lecturer ("foreign expert"). This I did in May 1980 and I went to China twice in 1981 to lecture at universities and to discuss scholarly exchanges. Each time I have encountered much warmth and receptivity. It reminds me of the kind welcome I have received from the leaders and members of the Chinese Historical Society of America over the years. One of the proudest moments of my life must have been the invitation by the Society to deliver the address at its annual meeting during America's Bicentennial Year of 1976. I am happy to recall that my parents were present to hear President Thomas W. Chinn introduce their son to the gathering in San Francisco. Later that same year, I presented a revised version of the same address, "Face to Face, Come from the Ends of the Earth," also in keeping with the Bicentennial Year, to the National Organization of Chinese Americans. The address concluded as follows:

> Many Chinese Americans express concern with identity and meaning, which is why many are tracing cultural roots and asking who they are. They realize that the old identities—China—or melting-pot-oriented, are unrealistic. . . .
> . . . the potential fulfillment of the centuries-old search for the meeting of East and West is in the hands of far-reaching societies such as the Chinese Historical Society of America, what happens in the community and in our very families, as well as in our own mind's eye. With a tremendous inheritance from both ends of the earth, we should celebrate this Bicentennial with the promise to better define, defend,

and extend a heritage that represents the best of all worlds.

The hope I leave with you tonight is that those who follow can celebrate that fulfillment during the tricentennial in 2076.

Should they assume the distinguished role before them, as I stated above, and fulfill it with farsighted understanding and sense of mission, Chinese Americans could represent the best of the East and the West. As citizens of a young democracy with freedoms, might, and resources that are the envy of the world, and as descendants of a great people and centuries-old civilization of awesome magnitude, Chinese Americans should take pride in their rich heritage. From the ancient philosophers to Thomas Jefferson and Sun Yat-Sen, Chinese Americans can bring to greater light and extend a magnificent history of global significance. In contrast to the sometimes contradictory, schizoid history of their past in America, their new blending of East and West as a conscious, purposeful effort can serve as an inspirational example and as an avenue to much social and individual harmony. What better mission can there be to ensure the brighter future they want for their young? Therefore, it is time that Chinese Americans recognize and accept their rightful mission and begin to find a strong sense of direction and ethnic identity of their own, a common search for meaning and relevance.

Plain Language from Truthful James*

Which I wish to remark
    And my language is plain
That for ways that are dark
    And for tricks that are vain.
The heathen Chinee is peculiar
    Which the same I would rise to explain.

Ah Sin was his name;
    And I shall not deny
In regard to the same
    What that name might imply
But his smile it was pensive
    and child-like
As I frequent remarked to Bill Nye.

But the hands that were played
    By that heathen Chinee,
And the points that he made,
    Were quite frightful to see.
Till at last he put down a right bower.
    Which the same Nye had dealt onto me.
And he went for that heathen Chinee.

*Bret Harte, *The Overland Monthly*, 1870.

The Twain Did Meet

Oh, East is East, and West is West, and never the
*   twain shall meet,*
Till Earth and Sky stand presently at God's great
*   Judgment Seat;*
But there is neither East nor West, Border, nor
*   Breed, nor Birth,*
When two strong men stand face to face, though
*   they come from the ends of the Earth!*
                RUDYARD KIPLING *(1865–1936),*
                The Ballad of East and West

A yet-unresolved controversy concerns the references to Huishen, a Chinese Buddhist priest, in the *History of the Liang Dynasty* (557–637 A.D.), a fifty-six–volume work written in the seventh century A.D. A short statement in the history credits to Huishen a report that in 499 A.D. he had returned from a voyage of 20,000 li or 7,000 miles to a land east of China that he called Fusang after a tung-like tree he found there. The Liang history briefly describes the people, their food and habits, and the foliage of the land. It also says that in 458 A.D. five mendicant priests from Jibin had journeyed to Fusang to convert the people to Buddhism and modify their customs. Based upon such references, J. de Guignes, a French sinologist, startled the West in 1761 with the publication of his paper *Chinese Voyages to the American Coast*, in which he claimed that the Chinese had discovered North America one thousand years before Columbus and had landed in the region known today as Mexico.

Research by Chinese historians supports the contention that Huishen and other Chinese had indeed explored Mexico and the American continent in the fifth century. Fang ZhongDu of the People's Republic of China lists a number of studies that contradict the accepted notion that Fusang was Japan rather than Mexico, and affirm that Huishen's descriptions of a faraway land and its people and surroundings could only be Mexico.* Many Westerners do not perceive China to have been a maritime power; their image of Chinese seagoing prowess is typically the practical junk we can still see today. However, as early as the first century, ships from China were sailing extensively through the oceans, equipped with magnetic compasses and sternpost rudders. In the third century, navigational skills extended to the calculation of sailing speeds and voyage lengths. Between 1405 and 1433, the Ming Emperor Yong Luo dispatched seven great fleets into South and Southeast Asian waters to bring that region under the imperial system of tribute. Under Admiral Zheng He, the first expedition sailed with 28,000 men on sixty-two ships, and traveled as far as India. By the seventh expedition, the Chinese had reached the eastern coast of Africa and even Mecca. We can better appreciate the advanced nature of Chinese seamanship by noting that it took Europeans until nearly a century later to sail around Africa to reach India. More than 400 feet long, the largest Chinese ships had as many as four decks and were capable of carrying more than three thousand passengers. It became fairly common for Chinese ships to sail to the Philippines and into the Indian Ocean. In 1979, James R. Moriarity III, an archeologist from the University of San Diego, reported two separate discoveries of 3,000-year-old sailing relics from China off the California coast. The dating was done from accurate measurements of the manganese accumulation on the

*China Reconstructs, 1980, 29(8):65–66.

ancient artifacts, including a large circular stone anchor with a hole in the center that was recovered from a depth of 1,000 fathoms off Point Mendocino.*

Without further verification of Huishen's journey and observations, there will continue to be speculation and disagreement. However, the Japanese Current that flows clockwise past Japan's eastern shores to the northeast, and along the western shores of North America have brought Chinese and Japanese ships and sailors to the West Coast in the past, as in the beaching of a Chinese junk and its occupants at Mendocino in 1852. Following the southern flow of the Japanese Current, Thor Heyerdahl and five other Norwegians tested their theory that ancient American peoples had populated Polynesia. They sailed from Callao, Peru, in 1947 in a great balsa raft named *Kon-Tiki* (after a legendary Inca god). After sailing about five thousand miles in the prevailing current of the Pacific, Heyerdahl reached the islands east of Tahiti three and a half months later.

Other scientists have pursued the theory of contacts between the Chinese and Japanese and the early American peoples through archeological and cultural studies. For example, pottery unearthed in Ecuador closely resembles the Jomon pottery of Japan (3000 B.C.). Also, there are cultural similarities between ancient China and the highly advanced civilization of Olmec in Central America and Mexico (1000–300 B.C.), such as many striking parallels in the use and styling of jade. Interesting too is the popular custom of the "China de la Poblana"—the colorful gown still worn by Mexican women for fiesta dances—which, according to legend, originates from a similar dress worn by a Chinese princess who visited Mexico in ancient times.

The case for early Asian travels to America was enhanced when on June 28, 1980, a forty-three-foot catamaran based on a 5,000-year-old design arrived in San

---

*For more on this, please see *Reader's Digest*, June 1983, pp. 148–152.

Francisco from Japan after a voyage of fifty-three days. Haruki Kadowkawa, President of the Kadowkawa Publishing Company in Japan, had become intrigued with research by Clifford Evans and Betty Meggars of the Smithsonian Institution in the 1960s that closely relates 3,000-year-old Ecuadorean pottery to Japanese pottery. By financing the construction of the catamaran and the successful voyage of the double-canoe craft, Kadowkawa proved that ancient seamen did have the ability and techniques to reach the Americas from Asia.

The first recorded stay of Chinese in the United States occurred in 1785 when the American ship *Pallas* landed in Baltimore with thirty-two East Indian and three Chinese seamen. Its captain quickly unloaded the ship's cargo and left the seamen stranded. No other records are available for the Chinese, named Ashing, Achun, and Aceum, so we do not know what became of them. Similarly, a crew of seventy Chinese sailors, carpenters, and helmsmen were part of an attempt by the British East India Company to forge a settlement in western Canada in 1788 under Captain John Meares. After the English force had built a two-story house and a forty-ton ship, Spaniards confiscated the property and dispersed the party. No further records exist to tell what happened to the Chinese. According to Western historians, it is the first recorded landing of Chinese on the West Coast. Until Sutter's gold strike in 1849, only a handful of Chinese were in California. Late in 1849, the gradually increasing number of Chinese led to a meeting of 300 Chinese at the Canton Cafe in San Francisco where the following resolution was adopted:*

> Whereas, it becomes necessary for us, strangers as we are, in a strange land, unacquainted with the language and custom of this, our adopted country, to have some recognized counselor and adviser, to whom we may all appeal, with confidence, for wholesome

*As reported by the *Alta California*, December 10, 1849.

instruction and advice, in the event of any unforeseen difficulties arising, wherein we should be at loss as to what course of action it might be necessary for us to pursue; therefore, Resolved, that a committee of four be appointed to wait upon Selim E. Woodworth, Esq., and request him, in behalf of the Chinese residents of San Francisco, to act in the capacity of arbitrator and adviser for them.

The appointed committee of Ahe, Attoon, Atung, and Jon-Ling obtained Woodworth's acceptance the very next day. Reporting on a meeting between Chinese and leading white San Franciscans on August 28, 1850, the *California Courier* reflected the general attitude of San Franciscans toward the first Chinese settlers as follows: "We have never seen a finer-looking body of men collected together in San Francisco. In fact, this portion of our population is a pattern for sobriety, order and obedience to laws, not only to other foreign residents, but to Americans themselves." The first several thousand Chinese came to the United States to work as merchants and traders. They paid their own way and were of a higher social class than the laborers and coolies who came later. Since this first group journeyed overseas to the United States despite the prohibition of the Chinese government against going abroad (Section 225 of the *Fundamental Laws of the Ch'ing Dynasty* prescribed the punishment of beheading for "proceeding to sea to trade" and emigration) and declared the United States to be their "adopted country," it should not be said that all Chinese who came to the United States were sojourners never intending to stay and live as citizens.

The abolition of black slavery created strong pressures for other sources of cheap labor in the second half of the nineteenth century. Following the pattern established by Cuba and Peru in 1847 and 1849, respectively, contract laborers or coolies were brought to the Hawaiian Islands in 1852 and to California through the 1870s but mostly from the late 1840s to 1860. The laborers supposedly signed a contract for two or more years of service, for which recruiters or "crimps" received seven to ten dollars per person. Hardly voluntary, the coolies "signed up" by being kidnaped, by selling themselves out of desperation to pay off gambling debts incurred through trickery, and by being taken prisoner in feudal wars. Brutal conditions aboard the ships that transported the coolies to the Americas, especially to Cuba and Peru, at times equaled the deadly mistreatment by slavers bringing blacks from Africa. Upon arrival, the contracts were auctioned or allotted to those who sought them. Even in the rough world of the 1870s, the government of Hong Kong in 1873 and that of Macao in 1874 responded to world appeals and took action to stem the coolie contract system.

Many Chinese emigrants to America, who could not raise the forty-dollar passage and would not accept the conditions of the coolie contract system, followed the credit-ticket system. Brokers in Hong Kong paid the fare which the emigrant would pay back out of his earnings in the United States. The contracts also provided assistance in finding work and getting established. The credit-ticket system became an acceptable channel of transport for many peasant men from the districts surrounding Canton, especially the region known as *Sze Yup* ("Four Districts"), an area sharing a common dialect which comprised the districts of Sunwui, Toishan, Hoiping, and Yanping. Until the end of World War II, 70 percent of the Chinese in California had originated in the *Sze Yup*. The early Chinese merchants described above had come from *Som Yup*, the three districts around and in the city of Canton, two of which (Namhoi and Punyu) lead the province in wealth and in their diversity of skills and income-producing industry, such as silk textiles, fish culture, tailoring, and ceramics. The vast majority of Chinese migrating before 1949 came from twenty-four districts of Guangdong. All spoke a dialect of Cantonese except for those from the

Hakka-speaking districts of Chikkai and Pao-On. After the *Sze Yup*, the largest percentage of Chinese in America came from the Zhongshan district. This district includes Macao and Pao-On (which includes Hong Kong), and its inhabitants had thus been in continuous contact with Westerners for some time.*

My own family originates from Toishan in the *Sze Yup*, which had the largest representation of any district in the United States through World War II. Of the Chinese-American population in the United States before 1949, 40 percent came from Toishan. Our people saw in the United States an opportunity to escape the tremendous social unrest and economic collapse of China brought about by the failure of the Chinese government to overcome the foreign imperialism of the Opium Wars, inflation, importation of machine-made products (especially textiles) from the West which undersold local industries, and the devastation caused by natural calamities, war, disease, and famine. The Taiping ("Great Peace") Rebellion, a popular revolt that failed but which is surely one of China's greatest and most unique rebellions, began in 1851 and lasted thirteen years. Under the leadership of Hong Xiuchuan, who believed he was the new messiah of Christianity, the Taiping Rebellion began in July 1850 near the West River in Guangsi Province southwest of Guangdong Province, when Hong Xiuchuan's soldiers engaged the imperial forces. Spreading throughout much of China, the Taipings captured 600 walled cities; more than 30 million died as a consequence of the rebellion's turmoil and devastation.

A remarkable coopcration between East and West helped to end the Taiping Rebellion when in 1864 the imperial government enlisted the aid of an American

---

*For more on the early Chinese in the United States, please read *A History of the Chinese in California* by T. W. Chinn, H. M. Lai, and P. P. Choy (San Francisco: Chinese Historical Society of America, 1969).

adventurer, Frederick Townsend Ward, who first organized and commanded a force of Western troops and
later an army of 4,000 Chinese soldiers called the "Ever
Victorious Army" that defeated the Taipings in more
than 100 engagements. Amphibious tactics on the
Yangtze delta and Western firepower proved highly
successful for the Western mercenaries, who were paid
handsomely by the merchants of Shanghai. In 1862,
after commanding for two years the troops he had
brought together, Ward died in battle. However, with
the permission of the British, an English officer, Major
Charles George Gordon, assumed command of the
"Ever Victorious Army." The Chinese government
granted him military rank, as it had done with Ward.
Gordon's army recaptured Suzhou and helped to turn
the tide against the Taiping forces. Returning to England in 1865, Gordon received a hero's welcome and was
dubbed "Chinese Gordon," a nickname he carried for
the rest of his distinguished career. Among the many
deeds for which General Gordon is remembered after
his success in China are the mapping of the Upper Nile
from 1874 to 1876 and, in the eyes of the British public,
his martyrdom at the siege of Khartoum in 1885. Before
achieving fame in the Taiping Rebellion as a young
army major, Gordon had participated in the occupation
of Beijing in 1860 during the "Arrow" War and had
personally supervised the burning of the Summer Palace as a punishment and warning against the anti-
foreign movement of that period. The war involved a
number of foreign powers who resisted the attempts of
the Chinese, particularly the Cantonese, to throw off the
intrusions won by the Westerners in the Opium War.
The "Arrow" War derived its name from an incident in
October, 1856, when police in Guangzhou seized a
Chinese-owned ship named the "Arrow," which had
British registration, and arrested its Chinese crew for
piracy and smuggling.

The preceding historical sketch illustrates the great social and political unrest of the mid-nineteenth century when many men from South China went to America. Such a background must have made the gold fields of California and the pristine beauty of the United States seem extremely attractive to the Chinese immigrants. No wonder that the Cantonese vernacular admiringly referred to the United States as *Gum San* ("Mountain of Gold") and *Fa Kee* ("The Flowery or Colorful Flag"), while the common name for the United States which is still used today has been *Mei Kwoh* ("The Beautiful Nation").

A History of Bias and Prejudice

Although Americans received the early arrivals from China extremely well, as mentioned earlier, the subsequent history of the treatment of Chinese Americans has been unfavorable. Despite their industry, lawful nature, and respect for intelligence and creativity, Chinese in the United States have had more discriminatory laws directed at them than at any other group in the United States relative to their small numbers. In 1854, the California Supreme Court heard an appeal by a white man who had been convicted of murder on the testimony of a Chinese witness. In its decision, the court observed that Columbus had landed in the New World in his quest for a new route to the Orient. Believing that the West Indies were islands in the Chinese Sea, Columbus called the natives he found Indians. Rationalizing that only three kinds of people existed in the world, White, Black, and Indian, the court decided that Indians and Asians were the same. Thus, because Indians had no legal rights, the court disallowed the testimony of the Chinese witness and ruled in favor of the appeal. Fourteen exclusion laws were passed against the Chinese between 1880 and 1924, representing the severest forms of racism. These restrictions, I believe, were caused by a fear of the Asians' great productivity. This fear continues today in cases such as the hostilities faced by refugee fishermen from Southeast Asia in the early 1980s and in the murder of Vincent Chin in Detroit in 1983. According to historian George M. Fredrickson's insightful work titled *White Supremacy*, the mobilization in the 1890s by white workers against the Chinese immigrants on racial, xenophobic grounds "was perhaps the most successful labor-based political movement in American history."* As a reporter for the *Territorial Enterprise* in Virginia City, Nevada, in the 1870s, Mark Twain made the following observation which characterizes the early treatment of the Chinese in the United States:

> Of course there was a large Chinese population. . . . it is the case with every town and city on the Pacific coast. They are a harmless race when white men either let them alone or treat them no worst than dogs; in fact, they are almost entirely harmless anyhow, for they seldom think of resenting the vilest insults or the cruelest injuries. They are quiet, peaceable, tractable, free from drunkenness, and they are as industrious as the day is long. A disorderly Chinaman is rare, and a lazy one does not exist. So long as a Chinaman has strength to use his hands he needs no support from anybody; white men often complain of want of work, but a Chinaman offers no such complaint; he always manages to find something to do. He is a great convenience to everybody—even to the worst class of white men, for he bears the most of their sins, suffering fines for their petty thefts, imprisonment for their robberies, and death for their murders. Any white man can swear a Chinaman's life away in the courts, but no Chinaman can testify

*New York: Oxford University Press, 1981.

against a white man. Ours is the "land of the free"—nobody denies that—nobody challenges it. (Maybe it is because we won't let other people testify.)

In California he [the Chinese] gets a living out of old mining claims that white men have abandoned as exhausted and worthless—and then the officers come down on him once a month with an exorbitant swindle to which the legislature has given the broad, general name of "foreign" mining tax, but it is usually inflicted on no foreigners but Chinamen. The swindle has in some cases been repeated once or twice on the same victim in the course of the same month—but the public treasury was not additionally enriched by it, probably.

In contrast to Mark Twain's objectivity, Bret Harte's fiction reflects hostile bigotry. Harte's writings intensified the growing climate of crude prejudice that the Chinese endured in the nineteenth century. The general attitude toward the Chinese in those rough times created the expression "a chinaman's chance," which meant having absolutely no chance at all. Without a doubt, the derisive expression carried a literal meaning. One still hears it today in daily conversation and occasionally on television, for the meaning remains extant. When I have pointed out the implied bigotry of the expression to people, even professors, who used it in my presence, they quickly claim that no slur was intended and are apologetic. Such experiences expose the insidious nature of anti-Chinese sentiments which seem well-ingrained in the United States, particularly in the western states. Bret Harte contributed much to the establishment of these sentiments and their lasting power.

A New Yorker who journeyed to the mining region of California in 1854, Harte made his fortune as an editor and writer largely through scurrilous, stereotypic portrayals of the Chinese. His talent took the form of describing touching, local-color scenes and attitudes, and his opportunistic nature made the most of the sino-phobia of the West. In 1870, the publication of *The Luck of Roaring Camp and Other Sketches* made him famous throughout America and Europe. That same year, he increased his popularity by publishing a poem titled "Plain Language from Truthful James," better known as the "Heathen Chinee" (reprinted at the beginning of this chapter), a pasquinading piece that carries no literary merit. Its sudden, widespread success comes from its obvious bigotry. In high school, my sophomore English teacher forced Bret Harte's short stories and poems on my class, which angered and frustrated me to some extent. I wondered then if the teacher, who taught Shakespeare's *Julius Caesar* in the same course, realized how a Chinese American might react to Harte's works. One might also wonder why a general literature course would include such trash in its readings. Per-haps it is because literary historians believe that such writings represent a significant period of American his-tory and literature, a point which I would reject simply on the basis of literary quality. At any rate, why are lit-erature courses structured to include both Shakespeare and Harte within the same semester course?

On March 5, 1981, I visited the National Portrait Gal-lery in Washington, D.C., to see a stimulating exhibit on the U.S. presidents. As I walked toward the exit, I spot-ted an exhibit on Bret Harte. In that show was the writer's portrait, which displayed a pompous and self-assuming character, along with several of Harte's writ-ings in their original editions. One of these was the "Heathen Chinee" accompanied by a sequence of car-toons of a silly-looking Chinese man and two white men. The final cartoon showed one of the white men kicking the pig-tailed Chinese quite forcefully. For fostering such a tribute or for even giving space and funds at all to such a person and his works, especially in an age of federal affirmative action and civil rights policies, I fault the National Portrait Gallery for its thoughtlessness. I directed a strong complaint to the gallery guards and their sergeant (who were black), all of whom blamed the directors of the gallery for the display. I calmly but forcefully asked them what they would do if Harte had directed his venomous pen at blacks. They did not answer the question.

It was 1969 and the Chinese Historical Society of America stirred with even greater energy and anticipation than usual, for the celebration of the centennial of the completion of the transcontinental railroad would take place on May 10. After 100 years, the 12,000 Chinese workers who had provided the manpower for the very difficult construction of the railroad line over the Sierra Nevadas would receive proper, official recognition for their courageous labors.

Leland Stanford, the Central Pacific baron, had said nearly 100 years ago that without the Chinese workers it would have been impossible to complete the western portion of "this great national highway." In later years, as a politician, Stanford repaid his debt to the Chinese by helping to pave the way for the discriminatory exclusion laws. Central Pacific's field manager, Charles Crocker, however, did not betray the Chinese workers whom he had learned to respect; he braved popular abuse and ridicule by testifying in their favor before an 1876 joint congressional commission studying exclusion proposals.

So, in 1969 the Chinese Historical Society of America produced two identical bronze plaques, one to be placed in Sacramento where the railway line started eastward and the other to be placed at the headquarters of the national historical site at Promontory, Utah, where the Central Pacific and Union Pacific met to join the cross-country line in 1869. Philip P. Choy, president of the Chinese Historical Society of America, designed the plaque. Thomas W. Chinn, executive director and co-founder (in 1963, with C. H. Kwock, Chingwah Lee, H. K.

Wong, and Thomas W. S. Wu) of the Society, composed
the wording of the plaque. P. C. Lee translated the words
into Chinese and also provided the calligraphy. The
bronze plaque reads: "To commemorate the centennial
of the first transcontinental railroad in America and to
pay tribute to the Chinese workers of the Central Pacific
Railroad whose indomitable courage made it possible."

At a grand celebration in San Francisco on May 4,
1969, with many civic speakers, the plaque was unveiled
by Thomas W. Chinn's mother, Mrs. Chinn Lee Shee
Wing, the ninety-eight-year-old daughter of one of the
Chinese '49ers, Lee Man Bien. In Sacramento on May 9,
there were many more speakers before the presentation
of the commemorative plaque. Congressman John E.
Moss of Sacramento gave the principal speech. He reminded the audience that the completion of the railway
line truly unified the country, and he paid tribute to the
workers who built it, particularly the Chinese pioneers.
Two special trains from the Southern Pacific Railroad
(the successor to the Central Pacific) were part of the
celebrations, one of which went on to the May 10th
ceremonies at Promontory. What follows is the main part
of the news account for the events on May 10, 1969, by
reporter Dale Champion, as published in the *San Francisco Chronicle*, May 12, 1969, with the headline, "The
Forgotten Men At Gold Spike Ceremony":

> Ogden, Utah—As history and rail fans by the hundreds
> headed for homes across the Nation in special trains
> yesterday, they were still muttering about the politi-
> cians who outsnorted the Iron Horse at the Promon-
> tory Railroad Centennial.
>
> A crowd of 20,000 turned out Saturday for the cele-
> bration, 56 miles from here, on the northern fringe of
> the Great Salt Lake.   So did four U.S. senators, seven
> congressmen, the governor of Utah, Federal Trans-
> portation Secretary John A. Volpe and John Wayne.
>
> The politicians so monopolized things that the au-
> dience, some of whom had come from Europe and

South America, sweltered almost out of patience under a hot desert sun, waiting for the Great Event: the re-enactment of the meeting of the Union Pacific and the Central (now Southern) Pacific a century ago.

Secretary Volpe, the principal orator, succeeded in infuriating the Chinese delegation from San Francisco by wholly ignoring the 12,000 Chinese who helped build the Central Pacific over the Sierra to Promontory.

"Who else but Americans could drill ten tunnels in mountains 30 feet deep in snow?" asked Volpe, speaking in a flat, nasal Bostonian accent.

"Who else but Americans could chisel through miles of solid granite?" "Who else but Americans could have laid ten miles of track in 12 hours?"

Sitting in angry silence at the rear of the bunting-draped platform were Philip P. Choy, chairman of the Chinese Historical Society of America, and his colleague from San Francisco, Thomas W. Chinn, founder and executive director of the society.

Chou Tung-hua, Consul General in San Francisco for the Republic of China, sat several rows forward on the platform, just behind the politicians.

Unlike Volpe, the three were well aware that none of the Chinese railroad workers were Americans. In fact, foreign-born Chinese were barred for years from becoming citizens.

Chinn said later that he and Choy were "very unhappy" at Volpe's chauvinistic slighting of the Chinese.

The injury cut particularly deep, Chinn said, because of the Chinese Historical Society's strong effort in conjunction with the Centennial "to correct various incorrect impressions concerning the Chinese and their role in building the West."

As part of the centennial, the society dedicated plaques at Sacramento and Promontory in tribute to the Chinese who worked for the Central Pacific. . . .

The *Stanford Observer*, Stanford University's alumni newspaper, printed a full-page article in its May 1969 issue to honor the Golden Spike celebration. It reflected the same chauvinistic attitudes and omissions in regard to the characteristics and origins of the workers. However, the *Observer* criticized those workers who had delayed the final construction and festivities by striking to obtain wages that were earned months before.

A century earlier, Judge Nathaniel Bennett had helped celebrate the completion of the railroad by declaring in a speech in San Francisco that the monumental work was due to the "proper origins" of Californians:

> In the veins of our people, flows the commingled blood of the four greatest nationalities of modern days. The impetuous daring and dash of the French, the philosophical and sturdy spirit of the German, the unflinching solidity of the English, and the light-hearted impetuosity of the Irish, have all contributed each its appropriate share . . . . A people deducing its origins from such races, and condensing their best traits into its national life, is capable of any achievement (*San Francisco Bulletin*, 1869).

The day following the historic event, the *Chicago Times* (1869) made slight but favorable mention of the Chinese workers "without whose aid it would have been difficult to complete the end of the road." In another article in the same issue, favorable mention was also given Chinese workers who gave "good satisfaction" as "profitable laborers" in Louisiana parishes. The article implied that "Chinamen" might replace "Ethiopians" whom "mistaken philanthropists and unscrupulous politicians" were attempting to enfranchise. The strong implication appears to be that the Chinese workers were competing with other sources of cheap labor and were delegated to the same social strata as blacks. The article also said that although a black would be accepted as "a hired servant" in the South, "as a voting citizen, however much politicians may seek to use him, he must expect to be forever despised." American society has traditionally pitted one immigrant group against another to compete for lower strata employment and acceptance into society. However, blacks and Chinese have faced definite disadvantages in America that persist to some degree today. Construction of the transcontinental railroad exemplified such ethnic competition; discrimination against the Chinese during and after the construction demonstrates some of the worst iniquities of nineteenth-century capitalism and bias.

People tend to perceive the Chinese in sharply contrasting terms, as H. R. Isaacs found in his exhaustive survey of media and national leaders. (*Images of Asia: American Views of China and India*):

> American images of the Chinese tend largely to come in jostling pairs. The Chinese are seen as a superior people and an inferior people; devilishly exasperating heathens and wonderfully humanists; wise sages and sadistic executioners; thrifty and honorable men and sly and devious villains; comic opera soldiers and dangerous fighters.*

To counter such stereotypic perceptions, Chinese Americans have been pressured to seek assimilation by fitting into a mold that is quite tailored and inflexible. In other words, tolerable behavior for them has become restricted. For example, Chinese who raise questions and are precise or critical are branded as "troublemakers," and those Chinese who run afoul of the law are given a disproportionate amount of publicity. In order to achieve their present level of social acceptance, the Chinese have attempted to be successful, larger-than-life Americans, especially through educational and professional achievement and through exceptional citizenship traits (they have the lowest rate of loan defaults and criminal records of any ethnic group in the United

*New York: Capricorn, 1962, pp. 70–71.

States). The Chinese have overcome bias largely through high achievement in the occupations they have entered, through cohesive family structures in which familial harmony and responsibility are maintained, and by being adaptable to social-environmental conditions.

My mother told me that a Chinese who sought work outside Chinatown had to be ten times better than an ordinary person in order to obtain and hold a job, but even that might not be enough. In the academic world where the rule is supposedly "publish or perish," Chinese professors statistically earn significantly less than their white and black colleagues, and receive promotions at a slower rate. Also, although a greater proportion of Chinese scholars may be found at major universities than the percentage of Chinese in the population at large, relatively few have obtained administrative positions, especially above chairing a department. Perhaps signaling a change, in 1983 Chia-Wei Woo assumed the presidency of San Francisco State University, the very same institution that I left in 1964 in part because of my frustrations with prejudice. Now that I am retired, I can say that my mother's advice was only too true. Time, however, may be bringing a brighter day.

Many Chinese Americans of my generation encountered attitudes in the public schools that seemed highly misinformed and prejudicial. As I entered their classes for the first time, some teachers would frown and make me feel unwelcome from the beginning. Often, they would say something such as, "Now I can have that unit on China." It is amusing how often I had to teach everyone in my classes how to use chopsticks. One of my sixth-grade teachers uttered remarks such as, "Some people with dark skins don't think they need to wash themselves." Besides myself, that class included one other possible person to whom she could have been referring: a Mexican-American fellow. I do not know if our teacher was talking about him or me, but I surely did not feel comfortable nor did I understand her attitude. A big, stocky woman, she would shake and scold the two of us on any pretext, it seemed. Our being darker-skinned seemed to aggravate her obvious bias against boys and partiality toward girls. Except for one effeminate lad, none of the boys volunteered anything in class. Instead, we relished the physical education lessons that the other sixth-grade teacher directed for the boys, and the rare appearances by the art teacher. Because I was so conscious of my sixth-grade teacher's domineering presence, I learned little that year. I remember being absorbed with having to be so aware of her every move, lest she grab me and shake me (I sat within arm's reach of her desk), that I would watch her bulbous nose throughout the day. I focused upon the teacher's big nose partly because it was relatively close to me, but that nose was fascinating in and of itself. Heavily powdered in the first hour, it would evolve during the course of the day as the powder faded and the pores grew increasingly prominent, all of which I watched in fascination. Teacher behavior during my youth frightened me, though several teachers seemed genuinely helpful and understanding. One helped me to overcome a reading handicap with her patience and some interesting activities, chief of which was a play in which I acted the lead, a bear!

In California schools, I read textbook generalizations such as: "The best American citizens have come from Ireland, Scotland, and England." That assertion was supported by showing how many presidents, congressmen, and senators had come from such heritage—an indisputable fact, but one which also requires definite qualifications as to why it was so. Furthermore, the fact does not support the generalization, which raises other improper and false generalizations. It does not allow people like me and many others to consider ourselves American. When I was a classroom teacher in the early 1960s, one of the popular social studies textbooks contained a picture of Marco Polo on his difficult journey to or from China. In the text, one had to search carefully to find a reference to Marco Polo's glorification of all aspects of China and to learn that China was the true objective of the European explorers who discovered the New World. American youngsters learned about the world and their nation's history from textbooks such as that.

From 1974 to 1977, I learned a great deal about school textbooks and their production through an appointment by the California State Board of Education to the Legal Compliance Committee. I chaired one panel of the committee, which reviewed 200 newly published textbooks a year for compliance with state requirements against bias, prejudice, and misrepresentation. Time-consuming though it was, the review process forced the publishers to modify their policies in order to have their textbooks adopted for use by the most populous state in the Union. Most people do not realize that textbooks are written primarily for profit and involve little or no input from professional educators. To produce profitable books, textbook publishers must have their books adopted as widely as possible. Textbooks, therefore, are written to avoid what may be controversial and unexpected. For example, publishers have eliminated mention of the United Nations, even whole chapters, because right-wing groups have campaigned against the coverage of the international body in the schools. Traditionally, the American Civil War is known as the "War Between the States" in social studies texts because that is what it is called in the South. With more straightforward, factual textbooks appearing now, we can see evidence that school curriculums are improving and that more enlightened publishers, educators, and parents are involved.

Pulp novels and cheap movies of the 1920s and 1930s

portrayed the Chinese in a highly distorted light, rang-
ing from the brutal and evil Fu Manchu to the romanti-
cized, chinadoll characterization of Anna May Wong.
What did Americans know about the Chinese or care to
know with the pressures of unemployment and poverty
hanging over so many people during the Great Depression? During hard times, people create scapegoats and
turn their frustrations against the stranger in their
midst. Yet how do we explain people's stereotypes in
more recent times? As a college student, I saw students
answering the instructor's question, "Why are there so
many Chinese?" with the answer: "Chinese babies are
born after terms of less than nine months, perhaps sev-
en." Also, I hate to think of the innumerable times that
I have confronted the pun about the reproductive structure of Chinese women differing greatly from that of
Western women. I grew tired of barbers teasing me
that they would sell my hair clippings to Chinese women.
The well-known "You like speechee?" joke goes over
because the situation seems actually possible. Other
statements speak for themselves: "This is not a Chinese
classroom, stop this noisy behavior!" "They were as
confused as a Chinese fire drill." "How long have you
been in this country? Your English is so good." "I met a
countryman of yours. Maybe you know him?" and "Is
this your first trip to the United States?" As patient as I
can usually be with faux pas such as those, the one that
brought me a headache (or heartache) happened at an
exclusive yacht club at which the university president
had invited me to speak. We encountered a member of
the university foundation board, whom I had worked
with for some time. The man complimented me on my
suit of the type I normally wore and said, "You look like
a real American."

Nevertheless, I can report a happy exception to the
negative routine which happened with children, the
object of all our hopes for the future. In 1955, after my

Army discharge, I found a job teaching in a rural school near Healdsburg, California. The county superintendent of schools told me later that after checking their records carefully I was the first Chinese to become a certified teacher in Sonoma County. My class combined youngsters in the fourth, fifth, and sixth grades, so I had my hands full. Even if I had had some experience, it would have been trying. The fourth-graders were to conclude their study of the California Indians with a dramatization for the entire class and we decided to make hand puppets for the show. As they molded the clay heads, several pupils asked me how to make the faces, "What did the Indians look like?" Suggesting pictures from the textbooks without success because the children wanted more authenticity, I suggested that they consider my features as a general model. We had studied the Bering Strait theory of the origin of the American Indians, which claims that they had Asian roots. So I said, "Well, put in high cheek bones like mine, since I'm Asian, a Chinese." Behind my words then and in my thoughts each day was the thought that a Chinese could not succeed as a classroom teacher. My elders said many times that the whites would not accept me and urged that I find another profession. When the children heard what I had said about molding their puppet's features after mine, they looked up at me from their circle around the clay basin and said, "We didn't know you were Chinese. We thought you were Mr. Yee." Oh, that they can remain so open and clear-minded!

Marco Polo and the Quest for Riches in the East

It is somewhat ironic that common people of the East and West confronted each other as Mark Twain described in the gold fields of California. For centuries, even before the birth of Jesus Christ, the Arabs, Greeks, and Romans had conducted trade with China. East-West trade became quite extensive after the first century, when the Han emperors restored China's control over Central Asia and a Chinese army crossed Parthia to reach the Roman Empire. The Romans craved all of the silk that could be obtained across the Central Asian route, which became known as the "Silk Road." Because of China's technological superiority, the Chinese enjoyed a trade surplus with the West which continued until the troubled nineteenth century. So great was the Roman demand for silk that Rome suffered a serious outflow of hard currency. In 658, the number of Arab traders in Guangzhou became great enough that they were able to burn and loot the city. The silk caravans expanded greatly during the Yuan Dynasty (1260–1368) of the Mongols, with the elimination of trade controls established during the Song and Jin dynasties. The wonders of China and fear of the Mongol rulers of China caused Pope Innocent IV and other Western leaders to send envoys and missionaries to Kublai Khan's court at Cambaluc near the present city of Beijing. Yet the most successful travellers came from Venice, Europe's most luxurious and powerful city of that period. In 1265, Niccolo and Matteo Polo found their way to China, where the Kublai received them handsomely and gave them a gold tablet that ensured them safe conduct on their three-year trek back to Venice.

In 1271, the two Polo brothers set off for China again—not with the 100 or so wise and holy men as requested by the Khan, but with Marco, a lad of seventeen, who became one of history's most significant figures. Becoming a favorite of the Emperor, Marco travelled throughout China and served the court in many important ways. Fortunately, Marco Polo recorded his observations of his seventeen years' service to

Kublai Khan from 1275 to 1292 in his book *Descriptions of the World.* The book, which he dictated in a Genoa prison, has stimulated profound Western interest in China across the centuries. It gave the West its first vivid descriptions of the riches and advanced civilization to be found in China. About Hangzhou, the famed resort city which President Nixon would visit 700 years later, Marco wrote: "Kinsai (Hangzhou) merits from its pre-eminence to all others in the world, in point of grandeur and beauty, as well as from its abundant delights, which might lead an inhabitant to imagine himself in paradise." Of Beijing, he wrote: ". . . everything that is most rare and valuable in all parts of the world finds its way: . . . for not fewer than 1,000 carriages and packhorses loaded with raw silk make their daily entry; and gold tissue and silks of various kinds are manufactured to an immense extent." Polo marveled at China's superior organization and system of communication, such as elaborate horse and runner relay networks. He praised the social system in which the people's honesty, civility, and good nature seemed perfect. Polo commented on the wonders of Chinese skills, such as their architecture: "The hall of the palace is so large that it could easily seat 6,000 people." A building this size was unknown in Europe at that time. The social and technological advances described in his book seemed so highly exaggerated and incredible to Westerners that, during the Middle Ages and even into the twentieth century, the name Marco Polo was synonymous with what we would call a "tall tale" today. However, we now know otherwise. The "black rocks" which he said the Chinese dug from the earth and used as fuel turned out to be coal. Six hundred years after his book was completed, Marco Polo's observations were verified. Even though some parts of his book seemed questionable to Westerners, his descriptions of China's riches were believed because they matched what had been known for centuries through

East-West trade, and they raised the hopes of ambitious men.

East-West trade by land continued for some time, but by the fifteenth century, expeditions were sent to find a speedier and less troublesome sea route from Europe to the Indies and China by traveling around Africa. Of great appeal but clouded by the ignorance of the time was an untested theory that if the earth were indeed round instead of flat, it would be possible to reach Asia by sailing west. Armed with Marco Polo's book, a tenacious and courageous but frequently dictatorial and delusive man named Christopher Columbus boldly proposed to the King and Queen of Spain that he could reach China by sailing to the west. Supremely self-confident, Columbus won the support of the Spanish rulers. In his preparations, he secured a letter of introduction from the Spanish court to the emperor of China and also lay a store of similar letters left blank so he could insert the names of other Asian potentates he might meet. His company included a scholarly Jew who could speak Arabic and whom, it was hoped, could serve as a translator with the Asians. Landing in 1492 on the shores of San Salvador in the Bahamas and later on Cuba and Hispaniola, Columbus believed he had found the island outposts of China, especially when he found a few gold nose pieces among the Arawak natives. He searched high and low in vain for greater evidence of and direction to China's imperial court and wealth.

Desperately undertaking three more expeditions, and returning from the third in chains after being relieved of command for his oppressive administration, Columbus found little to show for his efforts beyond slaves and the natives' habit of smoking tobacco, which in time would be worth "all the tea in China." Columbus fervently believed that one more voyage would find the elusive passage to the Chinese emperor and Japanese shoguns. In his copy of Marco Polo's book, which still exists today, Columbus wrote extensive notes, many of which attempted to tie his discoveries with those described by Marco. Even as he began to realize that he was exploring unknown lands rather than China, Columbus reasoned that this "Other World" must be a land mass tapering off of the Malay Peninsula. The pathetic admiral who had found the New World but dreamed only of Cathay, the "Earthly Paradise," died in 1506, disgraced and disillusioned. En route home after his first voyage, Columbus wrote a letter to Lord Raphael Sanchez, one of his patrons. Dated March 14, 1493, the letter names his objective and shows how he pressed his futile search:

> As soon as we arrived . . . I proceeded along its coast a short distance westward and found it to be so large and apparently . . . the continental province of Cathay. Seeing, however, no towns or populous places . . . I went further on, thinking that in my progress I should certainly find some city or village.

After Magellan's expedition in 1522 verified the possibility of sailing west to reach Asia, people began to realize that Columbus had discovered an unknown continent. Though the expeditions revolutionized the Western conception of the world, interest in the unknown lands themselves remained slight for some time. The Americas were regarded as a curiosity, a barrier in the search for the long-cherished safe and swift route to the "fabled realm of Cathay." After exhausting and costly expeditions around Africa, the Portuguese founded a trading port at Macao in 1557, an accomplishment which spurred greater efforts by other Europeans to find a western route to Asia through the New World. To avoid the extremely dangerous Strait of Magellan and the lengthy voyage around the tip of South America, route-seekers embarked on the costly and time-consuming task of exploring North America for a water passage through the continent. Commissioned by the silk merchants of Lyons to find the elusive passage, Giovanni da Verrazano explored the eastern coast of North America in great detail. Working northward from the West Indies in 1524, Verrazano almost reached the northern tip of Newfoundland. First to sight New York bay, the Florentine has been honored by having the world's longest suspension bridge, connecting Brooklyn and Staten Island, named after him in 1964. Four hundred and forty years earlier, Verrazano probably viewed the very same region as worthless, an impediment to the fulfillment of his commission. Most of the explorations for the northeast and northwest passages involved the English. Dutch and French enterprises in North America became significant, but the British eventually drove them away or diminished their influence through force. According to Walter A. Raleigh's *The English Voyages of the Sixteenth Century*:

> But indeed in these timid beginnings nothing was further from the purpose of England than to enter on a contest with other powers for the possession of America. The success of Columbus had set the court of King Henry aflame with the promise that it offered of a direct route to Cathay, 'insomuch that all men, with great admiration, affirmed it to be a thing more divine than human to sail by the West into the East, where the spices grow, by a way that was never known before.' Shortly after this it was ascertained that beyond America there lay a halcyon sea, yielding direct access to the promised land.*

What was the location of the passage to China and Japan—through or around the new continent—and how could it be found remained questions without any answers until 1566. In that year, Sir Humfrey Gilbert's

*Glasgow: James MacLehose and Sons, 1910, p. 13.

publication, "A Discourse to Prove A Passage by the Northwest to Cathaia," stimulated English interest and drive to find the legendary Strait of Asian passage to China. Francis Drake gladly accepted a commission to prove Gilbert's idea and sailed off in 1577 to round the Strait of Magellan and explore the west coast of North America. Probing numerous rivers, bays, and inlets along the entire Pacific coast from the Strait of Magellan up to 48° N near Vancouver, Drake was unable to confirm Sir Gilbert's hypothesis of a Northwest Passage. However, by returning to England in 1580 after a three-year voyage with his slight, 100-ton ship, the Golden Hind, overloaded with the spoils of a Spanish treasure galleon and a rich cargo of cloves from the Spice Islands, Drake returned to Plymouth, England, in triumph. The voyage made Drake the first captain to sail completely around the world, and he may have been the first European to sail through the Golden Gate into the Bay of San Francisco. Queen Elizabeth, who boarded the Golden Hind to knight the commoner Drake, reaped many more rich returns from her favorite's plundering of Spanish ships and possessions until his death at sea in 1596. Many years later, in 1936, a brass plaque was found near Bodega Bay, a few miles north of the Golden Gate. Its inscription corresponds with Drake's records of striking such a plate to commemorate his taking the territory on behalf of Queen Elizabeth and naming it New Albion (New England). After Drake's historic voyage, the English regarded the unknown land as a separate continent worthy of exploration in its own right, apart from the objective of reaching China and Asia by sea. Today, the dramatic and colorful Golden Gate Bridge in the West and the stately Verrazano-Narrows Bridge of the eastern American shores symbolize a unique and unsung theme relating China and Asia to the Americas and Europe. From Marco Polo to Francis Drake, the many explorers surpassed fiction in their courage and adventuresomeness.

China's Ties with the
American Revolution

While Drake was on the high seas testing Sir Humfrey Gilbert's theory of a Northwest Passage, Queen Elizabeth I consented to grant the same Sir Humfrey a royal charter in 1578 to discover "remote heathen and barbarous lands not actually possessed by any Christian prince or people ... and the same to have, hold, occupy, and enjoy," providing that all settlers who went out with him should "enjoy all the privileges of free denizens and persons native of England," and that any laws or ordinances he might pass for his colony "be as neere as conveniently may, agreeable to the forms of the laws and policy of England." Those key provisions of the charter set a historical precedent that would determine the independence of the American people and the birth of the United States of America. According to Samuel Eliot Morison, "the last two principles, new in the history of colonization, became basic English colonial policy," so that colonial leaders such as Gilbert intended to be (and Lord Baltimore and William Penn later became), "could not play dictator but must govern by English law."* The two provisions for the equality and freedom of English settlers in the New World according to the English system, therefore, laid the seed for the revolutionary sentiments of the American colonists nearly 200 years later. From Gilbert, who failed to carve out a successful New World colony himself, the royal charter passed through inheritance to his half-brother, Sir Walter Raleigh, the Queen's favorite courtier. The First Charter of Virginia, 1606, includes the following: "... all and every of the persons being our subjects, ... and every of their children . . . shall have and enjoy all liberties, franchises, and immunities, . . . as if they had

Oxford History of the American People (New York: Oxford University Press, 1965), p. 44.

been abiding and born, within this Our Realm of England. . . ." Raleigh spared nothing to colonize what he named the Virginia Colony after Elizabeth, the Virgin Queen, but the colony floundered from the start. Disease, famine, Indian attacks, and disorganization resulted in many deaths and regularly brought the colony to a state of near-collapse. After many years of dismal failure, the Virginia Colony found a way to success. John Rolfe, who had taken Pocahontas, an Indian princess, as his wife, crossed the local tobacco with West Indies tobacco in 1613 and produced a smooth smoke that became the rage in England. Within five years, 50,000 pounds of the leaf were being shipped to England annually.

By 1619, the military-like governance of Virginia had evolved into more of a representative system as the first legislative assembly of the New World was founded and began its work. The transition had been ensured by Sir Humfrey Gilbert's royal charter which established the pattern for future charters. In 1624, King James I annulled the Virginia charter two years after another bloody massacre of colonists by Indians, and Virginia became a crown colony with a governor. However, Charles I, who succeeded James I in 1625, maintained the Virginia House of Burgesses, the representative assembly, and the rule of common law. A century and a half later, in 1775, Patrick Henry would make his famous "Give me liberty or give me death" speech in the very same House of Burgesses where many American patriots, such as Thomas Jefferson, would deliberate the question of revolution. The stage was set for third-generation colonists to confront a hostile Parliament and King George III who could little understand their distant subjects, even if they had not been so preoccupied with Old World politics and conflicts. This historic setting came about in large part due to the farsightedness of a man whose primary goal was not the New World but China. Since the Boston Tea Party will be dealt with later, suffice it to say at this point that the tea dumped into Boston Harbor in 1773 came from Guangzhou, China, and that the act of protest went beyond the import duties imposed by England on the Americans. As the Declaration of Independence states, the colonists were especially incensed with the King's "cutting off our Trade with all Parts of the World."

The Unparalleled History of the Jesuits in China

The dramatic encounter between the East and West covered in this section rivals the most imaginative movie script. Learning the story of the Jesuits in China might lead one to speculate what might have happened had the service of the Jesuits in China continued longer than it did, or had their work in China never occurred. The relationship between the Jesuits and the Chinese began in 1583 when Father Matteo Ricci (1552–1610), a Jesuit missionary, was admitted to Macao where he began his life-long study of Chinese culture and language. From Macao, Father Ricci travelled to Zhaoqing, Shaognan, and Nanchang before settling in Nanjing. In 1601, he finally received permission to go to Beijing, the nation's capital. Unlike other travellers to China, Father Ricci and the over 900 Jesuits who entered China between 1583 and the end of the eighteenth century became diligent students of the Chinese language and culture. Their adaptability and learnedness brought the Jesuits far greater success than might have been expected.

Upon his arrival in Beijing, Father Ricci faced the seemingly impossible task of obtaining an audience with the Ming emperor Wan Li. Wan Li's reign began in 1582 and lasted until 1620. During those thirty-eight years, the emperor rarely dealt with affairs of state and the irresponsible ruler isolated himself and frittered his time away with amusements. The tall, personable Father Ricci appeared one day at the palace gate and stayed there. When the guards came to shoo him away, Father Ricci told them that he had something to present to the emperor and showed an elaborate clock he held, which the guards took into the palace. When in time the clock ran down and stopped, the court knew nothing of its mechanism and ordered the guards to locate Ricci and have him come to put it right. There was no need to search very far; the guards found Father Ricci waiting at the very same gate, as if he knew he would be summoned. Father Ricci obligingly entered the palace for the first time, rewound the clock, and departed. This happened several more times, until the emperor asked Father Ricci to stay and explain the clock's mechanism, as well as that of a second clock and a clavichord the clever Jesuit had also presented. In time, Ricci obtained imperial recognition as a scholar and his influence and acceptance grew so that he and his small group of Jesuits converted 200 members of the court to Christianity. Using the principle of working from the top of the government down, the Jesuits made use of their rank as mandarins. They donned the gown of Confucian scholars which under the Qing rulers included a colorful mandarin square positioned across the chest area of the gown. A bird insignia on this square and a colored button on the hat indicated the rank of scholar-official that had been conferred.

Working with another Italian Jesuit, Father P. M. Ruggieri, Father Ricci compiled the first dictionary translating Chinese into a Western language when the two completed a Portugese-Chinese lexicon. Father Ricci produced a number of books during his twenty-eight years in China. At ease with the Chinese intellectuals who befriended him, Father Ricci worked closely with the Ming scientist and Minister of Rites, Xu Guangqi. Xu became Father Ricci's student and with him translated Euclid's *Elements* to promote the knowledge of plane geometry in China. With the assistance of another outstanding Chinese scholar, Li Zhizao, Father Ricci translated the *Guide to Mathematics*, which gave China much information on Western methods of calculation. Six other important textbooks from Europe dealing with science were translated by Father Ricci and his Chinese assistants. As an author, Ricci wrote *On Friendship, The Twenty-Five Words, Western Methods of Memory, The Secure Treatise on God*, and *The Ten Paradoxes*. The latter two works attempt to interrelate Catholicism with Confucianism. Father Ricci's *History of the Introduction of Christianity in China* covered the history of the Jesuits in China with a record of his many years there and provided an introduction to Chinese economy, ideology, history, geography, politics, science and technology, culture, religion, and customs. The first carefully researched study of China by a Westerner, Ricci's *History* drew many readers in Europe after its translation from Italian into Latin.

When Father Ricci died in 1610, Jesuit centers could be found in three Chinese cities, and Christianity had the respect of many court members. Consisting of 7,000 volumes from Europe, the Jesuit library provided excellent reference material of which the hard-working Jesuits translated about 400 into Chinese by the end of the seventeenth century. The Ming court utilized Jesuit knowledge in mathematics, astronomy, architecture, armaments, engraving, and world geography. Astute, learned, and delightfully interesting in conversation, the Jesuits served throughout the palace as tutors, interpreters, medics, musicians, and painters. Jesuit astronomers headed the bureau in charge of the imperial calendar during the late Ming and early Qing dynasties. By 1701, the Jesuits had built 208 churches and chapels and had 70 mission residences.

While Marco Polo's acceptance by the Mongol court

in the thirteenth century involved a highly personalized
relation, the Jesuits' history in China spanned two dynasties, a number of emperors, and a total of 900 missionaries, thus involving a high degree of institutionali-
zation. To appreciate the highly unusual nature of
China's relationship with the Jesuit Society, we can attempt to imagine similar relations in European courts.
What would have been the consequences and how
would we view the relations of Chinese missionaries, say
Buddhists or Confucian scholars, to the courts of Elizabeth I, the Great Elector Frederick William, and Louis
XIV? Although the possibility of such East-West relations seems incredible, the reverse did occur with the
followers of St. Ignatius Loyola (1491–1556), who
founded the Jesuit Society. It is not very difficult to find
and understand the reasons why the Chinese did not go
to the West. The overall superiority of the Chinese during ancient times, as we know from Marco Polo, and
their self-sufficiency created no sense of mission in
China to seek relations with the West and concert with
European rulers. What religious urges the pragmatic
Chinese possessed did not cause them to proselyte and
seek converts. The Chinese sensibility was one of tolerance and passivity as expressed in the Confucian version of the Golden Rule: "Do not do unto others . . ." as
opposed to the Christian version of "Do unto others . . ."
Loyola's *Constitutions* of the Society of Jesus, which still
regulates Jesuit operations today for over 30,000 priests,
professed that above all, the apostles would be "ready to
live in any part of the world where there was hope of
God's greater glory and the good of souls." Therefore, if
improbable events were to occur, and in those days this
would seem more improbable than the moon landings
and space program of today, they had to be accomplished by the Jesuits, and they were.

Concentrating their attention on the emperors they
served, the Jesuits aimed to convert each ruler to
Christianity, from whence they would work to convert

the entire population with imperial assistance. Kow-towing prostrate before the Emperor as proper schol-ar-officials, the Jesuits worked assiduously to instruct and satisfy. Their close relationship with the Qing em-perors was unparalleled, as we shall see. Two Jesuits, one German-born and the other Belgian, stand out for their influence and special affinity with the imperial court during many significant years. The first was Adam Schall von Bell, who arrived in China in 1622, twelve years after Matteo Ricci's death. Father Schall would dedicate the forty-four remaining years of his life to service in China. Fleming Ferdinand Verbiest, who went to Beijing in 1660, worked in China until his death in 1688. The service of Fathers Schall and Verbiest over-lapped for six years, during which the young Verbiest learned much from the aging Schall. The influence of Ricci, Schall, and Verbiest spanned eighty-seven years of dramatic history. Shortly after Father Verbiest died in 1688, a group of six French Jesuits arrived in Beijing to carry on and extend the historic relationship between East and West. Since the Jesuit order remained in force until it was abolished for forty-one years beginning in 1773, Jesuits worked in China long past the outcome of the dispute between the Pope and Emperor in 1705. This section benefits from a number of sources, particularly personal communications with Father Francis A. Rou-leau, S.J., (who celebrated sixty years of Jesuit service on October 13, 1983!) and the book, *Jesuit Adventure in China*, by Eloise Talcott Hibbert.* The author, however, is solely responsible for any errors.

When visiting Beijing today, one can visit the spectac-ular Temple of Heaven (Tian Tan), the most famous temple in China, built originally in 1420. The emperor carried out two ceremonies at the temple each year that demonstrated his unique relationship to the heavens and his subjects. Only the emperor could perform these

*New York: Dutton, 1941.

rites, which at the first month of the year rendered homage and sought the confidence of the heavens so they would grant a good harvest for his people, and at the winter solstice informed the heavens of the vital events of the past year. Most imposing of all the structures at the Temple of Heaven is the Qi Nian Dian or the Hall of Prayer for Good Harvests, which stands on a three-layered, marble terrace with a balustrade encircling each layer. Twenty-eight columns made from trees laboriously transported from forests of the southernmost part of China, Yunnan, support the round hall, which has a diameter of ninety-six feet. Sixty feet high, the four largest columns stand in the center to symbolize the four seasons. Encircling the four pillars are two circles of twelve columns each. The innermost circle represents the twelve months of the year and the outermost circle the twelve hours of the day (the ancient Chinese divided the day into twelve hours instead of twenty-four). Not a nail went into the highly intricate framework and roof. Temple of Heaven rites, performed as late as the 1914 winter solstice when President Yuan Shi Kai wanted to restore the throne, give insight into the importance of the imperial responsibility to accurately maintain the calendar. This royal duty necessitated great skill by the court astronomer to accurately foretell the seasonal changes and position of the heavenly bodies.

In 1610, the court astronomers, who were then Muslim, erred by several hours in forecasting an eclipse. Seeing their opportunity to gain greater influence in the court, the Jesuits decided to import their own astronomer, thus bringing Father Schall to China in 1622. The last Ming emperor, Chong Zhen, took a strong liking to the scholarly and delightful Schall and appointed him the royal astronomer with the rank of a high official. When the Ming dynasty fell, Father Schall recorded for history how its last emperor hung himself in Coal Hill Park, just north of the palace, on March 17, 1644. Father Schall wrote that Emperor Chong Zhen, in utter defeat and despair, ordered the empress to strangle herself and sent his three sons to flee the city. Then, according to the Jesuit priest,

> Finally, he did not know what to do himself, so he left the palace once more but on foot; he went straight to the hill which is behind the palace to the place where once he had examined the cannons which I had cast. . . . He took off his boots and threw back his imperial headdress, then he hanged himself from a beam at the entrance to the above mentioned place.

The Qing conquerors did not harm Father Schall as the Chinese Christians had feared they might. Remaining in Beijing during the upheaval without the company of other Jesuits, he watched the city burn in a great conflagration which miraculously stopped at the edge of his church. He gave assistance throughout the city as best he could. When the Manchus ordered him to leave Beijing, Father Schall asked them in his excellent Chinese to be allowed to remain. Summoned to court to discuss his petition, Prince Jui, the regent, decided to ask Schall to continue as royal astronomer, a function he had fulfilled for the Mings for over twenty years.

Not long into the new dynasty, the Qing leader, Tai Zong, died suddenly without having named an heir. The six-year-old Shun Ji was chosen by the high officials to be the next emperor. During his youth, Shun Ji formed a strong friendship with Father Adam Schall. Tutored and entertained by Father Schall, the boy emperor often left the palace to visit the Jesuit residence, church, library, and grounds. The two conversed for hours about far-away places and foreign customs. In great respect, Shun Ji gave Father Schall the Chinese name of *Ma Fa* which in Manchu means "Venerable Father" or "Grand-father." At the age of thirteen, the young emperor ascended the throne and ruled for only ten years. His reign had prospered until his favorite concubine, Deng Guife, whom he loved greatly, died. In less than six months,

Shun Ji's death from smallpox was announced. However, a rumor spread that Shun Ji had abdicated the
throne and forsaken the world to become a Buddhist
recluse. Credence for the rumor has come from various
sources, most notable is the fact that Emperor Kang Xi,
who succeeded Shun Ji, visited a hermit monk in the
Buddhist monastery of the Wu Tai mountains over the
years and sent great sums in support of the monastery.
Father Schall had seen less and less of Shun Ji as the
Emperor turned more and more to Buddhism after the
Dalai Lama journeyed from Tibet to visit him. Also, a
definite falling out had occurred when the Emperor
followed the Chinese custom of having multiple wives
against Father Schall's advice.

Shun Ji made careful arrangments for his succession
and named his seven-year-old son, Kang Xi ("Unalterable Peace"), as the emperor-to-be. Shun Ji also appointed Father Schall to be Kang Xi's tutor. Father
Schall found the young heir to the throne to be extremely bright and inquisitive. While Shun Ji had listened intently to Western ideas and found them interesting, he had remained a devout Buddhist and did not
apply what he learned from the Jesuits. Kang Xi was different. He pursued the knowledge of both the East
and West and tried to combine them for the best
blend or synthesis possible. Kang Xi gave particular attention to scientific studies which he pursued all his
life. The Empress-Dowager, Bochita, encouraged her
grandson's studies with Father Schall despite the
fact that her Manchu heritage and conversion to Buddhism made her suspicious of foreigners. She cherished the aging Jesuit because he had once cured her
of a strange illness and because of his complete devotion to her son, Shun Ji, She wanted Kang Xi to remember his father and his ideals. One of China's greatest emperors, Kang Xi ruled for sixty-one years, until 1722.

In the interim, before Kang Xi took the throne at age
thirteen, the Jesuits found themselves in prison in

chains, accused by the regents of distorting the truth and plotting insurrection. The accusations were made by a Mohammedan mathematician who wanted to take Father Schall's place as royal astronomer. Bribing the most powerful of the four regents in control of the empire, the accuser succeeded in having all Jesuits in China arrested and brought to Beijing. Father Schall lost his official posts, and his disability due to apoplexy grew worse as he lost the ability to speak. In the same prison cell with Father Schall was a recently arrived Jesuit astronomer named Fleming Ferdinand Verbiest. The young Jesuit had reached China in 1660 after his first attempt to travel to the East was thwarted in 1656. En route to China with Procurator Father Marino Martini, who had recruited nine Jesuits to serve in China, via Malabar, where three other Jesuits and the Malabar Procurator were destined, Father Verbiest's Dutch galleon came under attack by a French privateer. After a bloody battle fought by cannon and hand-to-hand combat, the Dutch captain surrendered to the French pirates. Held for ransom on a small island near Provence, France, for about a month, Father Verbiest and the group of weary Jesuits straggled back to Genoa by circuitous routes, in rags and suffering from the terrifying experience.

No stranger to imprisonment, therefore, and incarcerated in Beijing with the probability of receiving the death penalty, Father Verbiest became the Jesuits' spokesman, even though he spoke only rudimentary Chinese. In this, as in other moments of crisis, Father Verbiest displayed cool-headedness and intelligence. The missionaries had been accused of conspiracy, teaching pernicious doctrine, and pursuing inaccurate astronomy, and Verbiest concentrated his efforts on refuting the last accusation. Of the three charges, its merits could be best challenged objectively. With references from Chinese and Western sources which he studied at length despite the chains and the prison conditions,

Father Verbiest prepared unequivocal challenges to the
accusers' logic and disproved all approaches they took
to discredit the Jesuits. In time, all Jesuits escorted to
Beijing from the provinces were sent to Guangzhou, and
Father Schall's three companions in Beijing, including
Father Verbiest, were banished to Tartary. This was due
to the fact that none of the Jesuits except Father Schall
had been in Beijing when it was alleged that Father
Schall had chosen the wrong day to bury the infant son
of Emperor Shun Ji and his favorite concubine. Even
though Father Verbiest's arguments during the three
months of deliberations won more than could have
been hoped for, the sentence of death by a thousand
cuts, a hideous punishment, was given Father Schall.
Learning of the sentence, Fathers Schall, Verbiest,
Buglio, and Magalhaens prayed for deliverance through
a miracle. A few days after their prayers for divine intervention, earthquake tremors suddenly shook the city
and brought great destruction. At that moment, the
court officials were convening in the palace for the formal confirmation of the death decree for Father Schall;
the earthquake shook the building with great violence.
Death warrant in hand, the Empress-Dowager Bochita
was about to tell the assemblage that it had her consent
to proceed with the execution when the palace walls
shook and the ground rolled and rumbled. Everyone
fled into the palace courtyard and in a short time, another wave of shocks took place. Bochita cried out, "A
pardon for all prisoners!"

Panic swept through Beijing and the populace said
that the Christian God had expressed his displeasure
and had given a dire warning that should be heeded.
The regents allowed Fathers Verbiest, Buglio, and
Magalhaens to return to their Jesuit compound but
kept Father Schall in chains. Father Verbiest refused to
leave the ailing Schall and remained in prison with him.
During the following months, a series of ill omens

occurred which finally convinced the regents to release
Father Schall. First, a comet appeared and the ominous
sight in the sky created fear because comets were
thought to foretell a change in dynasty. Next a strange
white bird the size of a sheep appeared on the roof of
the imperial palace. Finally, fire completely destroyed
the Empress-Dowager's living quarters.

After his release, the old man returned to his residence where he passed away in less than a year. Although the Jesuits escaped physical punishment in
the end, it was not until Kang Xi's reign that the severe restrictions placed upon the activities of the Jesuits were reversed. In the meantime, the regents put to
death five of the Chinese who had learned astronomy
from the Jesuits and become Christians.

With the support of his grandmother, the young Kang
Xi assumed the throne not long after Father Schall's
trial ended in 1666. The death of one of the four regents,
no doubt viewed as another punishment by God for the
mistreatment of the Jesuits, gave Kang Xi, though only
thirteen years old, the way to early power. The emperor
exerted strong and purposeful leadership from the start
of his reign, which was to be a highly constructive and
creative one. Kang Xi tried the most powerful of the
three remaining regents for conspiracy and put the duke
and his entire family to death as was the Chinese custom. Seeing that the Mohammedan astronomer, who
had replaced Father Schall as royal astronomer through
his false accusations, had made repeated astronomical
errors, the emperor sent courtiers to the Jesuits to make
unofficial inquiries regarding the errors. Father Verbiest's answers prompted Kang Xi to summon Verbiest
to him. The Emperor asked the Jesuit astronomer if he
could propose a suitable test to determine whose astronomical method was more accurate. Saying it would
be simple, Father Verbiest suggested that the test consist of predicting the noon shadow of three sticks placed

in the ground on any day the Emperor selected. Pleased with the proposed test of skill and theory, Kang Xi proceeded to carry it out even though Verbiest's opponent broke court etiquette and entered into a lengthy tirade against the Westerners. The Jesuits reported that Kang Xi maintained his self-control and composure despite the serious breach and the aspersion of his youthful inexperience. At the test the next day, the Mohammedan failed in three attempts to produce the correct calculation while Father Verbiest's results were successful. The emperor ordered the arrest of the Mohammedan imposter who had destroyed Father Schall and appointed Father Verbiest the new royal astronomer and vice-president of the mathematical tribunal.

After observing the Westerners for more than a year, even using a student spy planted in the Jesuit school, Kang Xi became convinced of the Jesuits' forthrightness and honesty. Aware of the highly political and xenophobic setting in which he worked, Father Verbiest did not take his position as royal astronomer for granted. He played his role with discretion and openness, as when he informed the emperor that he could not name an auspicious day for the reconstruction of a portion of the palace as he could for agricultural concerns. Doing their best to honor and satisfy the emperor, the Jesuits would produce interesting items, such as a book titled *Memories of the Occident*, which told of faraway places. They pleased the emperor with a calendar he had requested that covered 2,000 years, and gratified him further by adding Kang Xi's name in the finished work. In such ways, the indefatigable Jesuits gained the emperor's favor and support. Raising Father Verbiest to the rank of mandarin of the first class with the title of *ta jen* ("great man"), Kang Xi set aside a special study in the palace where Father Verbiest went early each day and stayed until night. The two conversed for hours and Verbiest explained Western mathematics, astronomy,

and engineering. In 1670, Kang Xi honored Father
Adam Schall posthumously and had his tombstone engraved to indicate the court's respect for his many contributions and good example. Fleming Ferdinand Verbiest served Kang Xi for two decades during which
these two extraordinary men with disparate cultural
heritages and equally disparate commitments maintained a close working relationship.

A rebellion erupted in South China in 1672 under the
leadership of Wu San Gui who had helped the Manchus
to defeat the Ming. Rewarded by the Manchus with the
title of prince and the independent viceroyalty of two
rich provinces in the south, Wu had, in time, grown
discontented. Many patriots yearned to expel the foreign Manchus from China and they finally prevailed
upon Wu San Gui to join in a revolution. During this
emergency, Kang Xi faced the problem of worn and
inoperative cannon armaments. To solve the problem of
the cannons, Kang Xi ordered Father Verbiest to over-
haul 300 worn fieldpieces. Although Father Schall had
cast cannons for the Ming, Father Verbiest felt uneasy
about such work. Nevertheless, he complied with the
royal request and rebuilt the fieldpieces so well that the
war minister complimented Verbiest highly. Though
repaired, the heavy armaments were difficult to transport, a problem Kang Xi asked Father Verbiest to solve
as well. Designing a smaller cannon that worked excel-
lently in all respects, Father Verbiest constructed more
than 300 fieldpieces, eight of which were ornamented
with the royal symbol of the dragon and were presented
to the emperor for his own use. Father Verbiest blessed
the cannons with holy water and gave each fieldpiece
the name of a holy saint instead of engraving his own
name as had been requested. Delighted with the eight
cannons presented to him, Kang Xi took them whenever
he went abroad to hunt in Tartary where he enjoyed
firing them to impress the nomads. As might have been

expected, the religious authorities in Rome criticized the armaments work and initiated ominous steps to restrict the activities of the Jesuits in China.

The Dominican and Franciscan orders had sent missionaries to Asia, some of whom entered China. In time, their reports raising severe questions about the accommodations made by the Jesuits, especially their tolerance of ancestor worship and Chinese rites in the Mass, eventually brought about the great Rites Controversy. The strongly contested dispute finally brought the Jesuit order a papal reproof and ended the work of all Catholic missionaries in China. However, before the grand history of the Jesuits in China ended during the reign of Qian Long (1735–1796) (the great-grandson of Kang Xi), Father Verbiest and the other Jesuits provided diligent assistance to the throne in hopes of someday converting the emperor to Christianity as they had successfully done with many members of the court and royal family. Father Verbiest even served as an interpreter and minister of foreign affairs with envoys from Holland, Portugal, Russia, and Siam, and he seemed indispensable to Kang Xi. At Father Verbiest's death in 1688, Emperor Kang Xi expressed his great grief and respect for his friend by conducting an unprecedented funeral with an elaborate procession through the city streets. The procession, which was prepared jointly by the court and the Jesuits, included a thirty-foot-trophy painted red on which Father Verbiest's name and titles were prominent; a huge Christian cross from which flags were hung, carried between rows of converts, dressed in white, holding lighted candles and handkerchiefs to dry their tears; drawings of the Virgin and other saints, also escorted by converts; and the Emperor's proclamation which read as follows:

> We seriously consider within ourselves that Father Verbiest has, of his own good will, left Europe to come to our domains, and has spent the greater part of his life in our service; we must say this for him,

that during all the time he took care of the mathematics, his predictions never failed, but always agreed with the motions of the heavens. Besides, far from neglecting our orders, he has ever proved himself exact, diligent, faithful, unalterable, and constant in his labor until he has finished his work.

On his death bed, Father Verbiest wrote with enfeebled hand the following last letter to Kang Xi:

Dread Sire, I die content, in that I have spent almost all my life in your majesty's service, but I beg your majesty will be pleased to remember when I am dead, that my only aim was to gain in the great monarch of the East a protector of the most holy religion in the world.

For over 150 years, China's leaders obtained the best of Western learning from the Jesuits, by conversing with them in fluent Chinese, and by reading the hundreds of publications they had translated into classical Chinese. Father Ricci had set an example by translating the works of Euclid and other mathematical works and by drawing a world map. In numerous letters and reports, which included drawings and engravings, throughout their service in China, the Jesuits gave the West detailed information about China, its rulers, and people, most of which was complimentary and influential enough to help stimulate the revolutionary Age of Enlightenment. One crucial theme of the age concerned the separation of church and state versus the principle of divine rule. To the Europeans, the Chinese served as an example of a natural society that existed very well or very poorly, depending on the bias of the many writers who made reference to China. Jesuit writings, such as Father Joachim Bouvet's *The History of Cang-Hy the Present Emperor of China* (1699), supported those who saw China as a society with a natural morality independent of religious structures and strictures. Deists, advocating morality and natural religion based on reason instead of revelation, and Physiocrats, French political economists who, anticipating the industrial revolution and the rise of the middle class, believed that governments should not be involved in the operation of natural economic laws, all found China, as favorably described by the Jesuits, to be a society from which Europe could learn much.

Especially prolific were the French Jesuits, six of whom Louis XIV (1638–1715) sent from his court in 1685 as his special ambassadors to Kang Xi. The two monarchs had many similarities; the fact that they were both strongly influenced by Jesuit court officials was one parallel.

After a difficult journey of almost three years, during which the xenophobic Viceroy of Nimpo imprisoned them until the ailing Father Verbiest obtained an order from Kang Xi for their safe passage, the six French Jesuits reached Beijing in January 1688, only to find that Father Verbiest had died before they arrived.

Father Jean Francois Gerbillon, a sophisticated courtier who was facile in languages, gave Emperor Kang Xi much assistance in diplomatic negotiations. Father Louis Le Comte wrote a history of China which provided interesting insights. Fathers Pierre Jartoux and Jean Baptiste Regis led the great mapping survey of the whole of China as ordered by the Emperor. Started in 1708, the atlas was finished in 1717 and a copy was produced in Europe. Besides writing Kang Xi's biography, Father Bouvet tutored the emperor in mathematics and science. Father Bouvet also served as Kang Xi's emissary by returning to France in 1693 to establish trade relations between France and China and to present Kang Xi's gift of forty-eight specially translated and printed volumes to Louis XIV. Although Louis did not appreciate the precious volumes, the books found their way to the royal library in Paris and became the nucleus of what is today one of the world's greatest collections of ancient Chinese works. Father Bouvet

brought new pleasures to the Beijing court when he
enticed the Italian painter Gio Ghirardini to paint in
China. Giuseppe Castiglione also joined them and these
European artists introduced Western art styles to China
and were in turn influenced by Chinese art forms.
Father Bouvet and Father Gerbillon became the leading
Jesuits in Kang Xi's court after Father Verbiest. They
obtained astronomical instruments, thermometers,
watches, clocks, and even a water fountain which
spouted a jet thirty feet high. They worked diligently
with Kang Xi as had their predecessors, even curing him
of malaria. Kang Xi repaid the Jesuits by building a
church for them and giving the French Jesuits a residence within the palace. Outstandingly trained as scholars and scientists, the French missionaries represented
well the high level of intellect and ability the Jesuits
brought to the court of China.

Well-connected with the French court and Western
intellectuals, the French Jesuits sent a tremendous
amount of information about China to a receptive Europe. Francois Quesnay (1694–1794), the prominent
French physician and economist who led the Physiocrats, wrote a book titled *The Despotism of China* (1767),
which gained him the nickname of "Confucius of the
West." Quesnay praised the Chinese, though he felt they
were despotic, for operating under the principle of natural law. Calling the society of China near-perfect,
Quesnay commended key features of China, such as the
absence of a hereditary nobility, and the fact that
property was passed from father to son but the son
could achieve the community's respect only through his
own efforts and deeds. The German mathematician and
philosopher Gottfried Wilhelm Leibniz (1646–1716),
who invented differential and analytical calculus, actually corresponded with Kang Xi and proposed cultural exchanges between China and Europe in his book
New Treatise on China. Through a translation of the
ancient Chinese classic *The Book of Changes*, Leibniz

found the principles of the Eight Diagrams (eight combinations of three whole or broken lines) developed by Fu Xi over 7,000 years ago to be mathematically generalizable. Leibniz extended the work which eventually led to the world's first mechanical calculating machine based on the binary system, a model of which he sent to Kang Xi. Francois Voltaire (1694–1778), the great French writer who crusaded against tyranny and bigotry, praised the governmental system of China most highly in his *Essay on Morals* (1756). He cited the facts that the first duty of government in China was toward the public welfare, and that the laws arising from the Chinese concept of the kingdom as a family not only stimulated public works and economic prosperity for all but also punished crime and rewarded virtue.

Based on the belief that mankind can find knowledge and happiness through the power of reason, the Age of Enlightenment created a new outlook on society and self-determination. The movement evolved from the sixteenth-century beginnings of the scientific revolution and from a return to ancient Greek philosophy, which championed human reason. Intellectual leaders challenged the old tenets of Christianity which permeated all aspects of society and which sanctioned a lockstep establishment of political rule through noble heredity and privilege. The Enlightenment, therefore, sought a separation between church and state and a distinction between religion and morality, views which created new perceptions of individual and social/political rights. Enlightenment writers in England, such as John Locke (1632–1704), greatly influenced American intellectuals and their philosophies were critical of the American Revolution. Educated colonials were well-acquainted with Locke's *Two Treatises of Government* (1690) and *Essays on the Law of Nature* (1690). Jefferson commissioned life-size busts of Locke, Francis Bacon (1561–1626), and Isaac Newton (1642–1727) for his home, Monticello, which can be seen there today. Jefferson, one of the greatest of the great himself, praised them as "the three greatest men that have ever lived, without any exception, and as having laid the foundation of those superstructures which have been raised in the physical and moral sciences."

According to the philosophy of natural law, the world operated through reasonable and discoverable laws of nature as set forth by God's universal plan. Locke wrote that people as natural beings had the capacity and freedom to arrange their lives. They should be able to handle themselves and their property according to their own desires and should also be able to institute systems of government through common consent to maintain an orderly and proper society. Such viewpoints made freedom of mind, conscience, and person inalienable, as Thomas Jefferson made indelible forever in the Declaration of Independence:

> We hold these Truths to be self-evident, that all Men are created equal, that they are endowed by their Creator with certain inalienable Rights, that among these are Life, Liberty, and the Pursuit of Happiness—That to secure these Rights, Governments are instituted among Men, deriving their just Powers from the Consent of the Governed, that whenever any Form of Government becomes destructive of these Ends, it is the Right of the People to alter or to abolish it, and to institute new Government, laying its Foundation on such Principles, and organizing its Powers in such Form, as to them shall seem most likely to effect their Safety and Happiness.

Jefferson and other early American leaders rarely referred to China in their writings, and their biographies merely mention in passing their trade interests and incidents involving China. For example, Dumas Malone's *Jefferson The President: Second Term, 1805–1809** talks about an episode in 1808 in which President Jefferson

*Boston: Little, Brown, pp. 596–597.

fell victim to a hoax by the financier John Jacob Astor. It appears that many American ships delivering cargo abroad sailed back to the United States in ballast (empty) because of the government's restrictions on imports to protect American producers. The embargo law gave the president some discretion to issue permits under special circumstances. While at Monticello in late summer seeking relief from Washington's heat, Jefferson had before him nearly 100 petitions for shipping permits, one of which was from a Punqua Winchong, supposedly a Chinese merchant and mandarin official. Winchong's visit to Washington received a favorable report from the *National Intelligencer* and a note from a New York senator introduced the Chinese dignitary to the president. Jefferson approved the request, "believing that the granting of this petition would amount to a diplomatic act and have favorable results in the mandarin's generally inaccessible country." However, Winchong turned out to be a complete impostor and no Chinese were connected with the petition. Some months later, after the import embargo had been repealed, the Beaver, a ship owned by Astor, returned from Guangzhou with a cargo worth a cool 200,000 dollars.

Jesuit writings from China, especially those by the French missionaries, provided much intellectual stimulus for Western intellectuals. Religious and language differences perhaps made it less likely that English philosophers would read the Jesuit reports for their analyses. Nevertheless, Chinese art and culture became a European vogue throughout most of the eighteenth century. Built in 1763 with a ten-story pagoda, London's Kew Gardens represents the best of a number of Chinese gardens constructed throughout Europe with the "back to nature" theme. Rococo artists found inspiration in the delicate arts of South China, and Chinese art and silk dominated the magnificent masquerades of the French court. Porcelain meant China, the source of the best, and the common name for porcelain in English

became "china," as it is still called today. The French
surpassed the English in their study and incorporation
of Chinese customs; this can be traced directly to the
French Jesuits sent by Louis XIV as ambassadors to the
court of Kang Xi. The French king even imitated the
Chinese custom in which the emperor would plow the
country's first furrows each spring. Invented in China
during the fourth century, the sedan chair or palanquin
won wide popularity in the West during the seventeenth
century. Also of Chinese origin, wallpaper was shipped
to Europe in great quantities in the seventeenth and
eighteenth centuries. Chinoiserie, a French term for art
styles reflecting Chinese motifs, became the rage in
Europe. It influenced architecture and furnishings such
as latticework and decorative Ming-style porcelain. By
the end of the eighteenth century, however, after the
American and French revolutions had succeeded, chinoiserie had faded from vogue. The Jesuit order had been
suspended by the Pope in 1773 (reestablished in 1814),
and Jesuit writings from China ceased their flow. The
Enlightenment gave way to nineteenth-century com-
mercialism and imperialism; China no longer represented a model for Western emulation.

Suspension of the Jesuits in 1773 followed the outcome of the great Rites Controversy. After many years
of study by fact-finding missions sent to China on complaints filed by Dominican and Franciscan missionaries,
the Pope made a final statement, the anti-Jesuit bull of
1715. Before the decree was made, Emperor Kang Xi
sent Jesuit delegations to Europe with many documents
to support the actions of the Jesuits in China. Kang Xi's
well-intentioned communications only brought a back-
lash of hostility in Europe when it was said that his
actions were arrogant challenges to the holy power of
the Pope. After additional Jesuit emissaries sent from
China to Rome by way of Russia were also denounced
by the Pope, Kang Xi terminated his long-standing
correspondence with the Pope. Papal emissaries sent to

Beijing to transmit the anti-Jesuit decree on the Rites
Controversy received hostile treatment from Kang Xi
when it became clear to all that their arguments for the
decision misinterpreted Confucius and the Chinese
classics. The first papal envoy, the Monseigneur Maigrot, made the mistake of pretending to understand
Chinese and its classics. Msgr. Maigrot's document
contained numerous errors and showed poor scholarship. Intolerant of any pretense to scholarship, Kang Xi
asked Msgr. Maigrot to translate the four characters
written over this throne. Unfortunately, the envoy could
explain only two of the four characters. The emperor
ordered Maigrot imprisoned and he was later dumped
aboard a ship headed for Ireland without winter clothing. Msgr. Maigrot returned to Rome nearly two years
later much subdued and changed.

Cardinal de Tournon had gone to Beijing to assist
Msgr. Maigrot, but his lack of training in Chinese language and culture harmed his cause as well. All foreign
missionaries received Chinese names upon their arrival
in China, and the name given Cardinal de Tournon was
To-lo, meaning "imbecile." His weakness and indirec-
tion before the Emperor brought further ridicule, although Kang Xi received him at first with great honor
and patience. In the end, the Cardinal was sent to a
Macao fortress where he died. Pope Clement XI sent
a third envoy in 1719 to study conditions in China.
Given the title of Patriarch of Alexandria, the Monseigneur Mazzabarba fared better than the earlier envoys. Kang Xi asked Msgr. Mazzabarba one question:
whether the Pope had revised his view toward ancestor worship. Learning that the Pope's earlier decree
had not changed, Kang Xi ordered the prelate to
leave China and take other Westerners with him. Kang
Xi permitted the Jesuits who had stood at his side for
years to stay and maintain their churches, provided
that they pledge never to leave China. Observing that

Catholics in Europe could worship as they please, Kang Xi issued the following edict:

> The church you propagate is neither good nor bad for China. And whether you remain or leave will make no difference. When de Tournon came, he listened to the missionary Maigrot who did not understand, who had no knowledge of literary Chinese and who could not even read. How could he determine the right and wrong of China's moral principles? Westerners are small-minded people. Henceforth foreigners are not to teach in China.

Thus the most remarkable relationship between East and West in olden times ended in China with a profound decline of respect for Westerners and all that they represented. There could be no ambivalence for the Chinese, unlike the pattern of other peoples. Yong Zheng, who ruled China after Kang Xi, from 1723 to 1735, belittled the Jesuits who remained in the empire and persecuted them from time to time. Reigning from 1736 to 1796, Kang Xi's great grandson, Qian Long, became, like his great-grandfather, one of China's greatest emperors. Emperor Qian Long revived the Jesuit adventure in China for a short period when he sought their mechanical skills and knowledge to help construct great waterworks.

Kang Xi's great regard for Western science and thought, as represented by his handful of Jesuit scholars, grew into disillusionment and disgust when his exposure to other Westerners in the Rites Controversy proved bitterly disappointing. His change of attitude during his final years would deter China's leanings toward the West and its modernization at the very time that Europe began to emerge anew politically and commercially. Emperor Qian Long's great compilation of the *Four Treasuries*, a 36,000-volume work produced by 15,000 scribes who worked for two decades, occurred in parallel with the suppression and destruction of thousands of writings judged objectionable to the Qing. The scholarship reflected the Qing commitment to the rich inherited traditions of China. The Qing also emphasized the development of public works; they instituted a system of state granaries and encouraged all types of industry, expressing a Confucian concern for the welfare of the people. However, their failure to reach for new ideas and go beyond the past left China illprepared for the nineteenth century.

Nineteenth-Century Imperialism and the China Trade

Westerners of the nineteenth century represented a different type of foreigner than the ones who went to China in earlier times. Traders, missionaries of diverse denominations, and soldiers went to China without the wonderment and respect felt by Marco Polo and the Jesuits. The new foreigners had no desire to accommodate themselves to the ways of China. Instead of being enthralled with what they observed, they found much that appalled them, such as the custom of binding the feet of females. The foreigners objected to the Chinese restriction of trade and began imperialistic moves with the rationale being in part that their interventions would improve the sorry state of the society. After Emperor Qian Long's death in 1796, his successors proved incapable of handling the problems of a population that was growing faster than production, factionalism and the spread of secret societies, and Western intrusions.

Wanting to improve its trade balance with China, the British East India Company began shipping opium to China in 1819. By 1839, Emperor Dao Guang, alarmed by the increase in opium addiction, especially in the army, and by China's great loss of silver, dispatched a stout-hearted official to Guangzhou to "cut off the fountain of evil." Commissioner Lin Zexu promptly took charge of the situation and besieged the foreign compound in Guangzhou. After three days, the British Superintendent of Trade, Captain Elliot, capitulated. Lin seized more than 20,000 chests of opium, including 1,000 chests owned by Americans, and dumped them on the beach at Bocca Tigris. It took more than 20 days to burn the confiscated opium. That gallant moment of victory for the Chinese, however, was followed by a military defeat in 1842 which the vacillating actions of Emperor Dao Guang helped to bring about. Dao Guang and his advisers blamed Lin Zexu for provoking the wrath of the British, and attempted to placate the enemy forces they greatly outnumbered. The Treaty of Nanjing, signed in 1842, surrendered $21 million in silver to England, as well as the territory of Hong Kong and trading rights at the ports of Guangzhou, Shanghai, Amoy, Fuzhou, and Ningbo. The trading rights included the fixing of tariff rates favorable to the foreigners. In 1844, America and France sought and received the same trading rights for themselves. After the Treaty of Nanjing, the breakup of China began. Foreign powers, overrunning China like locusts, competed with each other for greater trading and territorial rights, and in so doing they began the downfall of the Qing dynasty and old China.

With 1839 in mind, it is interesting to note that sixty-six years earlier in 1773, the tea dumped at the Boston Tea Party had originated from Guangzhou, where the patriot, Commissioner Lin Zexu dumped the British opium. Parliament, by granting the very same British East India Company a monopoly in the trade of the tea that the company obtained through the trading port of Guangzhou, caused Americans to think seriously of independence. Free trade, especially for China's goods, concerned the revolutionaries before and during the War of Independence. During the war, in 1779, Benjamin Franklin criticized American import spending, which amounted to half a million pounds sterling each year, and which, he said, went mainly for luxuries, "more than half of it for tea." The British East India Company's two historic losses of cargo, one into the waters of Boston Bay in 1773 and the other in the Pearl River in 1839, each produced different socio-political outcomes—the first brought liberty and independence for America and the second, foreign dominance and internal chaos for China. Both results, however, initiated revolutionary changes of tremendous importance, though China's overthrow of the Manchus through the revolution led by Sun Yat-sen in 1912 came 123 years after the Constitution of the United States of America went into effect in 1789.

At the conclusion of the American War of Independence, U.S.–China trade began in earnest and American enterprises in world-wide commerce became an immediate competitive force for the Europeans. The first American vessel to land in Guangzhou carried the distinctive and telling name *Empress of China*. Arriving in 1784 with a cargo of New England ginseng root, the *Empress of China* returned to New York loaded with tea and silk more than a year later. In Guangzhou, American ships traded hundreds of thousands of dollars in cash and goods such as furs and seal skins, sandalwood, dried sea slugs, cotton, lead, and quicksilver for the many goods available from China. After 1844, American ships carried ten percent of the opium entering China. Countless American ships sailed to China hoping to have fair winds for greater speed, and their choice of goods and quality. With the construction of the *Ann McKim* at Baltimore in 1838, the first tea clipper designed for swiftness, the Americans were able to outsail the British and other sea-going competitors in the China trade. The *Ann McKim*, 143 feet long and drawing 11 feet forward and 17 feet aft, sacrificed cargo space for its sleek lines, but ship designers believed it possible to have both speed and sufficient cargo space. In time, the *Rainbow*, built in New York with sharp lines and hollow bows and weighing 750 tons, made runs from New York to Chinese ports in an average of ninety days. In 1847, Captain William H. Hayes sailed the *Rainbow* from Guangzhou to New York in eighty-five days. From Smith and Dimock, the same shipbuilder that had built the *Rainbow*, came the *Sea Witch*, painted black with the characteristic bright stripe of American vessels and a figurehead of a huge gilded Chinese dragon to identify her as a contestant in the lucrative China tea trade. According to Daniel M. Henderson, in his *Yankee Ships in China Seas*, "Carrying clouds of canvas—three standing skysail yards, royal studding sails, large square lower studding sails with swinging booms, ringtail and water sails—she matched in speed the new ocean steamships and was for three years at least the fastest ship that sailed the seas."* In 1849, when the China clippers began a decline in importance relative to the shipping needs of the developing West Coast, Captain Bob Waterman brought the *Sea Witch* from China to New York in the amazingly swift time of seventy-four days and fourteen hours. One China clipper even carried the name *Houqua*, after the Chinese merchant whom the American traders respected most of the Guangzhou Hong merchants. The figurehead of the *Houqua* was, of course, a carved representation of the venerable Chinese trader-broker. By 1849, the British had had enough. New laws permitted British shipowners to purchase American-made vessels. Britain had twenty-four American-made tea clippers operating between her ports and China by the mid-1850s. Majestic

*New York: Hastings House, 1946, p. 171.

in full sail, the China clippers shipped huge cargoes of
tea, silks and other goods such as junk sails which the
Americans liked to use for floor matting. In Asian
waters, the clippers responded to the opium trade, and
ships such as the *Ann McKim* turned from tea to opium.
The market price for tea depended on the timing and
number of ships making port. The chances of making or
losing a fortune were great. American clippers raced
against each other and against those of the British,
especially to bring to market the first shipment of
China's annual crop of tea, which brought the highest
prices and a rich bonus prize at the London and American markets. The London tea merchants established a
prize for the winner of the annual race from China.
Cutty Sark, which won in 1869, set the record of 363
miles for one day's run.

According to the authoritative *Peter Freuchen's Book
of the Seven Seas*, the so-called tea clippers should be
known as the "opium clippers." According to Captain
Freuchen:

> The fact is that sailing vessels, which ruled the Seven
> Seas for most of the history we know, were perfected
> slowly over the years. They reached their finest in the
> last of them, and one type almost forgotten after its
> short period of existence were the opium clippers.
> These beautiful little ships with wonderful lines sailed
> so fast they managed to play a very important po-
> litical role in opening trade between China and the
> outside world. . . . The American and European
> smugglers hardly played a commendable part in the
> expansion of commerce. [Records] show how they
> entirely disregarded the moral aspects of their trade.
> They took terrible chances simply to earn great sums
> of money, not only for the big firms on shore which
> owned their ships but for themselves and their crews,
> who actually risked their lives. . . . Tea, slaves, opium,
> and later the California and Australian gold rushes
> were the reasons for the clippers—tea because it

deteriorated in the hold on a long voyage, slaves and opium because they were illegal, the gold rushes because miners were in a hurry.*

The true nature of the opium clippers was not known until twenty-two letters written by James S. Preston, captain of several opium clippers, to his brother in New York, the first written in April 1843, were discovered and made public by the Marine Historical Association in Mystic, Connecticut in the 1950s. No doubt it was because of the illicit and disreputable nature of the business that very few records exist. Prior to the discovery of Preston's letters, the China clippers drew romantic descriptions and heroic praise. Highly respectable English and American families, Indian princes, Parsee financiers, and Chinese merchants, such as Houqua, derived fabulous fortunes from the smuggling of opium into China. Though China suffered from the immoral opium trade, few Americans knew of it and opium was not shipped to America for trade.

Besides tea and silk, the U.S.–China trade consisted of feather dusters, kitchen utensils, wallpaper, furniture, porcelain, lacquerware, silverware, and pewter, most of which were made to order. Each morning, George Washington would have his porridge only from his bowl of Canton ware. In fact, U.S.–China relations were so important to President Washington that in 1786 he sent Major Samuel Shaw to represent the young nation's interest in China. Shaw had been one of the organizers for the sailing of the *Empress of China* in 1784 and he sailed on her to Guangzhou by way of the Canary Islands and around Africa.

Perhaps the most curious imports from China were the portraits and paintings that the Chinese craftsmen copied of popular American works. Many works by early masters, such as the *Battle of Lexington* and

*New York: Julian Messner, 1957, pp. 150–152.

Plymouth Landing, were copied as reverse paintings on glass by Chinese artisans. Reproductions of Gilbert Stuart's portrait of George Washington became so popular that the artist took legal action in 1800 against the importation of further copies from Guangzhou. Aiming to please, the Chinese painted Americana on china. At Monticello one can see a set of china that Thomas Jefferson ordered from Guangzhou for the White House, as well as brass handles on the dresser drawers in the Chinese bat design ("bat" and "happiness" are homonyms in Chinese). The Benjamin Franklin Hall of the U.S. State Department building, where formal receptions for foreign dignitaries are held, contains items of many Chinese porcelain on which are painted American designs and figures. During the Bicentennial celebration, exhibits in the Smithsonian Museum of History and Technology portrayed the wide use of Chinese porcelain in the earliest days of America's settlement, as early as the first colony at Jamestown.

As we learn from Walter T. Swingle of the Library of Congress, we are also more indebted to China and Asia than we realize for the food we take for granted:

> Few Americans realize that our chief agricultural creditor is China. We are indebted to the Chinese not only for the best varieties of oranges which we grow but also for many other fruits and vegetables grown commercially in the United States. The soy bean, whose extraordinary food values is now at last beginning to be appreciated throughout this country, was one of the five sacred grains believed to have been given the Chinese people by the semi-mythical Emperor Shen-nung, . . . about the 29th century B.C. Rice, wheat, proso (millet), barley, the other four of the five sacred "cereals," were grown in China many centuries before they were known in Europe; and the same can be said of many vegetables that we commonly regard as European. . . . As a matter of fact, all of our cereals

except maize, sorghum and some forms of oats originated in Asia. Almost all of our crops are Asian plants. All of our common temperate-zone fruit trees, except the pecan and the native persimmon, came from Asia, and all citrus trees too. Horses, donkeys, cattle, sheep, goats, hogs and chickens are all Asiatic animals. Our debt to Asia is enormous.*

Writing in the *Saturday Review* (1976, 3(17): 20–25), the historian-diplomat Edwin O. Reischauer expresses great concern that American students complete schooling with almost no knowledge of their country's history or the history of other nations. He writes: "Having little understanding of non-Western lands especially, they are no better prepared to face today's world than was an earlier generation of students who in their time of leadership marched us into the quagmire of Vietnam." Stressing the tragic misjudgments made by Americans in Southeast Asia and the radicalism of the late 1960s, Reischauer argues that "history to be relevant today cannot be so parochial but must encompass as much as possible of the total experience of mankind." One example he gives is the predominant emphasis the American founding fathers placed (and which most Americans still place) on ancient Greek and Roman ideals and history. However, Reischauer states that if the early American leaders

> had possessed a comparable knowledge of classical China, I daresay they could have drawn as many useful lessons from it. In fact, it is possible that the record of Chinese history during 2,000 years of close social integration and intimate experience with bureaucratic government holds more that is relevant to our crowded, bureaucratic age than can be drawn from our own, less bureaucratic past.

*"Our Agricultural Debt to Asia," in *The Asian Legacy and American Life*, A. E. Christy, ed. (New York: Asia Press, 1942).

During World War II, an anthropologist named Ruth Benedict received a government commission to write a study of the Japanese so that American political and military leaders would be able to understand the culture and people of Japan and act accordingly to win the war. Benedict, a famed scholar, had never been to Japan, had never studied the culture of Japan, nor could she read Japanese. Unlike Reischauer, it does not seem to have crossed Benedict's mind, though her resulting work* is generally regarded as a classic, that the very need for her to undertake such a study was a tragic judgment on American education and leaders.

Americans should reflect seriously on the fact that in the twentieth century their nation has fought three major wars in Asia and has been involved in a number of dangerous incidents. These might have been averted or concluded in less time with far less loss of life and destruction. But serious misjudgments, lack of knowledge and insight regarding Asian history and cultures, and a chauvinistic world view that highlights the West and neglects not only Asia but the many East-West relationships of the past have made America vulnerable.

Extending Reischauer's excellent point that Americans could understand their modern society better through greater knowledge of China's history, I would say that a search for the "best of both worlds" should be the objective. What has yet to be sought and developed is a blending of the East and the West wherever possible. As we have discussed in this chapter, the "twain" did meet, often in positive interchanges, over the centuries. A world map shows the United States and China facing each other across a shrunken ocean. Each should look to the other to find itself.

Chrysanthemum and the Sword: Patterns of Japanese Culture (Boston: Houghton Mifflin, 1946).

In War-Torn China, 1947–1948

China was once an exceedingly powerful and civilized nation, . . . with a standing higher than that of the modern Great Powers—Great Britain, the United States, France, and Japan. . . . Why did China once occupy so exalted a place and then "fall ten thousand feet in one drop"? The chief cause . . . : because we lost our national spirit, our state has day by day degenerated. So if we want to restore our national standing, we must first revive our national spirit.

SUN YAT-SEN, *Lecture 6 on Nationalism, San Min Chu I, March 2, 1924.*

(America's) worst disaster, however, came from the widening gulf between Chinese and American public feeling—in the postwar [World War II] years when ineptitude and corruption were thoroughly discrediting the Kuomintang in China, we were experiencing intensified alarm over Soviet expansionist aims and methods, particularly over the duplicity and ruthlessness of the Communist movement. As the experience of daily life continued to diverge in China and America, Communism seemed increasingly to be the only way for one people and the mortal enemy of the other.

JOHN K. FAIRBANK, *The United States and China*

Grandfather Yee (Kee Chong) and other elders of my family decided that the first son of a line of first sons needed a more extensive Chinese background, especially when he could hardly speak Chinese and seemed

overly Americanized. They decided that I should go to
Lingnan University, an American-sponsored institution
that some boasted of as the "Peking University of South
China."* Sending sons to Guangzhou for education was

*Established in 1888 as the Christian College of Canton, the Chinese
name of the school was changed to Lingnan ("south of the mountains") in 1903; it formally became Lingnan University in 1927. The
college was founded to teach western science, medicine, and religion, and had an American Board of Trustees in New York and a
Chinese Board of Directors in Canton. In the 1920s Lingnan graduates received, from the Regents of the State University of New
York, diplomas issued in Albany and transmitted to Canton. Lingnan
boasted many distinguished graduates, and had a flourishing American student exchange program in which several current members
of the Lingnan Board participated.

  After the founding of the People's Republic, Lingnan continued as
a private institution until early 1952, when it was incorporated into
the College of Arts of Zhongshan (Sun Yat-sen) University. Although
Lingnan University ceased to exist, the Lingnan Board of Trustees in
New York continued to support educational activities of various
kinds, including providing substantial funding for the development
of the Chinese University of Hong Kong. For more than 25 years,
however, there was no formal contact between Zhongshan University and the Lingnan Board.

  Huang Huanqiu, the president of Zhongshan University, and two
of his senior colleagues, Professor Gui Zhiyong, director of the president's office of administration, and Professor He Zhaofa, chairman
of the sociology department, visited the United States from May 5–
June 26, 1983, at the invitation of the Lingnan Board of Trustees.
The extensive itinerary included Pittsburgh, Boston, New York,
Washington, Orlando, Los Angeles, San Francisco, Vancouver, and
Honolulu. At the request of the Trustees, the National Committee
served as programming agency for the visit.

  In 1979 Huang Huanqiu, then Vice President of Zhongshan, came
to the United States to sign an exchange agreement with UCLA.
While in the United States, he met with Dr. Henry Frank, former
Lingnan provost and faculty member and now on the Lingnan
Board; this marked the official resumption of relations between
Zhongshan and the Lingnan Board. The Board made its first grant to
Zhongshan in 1981, and increased its financial support in 1982 and
1983. The Board has funded several Zhongshan faculty members for
study in the United States since 1981, and is currently assisting the
University in development of its Sociology, Economics, and Chem-
istry departments as well as with strengthening its administration.
(Footnote adapted from *Notes of the National Committee on U.S.-
China Relations*, Summer 1983, pp. 4–5, reprinted with the permission of the committee's president, Arthur H. Rosen.)

not unheard of among the Chinese Americans. Besides Lingnan University, the Toichin Middle School (a high school) also had students from the United States. Long expecting to enter the University of California, Berkeley, I resisted the decision at first ("But I've passed the Subject A exam and am cleared for full admission."). It was a sudden shift in plans, but in time I became captivated with the excitement of the long voyage and of going to school in China. Also, the events that were transpiring served as a rite of passage, i.e., a ceremonial change in status from youth to adulthood, and I had never felt such flattering attention from all simply because I was the first son. Surely a prince could not have felt more privileged, such was the influence and weight of the traditional Chinese family structure.

Wanamaker, the department store magnate, sent a handwritten letter from New York to inform me that as far as the university's trustees in the United States were concerned, my academic qualifications for Lingnan were more than satisfactory. He kindly gave his good recommendation and wished me well. School friends and town leaders also joined in the general excitement and expressed envy, though I did not know how to react when they remarked on how appropriate it seemed for a Chinese lad to live and study at a university in China. In my own thinking I believe I felt no different than my non-Chinese friends would feel if they were about to leave for China. Atypically, my father poured out funds for new clothing, second-class steamer fare, and health and dental checkups. The dentist took my father's good instructions to fix my teeth as well as possible quite literally and began to put in gold fillings. Modern dental care was hard to come by in China, but gold fillings seemed just too much. The dentist completed one such filling before father received the first dental bill and exploded. Years later, when I was in the service, the army dentist examining me raved over that filling and called other dentists over to see. One asked if I had been a patient for a candidate taking a state dental examination, when such elaborate work is done to prove proficiency.

Other relatives and friends showered me with gifts and things to take along, such as a granduncle who presented me with a broad-rimmed felt hat. An elderly lady gave me her precious Chinese language notebook, which her teacher in China had painstakingly written for her as he taught her character by character. She and her late husband had been missionaries in China for many years, and I can still see her kindly and deeply reflective face as she bid me farewell. Her face expressed both empathy with my youth and naiveté, and envy at my going where she had felt useful and been happy with her husband.

The shipside farewells and picture-taking in San Francisco climaxed several months of excitement and hasty preparations that had begun shortly after my proud graduation from high school in June. I shipped out the first week of August. Through the colorful, breeze-tossed streamers on the pier, the last person I could recognize among the large group of relatives and friends waving farewell as the band played "Auld Lang Syne" and the ship's horn blared was my dear mother. I knew then that I would not be the same when I returned. The innocence of my youth would have slipped away as the streamers were slipping from my sight.

Many American servicemen who shipped out from San Francisco will understand how the rolling tides outside the Golden Gate brought me back to earth in the first and worst seasickness of my life. Now missing only its guns, the S.S. *Marine Adder* had been a troopship during World War II, and I suffered three days before getting used to the ship's motions and military austerity. Two Chinese brothers from Chicago, one small, and the other husky and strong, if a bit dense, graciously took charge of me. They comforted me and brought fruit from their own meals. The big one told everyone in the cabin to "pipe down." It was as if I were the son of a Chicago gang leader, with two bodyguards. Since the two always seemed to wear suits and ties, I wondered if the other cabin mates thought the same. The three of us befriended an older Filipino passenger, also from Chicago. The brothers taught us cribbage, and we would play for hours. Learning that the Filipino man's birthday was coming, I asked the head steward to prepare an appropriate cake. At the surprise party, the man wept and to our own surprise said it was his first birthday party. The joy that our little gesture brought was many, many times greater than we had expected. Seeking aid from the ship's doctor for my seasickness, I was bureaucratically told my problem was seasickness, which I already knew. The doctor handed over a packet of APC pills and sent me off. A pretty coed acquaintance who was next in line described the exact same ailments as mine, but the doctor handed her a gown and asked her to change into it—a medical distinction I did not appreciate fully until later.

Since my family had planned that I would complete a bachelor's degree at Lingnan, we packed many suitcases, one huge crate, and one steamer trunk with clothes, books, and so on. My grandfather had helped me pack, then had brushed my Chinese name on red paper and glued the banner-like signs on my baggage. I would have brought far less if I had known that the entire load would be hauled to my dormitory by only two coolies, one a woman who strained so hard to earn a few pennies that she literally screamed out under the weight as if she were being whipped. The involuntary screams of that poor woman still haunt me. Her shrieks reverberated through the staircase of Man Foo dormitory, which had been donated to the university by the Tiger Balm tycoon. I could have realized then if I had been mature enough that China's ills were too great for the menthol and camphor ingredients of Tiger Balm to cure.

My first sight of China was of Shanghai, a city of imperialistic privilege and predatory economic exploitation by both foreigners and Chinese. Sin city of the world, Shanghai gave its name to the crime of kidnaping men to serve on ship crews, but any form of human deprivation could have been found in pre-World War II Shanghai, tragically representative of the old China's downfall and humiliation. Foreigners had profited and lived far better there than in their own homelands, protected by an imported military presence that included the Coldstream Guards of Great Britain and the U.S. Marines. Closed to Chinese patrons, the Shanghai Club had boasted of having the longest bar in the world. The city's parks had displayed signs that read, "No dogs or Chinese permitted." The various foreign nations, including the United States, appropriated a portion of Shanghai for their own territorial privilege and use. Along with the Aston Hotel tea dances, cricket, soccer, horse and dog racing, chauffeured limousines for the children, the French Catholic Cathedral, Anglican and American churches, symphony performances conducted by Maestro Mario Paci, cuisine of the greatest magnificence, educational institutions of world fame and pleasures of the flesh unequalled by any place in the world—for the privileged elite—the ordinary Chinese people of Shanghai suffered abject poverty and deprivation the likes of which the modern world has not tolerated elsewhere. According to the grim records of the Shanghai Municipal Council, 5,590 exposed corpses were collected in the streets of Shanghai in the nonwar year of 1935. In 1937, the year Japan conquered the city after a brave but fruitless defense by the Chinese, many of whom were students, 20,746 corpses were collected and buried by the unsung Chinese group, the Shanghai Public Benevolent Society. In 1938, the first year of Japanese occupation, the society buried 22,779 corpses, the health department of the municipal council cremated 55,511, and other agencies in Shanghai handled about 20,000 corpses, a total of over 101,000 corpses found abandoned in the streets. Such figures reflect the tremendous distance between the haves and have nots in China at that time and the terrible conditions that drove those with life remaining to forego the Chinese traditions respecting their departed, resulting in the grisly toll on the city streets.

The desperate conditions touched close to home one night for me and a group of ship friends whom I had joined in a search for nightclub dancing, when a thief rushed up to our group and tore the watch from a coed's arm, the force of which injured her arm severely. Another time, friends and I went ashore from the *Marine Adder* to talk with the ricksha pullers and beggars on the street. Looking thin and poorly fed, the men and boys talked about the war years when all had suffered from hunger and many had died. Without complaint or anger, they said they had seen some improvement in the two years since the war's end, but that they did not expect to live beyond age forty or to become wealthy. My Canadian ship friend, Eldon Andrews, asked them what they thought of Cantonese such as me. They said that the Cantonese and the people who lived in Shanghai were all Chinese, but that China was so divided and weak, the concept of one China was more ideal than fact. I studied a boy who was about fifteen and spoke intelligently and vigorously. His skin as far as I could see was covered with an ugly rash. A ricksha puller who was seemingly quite drunk came by and vomited against the dock wall. No one went to help him and he slowly weaved away into the dark street without saying a word. We took a ricksha ride, but on that first of many rickshas I would ride, I felt terrible having a man serve me as a beast of burden.

A group of us American students eagerly accepted the invitation of a kindly Englishman, a retired colonel aboard the *Adder* on his way to train soldiers in India. The colonel had proposed taking us to visit the sixteenth-century Yuyuan Garden, a famous example of Ming dynasty garden architecture located deep in the old Chinese part of the city. All of us had enjoyed the colonel's unassuming and witty company aboard the ship. He epitomized the military snap, humor, and delightful manner of a character like the one Ralph Richardson plays in the movie *Four Feathers*, which I had the good fortune of seeing as a youngster when I slipped away from home one night. Lining us up in two-person rickshas, the colonel took charge and we arrived at the garden after a long ride. Spending only about one hour at the garden, we were disappointed to find the works badly in need of repair and the tea of poor quality. Coming back, with a new set of rickshas and single riders this time, I rode last in line. The hustle and bustle of the busy, colorful streets captured my attention, and I did not see the crash coming. Another ricksha, not of our party, accidentally hit mine and we tumbled over. My frightened puller picked me up and set his vehicle in order again with anxious apologies and concern. I suffered a cut hand and tarnished clothing. However, our problem had just begun, for we had lost the rest of our party who were en route to the Park Hotel on Nanjing Road where we were to have tea. They had told my puller to follow the ricksha in front of him; all I knew was the English name, Park Hotel, which he and no one else he asked could understand, at least in English as I named it. Several hours passed, and I became more appreciative of the anguished efforts of the ricksha puller to get me home than of my possible danger. The puller asked almost anyone for help and I called out to those who might know some English. We were two Chinese yet so different; unable to understand the speech of the other, we were locked together in anxiety. Finally, by chance, we passed a familiar landmark—I believe it was a cathedral—and I directed him out of the old city into the Western area where we eventually came across Nanjing Road. Three blocks or so from the hotel, a Sikh policeman directing traffic at an intersection surprisingly knocked the puller to the street and began to beat and kick him until I jumped down and stopped him by shouting and getting in between him and the puller. I learned later that the melee occurred because no rickshas or pedicabs were allowed to enter Shanghai's exclusive Nanjing Road. Probably because of my English speech and American dress, the bewildered Sikh restrained himself and allowed us to continue on Nanjing Road. At the entrance to the hotel, my worried friends welcomed me with open arms and helped me reward the happy puller with a generous fare. I was lucky to have had such a reliable puller as that man, because if he had chosen to abandon me earlier, I would not have had the money to pay him. As I turned to enter the hotel, our happy reunion received an ugly jolt. Without warning, I suffered a heavy blow across the back that shook my whole body. Falling to my knees from the pain and shock, I could see the European who had struck me. Without speaking a word or looking back, he marched toward the elevator after striking me with his stick, no doubt feeling gratified that he had given a lesson to one Chinese for daring to stand in his way at the hotel entrance. Except for servants, Chinese could not even enter that hotel before World War II. Standing erect, the English colonel who had organized the Yuyuan tour prudently held back my friends with both arms outstretched and glared at the offender and then the closed elevator doors for several seconds. Speaking to my desire for retaliation while attending to my bruises, the soft-spoken colonel said, "Albert, his kind are fading away. It is you who have won. Pity the . . ." Although those words seemed empty then, I now know what he meant. In the Hong Kong of 1947 to 1948, I would witness examples of British colonialism that would be unthinkable today. I shed no tears when I left

Shanghai in 1947. The pre-World War II signs that had
read "No dogs or Chinese allowed" no longer existed
and Shanghai supposedly belonged to China once
again, yet the attitudes of the old, imperialistic days
remained, even then, in 1947.

In 1972, I went to the People's Republic of China on a
mission on behalf of the American Psychological Association to establish communication with the Chinese
psychologists and their national society (this visit is
discussed in the chapter titled "The First Fulbright
Scholar to the People's Republic of China"). During that
trip, I visited Shanghai and stayed at the Peace Hotel
(formerly the Repulse Hotel) for most of a week (located, like the Park Hotel, on Nanjing Road the Repulse
Hotel had also barred Chinese before World War II).
The many workers at the Peace Hotel, unlike their
counterparts elsewhere in China, were surly and treated
me with strange disdain throughout. The hotel personnel exhibited no warmth or courtesy. They would barge
into my room, even late at night, without knocking to do
something trivial and meaningless, such as closing or
opening the drapes and flushing the toilet. In the hotel
restaurant, on the top floor, I would have to ask for
utensils such as a fork to eat my meat or chopsticks to
eat Chinese food. In reply, the waiters would suggest
that I use the soup spoon instead. The hotel service
contradicted the friendly assistance of my guide in
Shanghai, and the openness and cordiality of the psychologists at the Shanghai Normal University and the
many students and teachers I met at Shanghai schools.
How strange it was to be so poorly received at these
Shanghai hotels, first by the would-be colonial in 1947
and then by the Chinese workers in 1972.

The Peace Hotel reflected its past in its British
tableware, furnishings, and fixtures. On the polished
brass plate near the elevator doors, I could read, "Gib-
bons, London and Wolverhampton." My room was
quite large and must have seemed lavish in the old days.

It had a huge two-room closet, totalling about twelve feet by thirty feet, the inner room of which once accommodated the foreigners' steamer trunks and cases. Well-built into the wall of the outer closet, at least twenty drawers dared me to try to find enough clothing to make use of them. Except for the warmth of the canopied bed, I shivered through much of my time in Shanghai whether outdoors or indoors. The completely tiled bathroom had fixtures of pre-World War II origin; ugly cracks marred the tub and washbasin and the toilet played a noisy leak for most of my stay. Fussing about with the plumbing, I could sometimes silence the toilet only to have a worker storm in to needlessly flush it, bringing the leak back. At night, cockroaches in the bathroom brought a shudder as I contemplated the ghosts of the past that must haunt such quarters. A large section of the main room, about ten feet by twenty feet, had its own separate entry from the outer hall and remained partitioned off by a long, shroud-like drape that seemed ominous to me. The space contained nothing at all and I speculated that it had been an area set aside for the children and servants in the old days. Weathered and rather shabby-looking, the hotel facade had faced and was facing still a history that seemed to carry more gloom than brightness. Since Shanghai represents so well China's woes of the past, I could not enjoy my several visits there in the 1980s, though I stayed at better hotels, the best being the Jing An (meaning "Silence" or "Quiet") Hotel, which had been built by the Nazis and used as a German billet.

One happy moment I shared in Shanghai took place in 1947, when my ship first docked. A ship friend, Phil Foisie, and I stood eagerly at the ship railing scanning the docks to find Phil's fiancee, whom he had met and fallen in love with when he entered Shanghai as a U.S. Army officer shortly after the Japanese surrender. Suddenly, Phil, who was normally sedate and humorous in a gentle way, exultingly shouted, "There she is!" She could not see Phil until the ship was quite close to the dock, and stood tall, with a lovely smile, her hands held tightly by her chest. Then she could see his wild waving and waved herself and joined in the joy of homecoming. They spoke only briefly, and Phil left shortly in haste to land. Can there be any greater happiness than in the moment of homecoming and reunion with loved ones?

Reaching Hong Kong from Shanghai in August 1947, I needed to arrange transportation to Guangzhou. Relatives in Hong Kong informed me that the Hong Kong-Guangzhou train suffered frequent raids by bandits. They gave gruesome descriptions of what the bandits did to gain prompt ransoms for those they kidnapped, their favorite targets being Chinese from abroad such as myself. To back up their demands for sizable ransoms, the bandits would send the captive's ears, nose, and eyes in succession. I required no further convincing, and booked a passage on the British paddle-wheel steamer, whose flag supposedly protected it from pirates. I would return to Hong Kong as often as possible in the following months. Unlike the crowded, noisy, bustling city of today, Hong Kong in 1947 to 1948 seemed to have a quiet, settled quality that the weight of British colonialism then enhanced. On my visits, I savored the cleanliness and the creature comforts that Guangzhou lacked. One thing that has not changed over the many years is the superb Star Ferry ride across the bay with a grand view of Hong Kong. Today, one cannot point a finger at Hong Kong from the Star Ferry without pointing at a tall building or a new one going up. Air conditioning did not exist then, at least not in Hong Kong, but they say that the place did not then have the added heat produced today by so many more people (more than 5 million), factories, vehicles, and machines such as air conditioners. American-built autos ruled the narrow streets in those days, but they have now so completely given way to Japanese and German-built cars that the sight of an American car in Hong Kong at

all deserves a second look. On the Kowloon side of Hong
Kong harbor today, I truly miss the little, uniformly
black Austin taxis that one could once find lined up by
the Ferry Building. One excellent feature of modern
Hong Kong must be the far greater role that the Chinese
people now play in the daily life of Hong Kong. It is
largely due to their enterprise and creativity that Hong
Kong has become a major industrial, trading, and tour-
ist center of the world.

In the old days, the British seemed to have their way
and as colonials they were not often to be admired. I
frequently saw Britishers, perhaps constables, scream
out at someone for an infraction on the streets and
literally whip the person with their stick. Once when I
came out of a theater, a car sped by so fast that it almost
crashed into my party of friends. I shouted out that he
should watch his speed, which would have been normal
behavior in the United States. My friends told me that I
should not have done that, and sure enough, the Brit-
isher who had been driving the auto came up to the taxi
we had boarded. My friends froze and stared into space.
The man took hold of the taxi door and said, "Who was
it that shouted?" I identified myself and told him he had
been driving dangerously in a crowded area. The man
lost his temper and I thought he might drag me from the
taxi. He accused me of insulting a constable and
screamed that he would take me to the station. I agreed
that we should proceed to the station, but in my view it
was he who should be booked. In time, perhaps realizing that I did not sound like a local Hong Kong type, the
policeman tapered off, saying things like, "You should
watch your step and mind your tongue," before retreating. My friends took a deep breath after the constable departed and, rather than congratulating me for
winning the argument, told me how lucky I was not to
have suffered more than harsh words. The behavior of
that constable would be unthinkable today, I am happy
to say.

I saw Guangzhou for the first time as the paddle-wheeled steamer negotiated a bend on the Pearl River. This was the city that Friar Odoric de Pordenone, who followed Marco Polo, had described as being "as big as three Venices . . . and all Italy hath not the amount of craft that this one city hath" upon his return to Italy in 1330 after thirteen years in Asia. Through the dark, overcast gloom of the day, across the broad expanse of the Pearl's blackish water, I could see an imposing sky-line of ghost-like buildings about five miles ahead. From that distance, I could see no lights or movement and it seemed the polished, white steamer flying the Union Jack was my last link to the world I knew. As we moved closer to the bank, the largest buildings loomed before us as silent, empty hulks. Someone said that they had been destroyed by Japanese air bombings during World War II. Both close by and far beyond the steamer's dock, innumerable sampans with quaint little lamps wobbled and clung together invitingly. The sampans, with their sleek, dark decks and bamboo-slatted canvas canopies that curved over the middle half of the boat, seemed quite romantic and pleasant at first, but almost all first impressions of China proved to be false, it seemed. In time, I learned that the sampan dwellers were especially deprived and that most rarely touched land. Great wooden barges with aft and fantail superstructures similar to those on old sailing ships also lined the docks. Such craft carried passengers and cargo up and down the rivers and, being without engines, were towed by slender, low-lying boats that were armed to the teeth with cannon, machine guns and armor and fitted with powerful engines. Yes, Guangzhou appeared to be another world altogether, perhaps what other cities of the world had been like centuries ago, I thought.

Landing for the first time in Guangzhou, I could see from the steamer's upper deck that all manner of people and small vehicles crowded the docks and streets. On the riverfront, the sampans huddled tightly together and, closer up now, I could see their pitifully cramped space. Under the curved roof of mats, I could see the prominent double paddles that ingeniously allowed one person standing toward the rear of the sampan to propel and steer the boat with a cross-oar, push-pull motion that seemed relatively relaxed and efficient. Most sampans looked neat despite being crowded with miscellaneous baggage and goods, half-naked children, clotheslines, and charcoal burners for cooking. Adults on the sampans, mostly women, would call and shriek out, for what purpose I did not know, perhaps for passengers to ferry across the river—so much life in a space no more than twenty feet by five feet.

Ashore, the land equivalent of the sampan people seemed to be the ricksha puller standing or sitting darkly between his two pull-bars waiting or bargaining for riders. En route home in 1948, I posed as a sailor and went ashore with a crew member in Yokohama. Reaching Tokyo's Ginza, we rode high-wheeled, lacquered rickshas, called jinrikishas. The Chinese vehicles lacked their attractiveness and size. The Guangzhou puller typically wore a peaked straw hat large enough to keep the rain off his shoulders, crude cotton shorts and T-shirt, ribber-tire-soled sandals and, around his neck, a sweat rag. The ricksha's cab could hold one adult comfortably and had a rubberized canopy that folded out if it rained. The cab's cleanliness and comfort contrasted greatly with the miserable wages and life of the rickshaman, running miles through heavy traffic in all weather for a fare of ten cents or less. Pedicabs, three-wheeled taxis capable of carrying two persons, cost almost one-third more for greater safety, speed, and comfort. The pedicab drivers seemed a little less pressed than the pullers, but rental or loan charges for their vehicles were higher. In the following months, I rode many pedicabs and rickshas, which made me uneasy at times, especially when it rained. Under the canopy and its flap in front, I could see only the passing wet pavement, the watery potholes, and the pathetic pace of the man-slave's feet and legs.

Negotiating the steep, narrow gangplank from the ship to the dock, I suddenly realized that someone in the noisy, pressing mass had stolen my wallet. A second later, a man ahead of me cried out to stop a thief who had grabbed his fountain pen and fled as fast as he could. A crowd of people dragged the desperate person back and pummeled him until it seemed he was dead. If he was still alive, a soldier wearing a large raincoat did his mighty best to finish the thief off with a heavy thrust of his rifle butt against the man's head as he lay on the dock. That explosive violence, the colorful diversity and tumultuous density of the masses, the humid, rusty atmosphere of the Tropic of Cancer, and the war-torn, ghost-like buildings across from the dock seemed stifling and far too much to absorb at once. My head spun and I felt faint. A sense of loneliness and being lost swept over me.

Culture shock, the clashing confrontation of one's cultural awareness and familiar life-patterns with an alien, unexpected way of life and social history, would be a simple, catchall explanation of my reaction to the scene. I felt that all eyes were on me, and that self-conscious feeling unnerved me even more. A typical American approach (which tends to be phenomenological) would be to offer an excuse acceptable to people back home, such as culture shock, in order to brush off my naiveté and ignorance and explain feelings at that point. One can see this in the way that most Americans, who are the world's greatest travellers (at least before the Japanese), relate to others what they saw and did in foreign places. All too often, Americans assume that others will accommodate them by speaking in their tongue and accepting their standards and wants as superior and proper. Americans tend to dichotomize social perceptions into black and white, and are prone to critical and judgmental observations, rather than objective ones, as Alexis de Tocqueville insightfully described in *Democracy in America* (1840). These inclinations can be attributed to a tendency to particularize and partition, coupled with a peculiar insularity. Despite the high standard of living in the United States, which makes enlightened education so possible, and despite the immigrant origins of Americans, the dissipation of ethnocentrism in the United States into a more cosmopolitan outlook has yet to occur (please see the last chapter, "Race versus Ethnicity"). Only recently have educational programs been developed to help Americans acquire an awareness of their basic customs and values in relation to those of other countries.

In 1947 to 1948, China had not recovered from the devastation of World War II and its turmoil increased steadily as the Civil War advanced. Criticizing the lack of a national loyalty and the inability of the leaders to reorganize China's socio-political structure after the 1911 Revolution, Sun Yat-sen said: "The Chinese achieved in their revolutionary effort only the work of destruction, and were not able to carry through the work of construction. That is why, as a result of our struggle, we have today the name, 'Chinese Republic,' and nothing else."* The abject poverty, corruption, and chaos of Nationalist China prior to the victory of the Communists brought me to a naive view which said, "If this is China, thank God, I'm an American!" What I saw in China seemed so alien and tragic that instead of identifying with China as my family wanted, I separated myself from it. I felt some compassion and sorrow but only as a detached and uninvolved observer. I crossed over and passed starving people in the streets and saw corpses of babies floating down the Pearl River, victims of famine.

---

*Sun Yat-sen, *Memoirs of a Chinese Revolutionary* (London: Hutchinson, 1918), p. 138.

My first encounter with a corpse came on the evening of the Moon Festival. The evening being warm, I went boating with several coeds and fellows from the university to cool off and eat the traditional moon cakes that celebrate the great day. In the moonlight, I saw what I thought was a log at first, but then I felt the horror of seeing the legs and then body of a baby. All of us froze as the body swept past with the current and one of the students quietly said there was a famine at a certain area up the river, to which the others nodded passively.

Being China-born, the other students had seen many similar sights. They quickly recovered and resumed their humorous conversation. Stunned, I could not shake the experience for several days and still recall the floating baby's body only too vividly. Fortunately, my memory of China in 1947 to 1948 remains clear. I am much more reflective today upon those events than then, when I developed a front of being as hard-boiled and blasé as the other students. For example, a mob of ricksha pullers and pedicab men would rush up to solicit a rider when the university bus reached the Sun Yat-sen Medical School Hospital, its final stopping point in the city. We would bargain with them for the lowest fare and some were keen enough to do it with finger signs, which seemed in good humor. Those ragged men, poor wretches, seemed like slaves as I remember them today. We were not intentionally cruel—our behavior toward the ricksha men was all wrong, but it was in accordance with social expectations and ancient practice.

What Americans would have found abominable and intolerable in the raw life of China can be shown in the social acceptance of a scene that I witnessed. Near the same Sun Yat-sen hospital gate, a ricksha man was hit by or fell in front of a heavily loaded bus. Hearing the painful shrieks and commotion, I came upon the accident and found that the poor fellow was pinned under one of the large wheels of the bus. He was terribly mauled and bloodied and in great pain. Instead of rescuing the man as quickly as possible, a policeman reprimanded the ricksha puller for delaying the bus and causing a scene! The scolding continued at length even though the man seemed seriously hurt. I hurried away from the crowd in disgust. Gathered about the accident, the crowd showed little indignation or anger. Yet Americans too have turned their eyes and ears away from problems they could have addressed, such as ignoring the screams of a woman crying for help against a rapist or murderer. This occurred in the famous case of Kitty Genovese in New York, who died screaming for help from her murderer in 1964 while neighbors and people in the streets turned a deaf ear. Such incidents occur in the United States and all urbanized societies more regularly than we would like to admit. We see another instance of inhumanity in the example of Bessie Smith, the "Empress of the Blues," who is still acclaimed as the greatest female blues singer of all time. Refused treatment by a white-only hospital in Clarksdale, Mississippi, after an auto accident, Bessie died in 1937. Similar to the bus accident in Guangzhou, Bessie's auto accident happened close to the door of a hospital. In 1947 to 1948 I particularized inhumanity to what I saw in China. Time would show my error.

Mounting a pedicab or ricksha, we would find a swarm of beggars surrounding us and preventing us from moving. In time, I recognized certain beggars, especially the youngest, whose sores and wounds must have been kept open on purpose, since I saw no change over many months. Their pathetic shouting and pleading shook me at first and I would hand over most of my wallet, which for me was a shoulder-strapped camera bag used to carry the large wads of bills necessary in China's inflation-ridden economy. To avoid the beggar mob at the university bus stop, friends taught me to accumulate near-worthless bills, such as ten-yuan notes, and toss a handful up into the air to the rear of the ricksha for the beggars to pounce upon and thereby free the passage for my ricksha. All of this took place daily at the gate of the Sun Yat-sen Medical School, ironically named after China's revolutionary father.

Students at Lingnan University came mainly from well-to-do families in Guangzhou, Hong Kong, and other South China cities. Almost all students lived in university dormitories, and the quarters were spartan though adequate. I shared my first room with four local fellows who treated me very well, perhaps because of my seemingly exotic American ways and speech. They appeared glad to have the opportunity to improve their English, though I tried in vain to get them to help me improve my Cantonese. Each student had to supply his or her own furniture, and I promptly went into the city and bought a dresser with mirror, cot with springs, a mattress, a study desk and chair, a study lamp and a transformer for use with the weak current, and a sleeping net. What seemed to be a small set of basic furnishings took up almost one-third of the room's space. I tried to squeeze it in as tightly as I could but it resulted in my seeking a room with more space the next semester.

All of us in the three-story dormitory, which was being reconstructed into four stories, depended upon an old servant who lived in a small cottage across from the dormitory. He stored our trunks and suitcases, kept the hallways and grounds fairly neat, maintained the supply of boiled drinking water in a centralized urn, and served as security guard over our area. He also delivered the mail, and did so most cordially. He looked old enough to be our grandfather with his gray hair and slight hunch. Bringing a letter to the room, he would seem almost reverent, as if receiving a letter and being able to read it deserved great respect. When the water urn dried out, he and the students would curse each other, and I must say his bittersweet existence with the lot of us seemed to be at his expense and typical of the ever-present servants in China., His age no doubt sheltered him from physical abuse and allowed him some degree of verbal retort. I never thought he cared much for me until he appeared genuinely sad to see me leave in 1948. He brought my big steamer chest and shipping crate from storage by carrying them on the ends of a long bamboo pole. Rhythmically half-trotting as the coolies did, he balanced the load on one shoulder and steadied the chest and crate with his hands. The trick in this is to wobble one's hip in coordination with the feet and the heavy loads dangling from the pole's ends. From my second-story window, I could see the old man coming up the red clay pathway with my luggage and wondered how many times he had made the same circuit.

Most of the students rode slim, black-colored English bicycles with hand brakes, and I bought one to ride about the large campus. In the hot, humid nights, it was exhilirating to ride a bike as fast as the uncertain pathways would allow to the campus village for a papaya slice or some other fruit. Thieves, dressed as students, would come to the campus at times to take bicycles, which cost about $75 new, and other goods. The campus police would often catch the thieves and give them a terrific beating in the station house behind our dormitory. The commotion would draw our attention and callous cheers. I went over to the station house once and never went back. Common criminals caught redhanded received severe and immediate punishment from the police in old China, but the corrupt leaders who beguiled the nation never suffered the pain of arrest.

Walking together as a group, the fellows would often hold hands and did so quite naturally. I never got used to such hand-holding and found it embarrassingly unmanly, though I realized it was a friendly and common practice there. What struck me besides the practice was the slender, soft hands of the local fellows. Their high-class status did not permit them to perform manual work. Packing a bunch of books or a bundle of laundry for myself, I would be told by my roommates to get the old dormitory servant to carry it for me. I would respond that it was no problem, that I would do it myself in order to get the job done sooner, and that the servant had enough to do. The fellows no doubt regarded me at times as an impulsive American who did not understand class distinctions and other matters that they took for granted. Despite my shaky acquaintance, for better or worse, with the local boys, my record box of dance music from the United States brought many invitations to parties.

The coeds at Lingnan were of all shapes and personality types. Almost all were slim and attractive and quite enticing in their quiet manner of deferring to the fellows and studying seriously. Unlike the local boys who needed music with a strong beat before they would take a turn on the dance floor, I was often the only one dancing, which seemed to impress the gals as much as it depressed the fellows. I dated a number of coeds and found most of them excellent companions. They seemed interested in me or at least pretended well enough to make me feel so. Their charm and grace were subtle and hypnotic. Light and lithe on the dance floor in their form-fitting high-collared *cheong-sam* gowns, they made any clod believe he was Fred Astaire. Every one had a nickname, it seemed, and my nickname became *ond foo*, which means "short trousers" in Chinese. The appellation came during an evening meal which my roommates and I had hosted for an equal number of coeds at the campus pavilion cafe. Toward the end of the ample meal, I announced to all, "I'm full." A puzzled coed, whose crossed eyes augmented her look of puzzlement, asked me about the statement, which I explained meant having eaten to capacity. After a brief pause, everyone had a good laugh; they were not familiar with the American expression and thought I was referring in Chinese to my tailored tropical shorts —*ond foo*.

George became my best buddy. Tall and handsome, George had the physique and dress of a collegiate American. I asked him on first sight if he, too, came from the States. He smilingly replied, "In a way; I lived in Hollywood many years." As it turned out, George's father was Universal Pictures' head distributor in China, and that position must have paid quite well. My friend's childhood classmates had included Shirley Temple, Jackie Cooper, and other young stars. During World War II, George had been a captain in the Chinese army and served as a liaison officer for an American combat group. Often supercilious, he encapsulated his dashing wartime exploits in stories of speeding by jeep into captured villages in Burma, shooting pistols with both hands along with his American buddies, and "raising hell" in general.

George and I raised hell together in our way, for we both loved a good time. Once we found a farmer with a small crop of sweet corn and, purchasing some, feasted on corn on the cob after painstaking work to boil the corn undetected in the dormitory. We often went into the city for an evening's tour of the cabarets where the gals, in their *cheong-sam* gowns, got to know us fairly well. I would not characterize our behavior as boisterous or rowdy. In fact, we attempted to present an air of sophistication and worldliness which I adopted so thoroughly as to order gimlet cocktails, pretentiously handle cigarettes, and carry an engraved cigarette case and lighter. George and I acted as though we were the Chinese version of the "Lost Generation," F. Scott Fitzgerald's era of the 1920s. Having some sense of beauty and ugliness, and feeling detached, superior, and ephemeral, we lived day to day, with seemingly little commitment and objective. Our taste for light music, cuisine, drinks, and women being more discriminating and foremost in our lives than our political and social interests, we two playboys floated along in an enticing dreamworld.

At a cabaret, we would often share the same dance partner, whom we found an interesting conversationalist and dancer. I suppose the ladies we preferred increased their billing by being able to say that Lingnan University students craved their attention. One night, one of our favorites, a particularly attractive gal but not a young sprout, seemed unusually distant and upset. Contrary to her usual coquettish charm, she alarmed the two of us with a deathly, tragic air. Towards the closing hour, she gave in to our probing by declaring an intent to kill herself that evening because a wealthy patron had given her up. George and I said everything possible to change her mind and brighten her view, but she persisted in her sorrow and suicide threats. At closing time, we insisted on staying with her to prevent any attempt at suicide and accompanied her to her suite, several floors below the top-floor cabaret in the Guangzhou landmark next to the Pearl River, the Oi-Kwan Hotel.

Throughout the night, George and I alternated duty in staying awake, watching her fitful sleep and quieting her emotional tirades. Neither one of us got much sleep. By dawn, George and I were simply exhausted, groggy-eyed and woolly-mouthed. The gal to whom we had devoted ourselves so gallantly slept soundly and we finally did too for a couple of hours. At about 9 A.M., as bright sunlight streamed through the window, she woke the pair of us, fully dressed, bright-eyed, and full of good cheer. Red-eyed and worn out, George and I asked her how she felt and if she still wanted to die. She laughed and skippingly proclaimed that the day was a new one to make the most of and teased us for being so sober. She suggested that we were too serious. George and I stared at her, at one another, and then at the floor, before we began laughing uncontrollably. Somehow, we crawled out of there and got ourselves back to the university on the first launch. I took a picture of that morning's awakening scene and wonder today where that woman and my buddy are now. George and I lost contact after my return to the United States. Neither one of us seemed to have the heart to write after my return to the United States, being so far apart without much possibility of seeing each other and living in contrasting worlds.

Other overseas Chinese attended Lingnan too, coming from every English-speaking country of the world, it seemed. Wherever they may have settled, the first-generation immigrant parents saw Lingnan University as a way to combine their sons' and occasionally their daughters' higher education with Chinese acculturation. Fellows from the British colonies and Commonwealth countries spoke with an English accent and wore secondary-school blazers with their particular school insignias on the chest pocket. Meeting fellows from Hong Kong, Burma, Malaysia, Singapore, Jamaica, British Guinea, the Fiji Islands, and Canada, I was astonished by the remarkable influence of the British upon the world, though the United Kingdom has had to grant independence to almost all of its once-great empire. The worldwide influence of the British as shown by such schoolmates seemed to me more telling than the famous expression, "The sun never sets on the British Empire."

Of course, fellows from the United States also spoke the same basic tongue of English. However, we Chinese Americans varied greatly among ourselves. Some of us were third- or fourth-generation, but most were first- or second-generation. Our English instructor, Polly Walker, had to divide the overseas students into two parts—one for those who lacked high school proficiency in English and seemed more Chinese than American, culturally as well as linguistically, and the other section for about seven of us who appeared ready for regular freshman English composition and literature. Those from Southern states spoke with heavy drawls. One, for example, from Mississippi became so enthused over a

coed, he said to me, "Eyes so wilde w'love for her, Al-
Bert, eyes jus' can't sleep! You all understan', don't
you?" No matter where we came from, our fathers typically ran stores and restaurants. Few had made it into
the professions, and most came from peasant backgrounds in South China, where most of the overseas
immigrants came from before 1949.

Without a doubt, the most interesting group of overseas Chinese came from Jamaica. The British had
brought their great-grandfathers into the West Indies as
contract laborers, the first arriving there in 1854. In time,
the Chinese overcame their lowly coolie status and became merchants. Because of the strict immigration laws
that prohibited the importing of brides from China,
many of them married native Jamaicans. A mixture of
black and Chinese, the students from Jamaica had ne-
groid hair; some had hair that was very kinky and some
had straighter hair. Some had reddish hair as is not
uncommon in black-white mixtures. Taller than any
other group, the Chinese Jamaicans showed high intelligence and a good educational background. With little
loyalty to the British, they seemed to have less of an
identity problem than one might expect, which seemed
also to be the case for others from the British colonies
and Commonwealth nations. I suppose this was because such places left no doubts as to the social status of
Chinese and non-whites, which was lower than people
of European background. Though well-mannered and
mature people, the Chinese Jamaicans confronted prejudice at Lingnan. The tradition-bound Chinese in general found their mixed blood somewhat shocking and
left them to themselves in their out-of-the-way dormitory. I liked those Jamaicans very much and enjoyed
their intellectual humor and wit.

One Chinese Jamaican named Reuben had been an
amateur welter-weight boxer in the islands, and we
talked him into entering a Guangzhou boxing tournament. Reuben went easily through the preliminar-

ies to the finals. I served as his manager but was actually more of a towel waver—what could I possibly tell Reuben about boxing? A pacifist and gentleman, Reuben never punched harder than necessary to win a match from an opponent, disappointing blood-and-guts boxing enthusiasts. Reuben utilized fancy footwork, dancing skillfully around his opponents and scoring with stylish, laid-on blows that his opponents could not ward off or return. At first I thought the judges might deny our man points for lacking aggressiveness, but so clear was Reuben's superiority that he was never challenged. The local newspapers made a big deal out of the boxing tournament, and Reuben was for a while the toast of Guangzhou. His handsome, mustached face appeared in the local newspapers in many articles we ironically could not read because of the language. A Jamaican had never risen to such popular acclaim in Guangzhou before and never has since, I am sure.

In the second semester, I moved into another dormitory room at the invitation of its two occupants and obtained the additional space I wanted for myself and my furniture. Since there were only three of us and ample space remained, Reuben moved in on my invitation and we had long talks at night about the United States, Jamaica, and our impressions of China and Lingnan. After lights-out, we tried to count the mosquitoes and June bugs that probed our respective sleeping nets—the latter hitting the top of the net and sliding down to the floor with a slight, dull, scraping sound as they struggled to right themselves off their backs. At my study desk, I keep a large bottle of June bugs that I had captured around my lamp. In the day, the night creatures, except those in my bottle, vanished as did the ghosts of the "Night on Bald Mountain" segment of Walt Disney's *Fantasia*. Reuben and I spent many a night trying to outdo each other in telling fantastic stories involving Rube Goldberg-like contraptions and science fiction as well as experimenting with mental telepathy, which brought surprisingly good results. Monsters became one of our favorite topics for tall tales, no doubt prompted by the persistent night creatures.

Perhaps because our conversation exceeded their command of English, the two original inhabitants of the room began to make us feel less welcome. They directed their hostility mostly toward me, because they said I had brought Reuben in without their full permission. I found them to be more than just naive, as I had originally thought, and they were far less likable than at first. One was a duckfooted popinjay who boasted of his wealth, clothes, guns, and so forth. The other fellow seemed to be the other's lackey and only friend. I pitied him. With limited funds, he saved money by cutting as many corners as possible, including coating the face of postage stamps with mucilage that would wash off so the stamps could be used again. With the exasperated permission of the university administration, he also delayed paying his tuition until the last moment, by which time the continuously escalating inflation made his payment about half the original cost. Other students did the same, but only if they had to.

One evening, after having lived in the room for several months, I noted a slight stir behind the wall of dressers and their tall mirrors, which were arranged to divide the space among ourselves. Curious, I poked about and through an opening, I saw a little light and then a hand holding a book, all within six feet of my cot. My scalp tensing with apprehension, I forced myself to look again. Yes, someone was there! The shock so overwhelmed me that I broke our mutual silence and asked the popinjay if he saw the same. Without hesitation or looking up, he said that it was a student who slept there each night who was so impoverished, with barely enough to survive, that they had walled him off long before Reuben and I arrived. The isolate came in late at night to sleep and left early in the morning. Apparently, he had returned earlier than usual that evening. Since the space left to him barely left room for his cot, and since he was shunned by his roommates, I could see why the poor fellow stayed away.

Reuben and I could hardly believe that a fifth person was living in our room without our knowledge. We protested his treatment to the other two. They responded with much prejudice toward the isolate and described him as weird in addition to being near penniless. Reuben and I decided the arrangement should end, and we proceeded to liberate the "prisoner" by opening up the wall. Silence pervaded the room as a dingy-clothed student exchanged surprised stares with his "liberators" and two other roommates for several long seconds, as if we had uncovered an animal's lair. Instead of expressing gratitude or even some light pleasantry to ease the tense moment, the fellow cursed us out for our efforts. Accusing us of disturbing him, he quickly set up the wall as before. Perhaps he had had enough of the room's occupants already or he was like Lord Byron's Prisoner of Chillon, who grew protective of his cell's safe security and the sanctuary of limited but familiar bounds. The atmosphere of the room seemed sick and spooky after that and I began to extend my stays away, especially overnight to Guangzhou and Hong Kong.

Most of us, I suppose, form our own kind of cell within which we work out accommodations with others and ourselves so as to survive with some kind of inner meaningfulness, even though the premise may be partly irrational. That solitary roommate resembled a private I knew years later during the Korean War whose main duty was making the garbage runs each day. Large, with more fat than muscle, a high-pitched voice and a moronic sense of humor, he would laugh and wheeze in his dark corner of our tent. We skirted his corner of the squad tent, afraid of the unknown bugs and contagion that we were sure surrounded such an unkempt and foul person! Unfortunately, the captain punished him for malingering and black-marketeering with a sentence

of two months' restriction to the tent. Of all the punish-
ments possible, the captain picked the very one that fed
the garbageman's greatest weaknesses. Day after day,
except to eat, he lounged in his corner with a shortwave
radio blaring away. His filth and debris accumulated,
and we finally built a partition around the unsavory
fellow and his bad sounds and smells. Finally, fed up
with his taunts and fearing as much for our own health
and well-being as for his, we broke down the barriers
with the captain's approval and dragged the fellow to
the shower station. We scrubbed him with soap and a
brush, then burned his absurdly dirty clothes and
moved our tent to a new location. Any enemy sniper
observing our actions would have scratched his head
and had difficulty explaining our behavior to his superiors. The long flow of mournful sobs, cursing, and
screeching from the man long afterward indicated that
the situation went beyond what met the eye (and nose).
Perhaps we had destroyed a precious existence for him,
one in which he had the greatest sense of well-being and
satisfaction. If so, intervention was still justifiable, but
which method was right? Our means gave swift exor-
cism that satisfied us, the instigators, none of whom
gave any thought to the psyche of the garbageman. At
Lingnan, Reuben and I acquiesced to the status quo,
crazy as it was. In Korea, my tentmates and I overthrew
the situation. In both, I wish I had had the time and had
known enough to try to counsel the individual, to
change his way of thinking. My concern, however, is not
due to soft-heartedness or idealism, but to an interest in
the ways that people develop psychic closets out of their
own pride and self-deception. As we seek meaning and
security for ourselves, while at the same time accom-
modating the rights of others, the question could be
raised, "How much freedom and control can we allow
ourselves and to those about us? What form of cell do
we make and accept for ourselves?" Of the students I
met at Lingnan, the one whose behavior made me most

introspective was the little prisoner we could not free. Independent and isolated, he may have felt freer than we did.

In its vastness and human multitude, China seemed to me a massive prison. No one could say that he or she was free of the increasing degradation of the Nationalist position under Chiang Kai-shek and the undeniable advent of the new order. The severe economic inflation in China reflected the steady collapse of the Nationalist government and the people's faith in it. Once in China I rapidly learned the basics of inflation, money changing, and self-protection. Thank goodness I did not make the same error as my friend George, who out of patriotism deposited most of his cash into a local bank upon his arrival in Guangzhou. In no time at all, the value of his deposit eroded in the mounting inflation. Whenever we went out, therefore I covered the tab and did so gladly in order to have more of George's company.

Passing through Shanghai by cargo freighter on my way home in 1948, I had to surrender about one million yuan to a ricksha man who would not let me go until he was satisfied. His manner contrasted sharply with the Shanghai ricksha man who less than a year earlier had been so patient and worked so diligently to return me to my party of ship friends. The wild man in 1948 characterized the desperate, chaotic state of the city and collapsing nation. The fee of a million yuan, which was an extremely high fare but which equalled only about fifty American cents, showed the inflationary chaos of the Republic of China. Upon my arrival in China in August 1947, the exchange rate was 10,000 yuan to one American dollar or $5.50 Hong Kong. By June 1948, the rate had skyrocketed to two million yuan to the dollar and would go beyond 10 million in several more months, until the bills finally became worthless when the Communists broke through the final Kuomintang defenses. The Nationalist government paid dearly to print new issues of bills in the United States. The crisp bills which bankers and storekeepers could count so rapidly, flip-ping one corner of the stacks like animated cartoon books, were worth saving as souvenirs. I saved a good number and brought them home, but later lost them to a fellow teacher who "borrowed" them for "only a little while." By the time I recalled the loan some months later, I had lost touch with the teacher. To con-ciliate myself, I reasoned that the inflation rate under which they had been issued destined their eventual disappearance.

In Guangzhou, inflation taught me to possess no more yuan than might be spent in one day. I learned to con-vert money from home (in the form of a cashier's check) to Hong Kong dollars, which I would hold and convert to Chinese yuan when needed. Goldsmith shops were the best places to change currency, though exchanges were supposedly illegal. One would approach a man sitting by an abacus behind the shop counter and softly ask what the going rate for Hong Kong dollars was. The man would usually reply by showing a figure on the abacus. Should it be acceptable, the two would proceed to the shop's rear or behind a screen for the actual exchange of bills. Apprehensive at first, I got quite used to the routine and was seldom turned down. The Hong Kong dollar of those days was sound and more easily exchanged. With Guangzhou's proximity to Hong Kong, its bills were more acceptable for trade than American greenbacks, and their value—about eighteen cents then—meant I would not have to convert a whole American dollar. Three to five Hong Kong dollars would easily cover a good time in Guangzhou.

Another event illustrates the tensions and mood of 1948 China. In the spring, Hong Kong police uninten-tionally killed and wounded some Chinese squatters during an incident in the disputed "Walled City," a por-tion of land that the Chinese have claimed was not part of the ninety-nine year lease for the Kowloon Peninsula. After the bloodletting, students demonstrated against what they called latter-day imperialism. Student leaders rallied the students of Lingnan University together and demanded that all march. I offered mild protest and resistance at first because of my American citizenship, but my inner curiosity and eagerness to observe the action prevailed. I had little hesitation about joining the demonstration after student leaders said everyone was to go. However, the Jamaican students did not join in the march and almost all of those from countries under the Crown resisted going because the action could have been interpreted as traitorous.

We marched to wooded Shameen Island, the notorious foreign compound where signs in the nineteenth century announced "No dogs or Chinese allowed." Part of the Opium War concessions to foreign powers, Shameen contained the offices of foreign businesses, legations, and residences. A proper nineteenth-century stronghold, the island was sheltered on one side by the Pearl River and by a wide and deep moat around the other sides. From across that moat, British rifles had wounded and killed a number of Chinese in crowds protesting the abusive signs at the turn of the century. Today, big posters on Shameen remind the people of the many years of rule by imperialists "when China was weak and could not defend herself."

Luckily, when my line of march reached the British consulate, no military opposition had yet appeared, and the bridge guards were strangely absent. Through the banyan trees on the narrow walkway, I could see that the British flag pole had been bent so it looked like an inverted "U". Students within the buildings tossed quantities of papers from the office windows, and furniture and dishes crashed to the ground, strewing the shaded, park-like grounds with great heaps of debris. Bonfires poured out streams of smoke. As we hurried past, the consulate and a whole block of British buildings were set ablaze. I took photos but they came out poorly because I had forgotten to remove a close-up lens. Shortly after my line of march had passed, Chinese troops arrived and arrested some of the lingering students. Although the Guangzhou students felt they had won a victory against imperialism, students in Shanghai decided that the Nationalist government had orchestrated the "national outrage" as a propaganda ploy to divert, at least temporarily, the people's attention away from the worsening war situation. I have been told that the Shanghai university students demonstrated against the Kuomintang instead of the British at that time.

Occasionally, I would visit Shameen to pause by the American consulate and see its large flag. The desire I felt to embrace the Stars and Stripes encapsulated the ambivalence I felt toward my Chinese heritage. What I observed of China's chaos reinforced my American identity and my wish to belittle my ties with China. My family's intention that I become more Chinese by studying in China began to backfire and have the reverse effect. Soldiers of the Nationalist forces, wearing baggy, dingy brown uniforms, seemed everywhere. Lines of troops paced through the campus almost daily, some carrying weapons but mostly without. Looking impotent and spiritless, they seemed to be strangers themselves in a hostile, alien land. Treating them more like foreign occupiers than their defenders, students shied away from the soldiers. Waiting with friends in line at a downtown matinee showing a Joseph Cotten romance, I watched the theater empty of its full house of troops. The soldiers moved out smartly enough wearing cotton-padded jackets and trousers and rubber-soled shoes. They filed out through the lobby, saluting an officer sitting patronizingly in a big stuffed chair. I wondered how bewildered and amused they must have been with the movie, since my educated friends from Guangzhou could not grasp the meaning of the romantic film themselves and generalized gigglingly that it was just "too American" for them. The Western love story, which contrasted sharply with Chinese ways, helped the soldiers and even my friends confirm their own culture-laden perspectives toward the West. What must those friends have thought of me? What is the Chinese equivalent of Joseph Cotten and Teresa Wright?

Culture affects military life as it does anything else. In the old China, the lowest form of employment was soldiering, which was nearly synonymous with banditry and being a social misfit. Peasant conscripts made up the Nationalist armies. Most had been forcibly taken from their villages, with ropes around their necks, to serve in an unfamiliar province, an old Chinese practice. Unable to converse with the people where they were stationed because of dialect differences, such troops seemed disrespected by the populace. The social distance supposedly made them better soldiers. It was common knowledge that commanding officers gave their troops little of the allocated wages and food, that weapons and ammunition vanished through graft and corruption, and that the troops in turn eked out their existence through subjugating the poor. During World War II, an American watching Chinese troops passing by on a road toward battle, some leading dogs on a leash, said to a Chinese companion, "Soldiers are the same everywhere. Look at those fellows with their pet dogs." The Chinese informed the American that the dogs were not pets but were destined for the makings of the soldiers' "chow."

Some Nationalist armies developed outstanding reputations from their American training in India and Guilin and from their success in Burma during World War II under General Joseph Stilwell. Supposedly well-trained and well-equipped, these elite forces became Chiang Kai-shek's best hope against the Communists. One group of these troops passed through Guangzhou and I saw some of the officers. They did look tough and seemed on a par with American GI's in their physique, dress, weapons, and most significant, in spirit. Their arrogant and brusque demeanor, however, made one wonder, as do some television crime and spy shows, whether they were the good guys or the bad guys. You could say that the ones working for you are the good guys. But there was some doubt on that score. We at Lingnan lacked confidence in the allegiance of strangers, and thus all soldiers were to be avoided. However, the air force pilots, most of whom had been trained in the United States, had become the glamour corps of Nationalist China, though U.S. Army observers, such as Major General David Barr, condemned the Chinese Air Force most bitterly. General Barr, the chief of the U.S. Advisory Group to Chiang Kai-shek, reported in 1949:

> The Chinese Air Force, consisting of 8-1/3 groups, is far in excess of what a country bereft of gold credits can support. Although it has among its personnel over five thousand United States trained pilots, it accomplished little, other than airlifting troops and operating its transports for personal gains. There was an ever-present reluctance to take a chance on losing equipment or personnel, which was clearly reflected in their constant refusal to operate at other than high altitudes. There was an ingrained resentment in the Chinese Air Force against killing Chinese Communists who had no air support.

Visiting friends at the campus, the pilots, wearing American uniforms with the "pink" trousers, did look straight out of the U.S. Air Corps. Said to be skilled with modern aircraft such as P-51 Mustangs, the fliers definitely made a hit wherever they went in the city. One got after me for dating a coed he had his eyes on, and I paid little notice until he added his Colt .45 to his belt and coolly reminded me of our earlier conversation. If I had had General Barr's report then, perhaps I would have called his bluff.

Manned concrete or brick emplacements, sometimes concrete pillboxes, occurred at regular intervals along the roads. Especially at night, one could not walk for

long on the potholed road by the university without
encountering a sentry who stood his duty without ceremony. Their rusty rifles appeared to be Japanese rifles
left over from World War II. Though the sentries may
have lacked the ability to fire, their bayonets looked
sufficiently menacing. Following the lead of the Mary
Knoll fathers who taught at the university and had invited me for dinner my first month at Lingnan, I froze in
place and complied when challenged. When someone
has a gun pointed at you, he is the ultimate master of the
moment. Answering "Lingnan student" to the harsh
challenge of the sentry, we would be allowed to pass in
the dark. At times, the university bus would be stopped
for a look-over. I still wonder at the usefulness of the
procedure, since anyone could have answered as we did
and passed safely. That bit of military illogic illustrates
the civil-military inefficiency of Nationalist China.
However, as I would learn later (see the chapter titled
"GI American, 1952–1955") the American army, and no
doubt all armies, forces their men to perform almost
meaningless tasks. As an older major once confided to
me, "Keeping the men busy and out of trouble is about
the toughest job of company officers." That helps to
explain why my company was ordered to take the
knives from the messhall after breakfast and to line up
on a grassy field in formation. On command, we bent
down and proceeded to "mow" the grass.

I came across some unforgettable characters in
1947–1948 China that remain unique in my experience.
For example, one day in August, during my first weeks
at Lingnan, I decided to go shopping in Guangzhou and
seek relief frm the unbearably hot and humid weather.
Waiting for the bus at the university stop, I heard and
then saw a powerful motorcycle approaching on the
red-soiled road. Astride it sat a well-built Englishman
with a bright red head of hair and a full handlebar
mustache. His skin seemed far more pink than white
from the heat. Wearing white tropical shorts, a shirt,

and shoes with calf-length stockings, he looked the spitting image of the immaculate and authoritative colonial. Taxiing up to me, he asked in a heavy accent if I spoke English. I answered, "You may be surprised, but I speak English far better than Chinese." On hearing that, he relaxed a bit and eyed me sympathetically. Whatever he wanted, I was too ignorant of the area to be of help. He asked where I meant to go, and I told him my objective of purchasing a present for a baby's one-month birthday party. He told me exactly how and where to get a gold, inlaid bracelet for a fair price in Guangzhou, and the information he gave me proved accurate.

About three months later, I saw the same Englishman walking briskly, head towering above the crowd. Interested in knowing him better, I rushed off the bus and caught up with him after a run. He remembered our meeting and invited me to have a drink. As it turned out, the Englishman had been in China for most of his life and had been captured with the Hong Kong garrison by the Japanese. He and other British prisoners of war had been herded through the streets of Hong Kong daily by the Japanese to show the Chinese the degradation of their former rulers. My friend told me that the Japanese beheaded Chinese prisoners on the spot when captured—their punishment for resisting the Asian Co-Prosperity movement of Japan. It did not take me long to realize that the man remained disturbed emotionally from his years of imprisonment. He described quite vividly how he had stood up to the prison guards several times for want of rest and food and had been terribly beaten down each time. A Eurasian friend of mine in Hong Kong, also a former prisoner of war, confirmed the Englishman's story later on, but he scorned my friend for often upsetting the Japanese with taunts and tirades that brought trouble and suffering to all of the prisoners. The Eurasian had his share of emotional problems for which his doctor prescribed prostitutes, but he could not take such medicine, and attended to his wounds in drink and gloom.

Japan's attack upon the British crown colony of Hong Kong had coincided with its bombing of Pearl Harbor. Faced with heavy naval bombardment and Japan's superior forces, the Hong Kong defenses on the island fortress held out until Christmas Day, 1941. Without naval reinforcement, the defenders lasted longer than would have seemed humanly possible. In 1948, I could see the burned-out shells of residences on the slopes along Stubb Road around the island and I poked about the concrete defenses still standing at Repulse Bay with three or four gun-ports each. The crossfire of those strong emplacements must have been devastating if their cannon and machine guns had sufficient ammunition. Stouthearted soldiers had manned those positions. With streams of barbed wire and obstructions in the water and on the beaches, I imagined the repeated waves of Japanese barges swarming in and landing the troops, who bravely stormed ashore over the wire and their dead comrades. I could imagine the defenders being overwhelmed by the sheer numbers of the enemy and by the devastating firepower of the naval guns. Perhaps the lucky ones had died during the fighting, because they perished quickly instead of suffering the slow torture of four years' imprisonment under the Imperial Army.

Above Repulse Bay Beach, which is a lovely expanse of light-colored sand gently sloping from the rolling waves, stood the Hong Kong Repulse Bay Hotel. In 1948, it looked quite the same as it might have before World War II, though it needed paint and much repair. Before its crude demise in 1982 to make way for an apartment building, the hotel had been renovated splendidly, the high-ceilinged fans had been supplemented by air conditioners and modern hotel wings ambled up the foothills, coated now with high rises. It is remarkable that the structure survived the Japanese invasion and occupation. Victorian colonial style, with high columns and a long front veranda where an old world-style breakfast was served on Sundays, the building provoked images of ladies wearing floor-length gowns and fluffy hats and carrying parasols and gents in straw hats and summer suits strolling through the great rooms and along the veranda, some taking tea served by Chinese servants. The concrete gun emplacements looked out over the gentle waves and blue-green waters of the bay. In 1948, I envisioned the fierce chattering of the machine guns and the clamor and shrieks of the bloody battles on the beaches of Repulse Bay. The Japanese soldiers came in wave after wave, falling and dying on the barbed-wire barriers, making footprints for later waves of men storming the beaches. If my English friend in Guangzhou had been one of the defenders at Repulse Bay, he would have had a full view of that famous hotel as he came out from the rear of his pillbox with hands held high and with perhaps a white cloth of surrender over his blazing red hair. In 1980 when next I visited Repulse Bay after 1948, the fortifications were gone and sunbathers filled the sandy beach.

It was exciting being with the red-haired Englishman, for the man was hardly the cool and proper colonial that his natty surface made him seem at first. He was employed on and off and he must have had a military pension to survive at all. We became good buddies and a typical night's activity with him would go as follows: He seemed to know instinctively where the closest gin gimlets could be found and the places were usually cabarets where hostesses would come to entertain and dance for an hourly fee. Many of the cabarets would have compared favorably with American night clubs with their softly lit decor and furnishings. Filipino musicians provided excellent Western and Chinese dance music. The popular music composed and arranged in China surprised me at first since I did not know of its existence before going to China. It rivaled dance music from the West. I thought its Chinese touch made it all the more exotic. I took a good number of Chinese dance records back to the United States and played some for a musician friend who arranged music for leading dance bands, such as Stan Kenton's, but he seemed disinterested. Yet shortly afterwards in 1949, one of the Chinese songs, "Rose, Rose, I Love You," became a national, hit-parade item with the lyrics in straight translation and the music taken intact.

My English friend and I danced very little during our evening tours, saving our time and cash for the drinks. Alternately stretching his big frame upright on his chair and hunching over to tell me something in a loudish whisper, he had the servants scurring about as in the *pukka-sahib* days, or he tried to, anyway. He labored over the telling of astonishing stories, for example, remembering some woman across the room from long ago and not wanting her to see him ("Oh, my God! I do hope she doesn't note my bloody presence. No, let's stay and have another gin. All right, sport? I'll tell you about her. . . ."). He would elaborate on past sex and spy exploits with the woman, and it seemed ludicrous that the person concerned did not notice the presence of a big, red-haired Englishman. Some of the escapades that he described seemed mad as hell. One night, the main objective of our evening out became a plot to steal the many congratulatory baskets of flowers surrounding the walls of a newly opened night club. Planning it in great detail, he worked out a strategy in which we would swoop up all the floral baskets at closing time and rush off in separate rickshas to our hotel. Imagine the two of us whooping it up on fleeing rickshas, loaded down with flowers, baskets, and flowing ribbons on which good wishes and hopes for prosperity had been written. The exploits went well; we never encountered the law. However, as far as my friend's state of mind was concerned, I did not know why he did such things and could offer no solution for his inner torment. Drunkenness was not the cause, yet it probably removed what superficial inhibitions remained. As an eighteen-year-old, I was fascinated and persuaded by his words and behavior, though I had many doubts about their purpose other than relieving and acting out his POW scars. I followed suit more as an observer than as a participant. Though pained by prison memories, he also frolicked as might a soul reprieved from hell who did not know why he should have survived when so many others did not. Reality and illusion were terribly confused for him; his mind seemed as schizoid as possible without his being completely dysfunctional. At one moment, he could coolly describe details of a water torture or other punishment to rival Edgar Allen Poe and in the next moment, become as straitlaced as a colonial judge. The poor fellow would often go into the back country on engineering sales jobs, returning after several weeks. After one especially wild farewell, I never saw him again. Definitely an exception to the white *bwana* stereotype, he illustrated the degree of tolerance that foreigners received in China, which I never would have seen without having made his extraordinary acquaintance. Wherever he may be now, I hope he has found some peace of mind.

As the experiences with the schizophrenic Englishman suggest, I spent my time in 1947–1948 China as both a playboy and a wide-eyed observer. I was on my own in a society that was very different from the one my elders had known, and I was without my own set of goals and values. I suppose some would characterize my youth as being what the sociologist Reisman defines as "other-directed." In my opinion, however, the term does not apply, since an "other-directed" person follows the changing fashions and modes of behavior of others without reflection and ultimate judgment. Having had a wide range of experiences, I can now reflect on them and formulate meanings. Thomas Jefferson, one of my two personal heroes, the other being Sun Yat-sen, wrote to his teenaged nephew Peter Carr in 1785: "An honest heart being the first blessing, a knowing head is the second." He went on to say that it was time for young Carr to begin a course of serious readings and study that would continue throughout his life. During my stay in pre-1949 China, I had an "honest heart" like Peter Carr. I meant well even though my actions on behalf of other people were almost nil. Naive and unknowing, I lacked the understanding and means needed to serve others. Yet it is encouraging to remember that I did furnish blood at the medical school at least five times. Through urgent messages pinned to my dormitory door, the M.D.'s called me so often that I became, as they put it, "anemic in relation to U.S. standards but not Chinese standards." The Chinese by tradition did not believe in blood transfusions, and the medics would summon me for the most desperate cases. As far as I know, my donations did not save the five or so people who were given my blood as a last resort. I recall that one patient had been shot clear through the pelvis by pirates who had attacked his junk. The faces of the recipients and their relatives seemed to express more pity and amazement toward me than gratitude for the act. That difference in attitude reminds me of the moment in John Hersey's novel *A Single Pebble*, when the cook on a junk watches an American engineer "deposit two blasts of nasal phlegm in a square of cloth and treasure these excreta in one of (his) pockets."* Shocked at such peculiar, unnatural behavior, the Chinese cook urges the skipper to put the American ashore at the next port.

*New York: Bantam, 1956.

The Nationalist cause grew bleaker every day. Reports of Chiang Kai-shek's gains seemed like so much propaganda; they contrasted with all other sources to the point of ridiculousness. For example, the Nationalists highly exaggerated the significance of the capture of Yanan, the Communist capital, in March 1947, which Mao Zedong's forces had evacuated. People hoped aloud that the United States would send troops to stem the Communist tide. However, the Truman administration had complained for some time to the Nationalists that despite massive military assistance from the United States, they appeared to be on their way to defeat as the Communists dominated the civil war. In July 1947, Truman sent Lieutenant General Albert C. Wedemeyer to China to appraise "the political, economic, psychological and military situation—current and projected." Wedemeyer bluntly criticized the Nationalists in no uncertain terms for a defeatist military effort and the pervasive corruption and inefficiency of its government and armies. General Wedemeyer's parting statement on August 24, 1947, as contained in then Secretary of State Dean Acheson's *The China White Paper*, was: "In China today I find apathy and lethargy in many quarters. Instead of seeking solutions presented, considerable time and effort are spent in blaming outside influences and seeking outside assistance."* Stressing great urgency, Wedemeyer urged the Nationalists to reverse their policy, and to "win and retain the undivided, enthusiastic support of the bulk of the Chinese people by removing incompetent and/or corrupt people who now occupy many positions of responsibility in the Government, not only national but more so in provincial and municipal structures." Pointing out the great patience and ethical nature of the people and many of the leaders, notwithstanding the greed and incompetence in the Nationalist

*Palo Alto: Stanford University Press, 1967.

hierarchy, Wedemeyer said that China could be saved only through "inspirational leadership" and immediate "drastic, far-reaching political and economic reforms" in the form of action, not promises. "It should be accepted that military force in itself will not eliminate Communism."* The unequivocal report of the Wedemeyer mission to President Truman and Secretary of State Acheson remained secret until *The China White Paper* was first published in 1949. It confirmed much of what had been said eight months earlier by General George C. Marshall, whose mission to China, in an attempt to settle differences and form a coalition government, ended in frustration after several years of false starts, hostilities, and broken negotiations.

Following Marshall's recommendation, Truman finally recalled the great general, author of America's massive program to rehabilitate Europe after World War II and 1953 winner of the Nobel Peace Prize. On the day he departed from China (January 7, 1947), Marshall had already completed his appraisal of the situation in China for the president. According to Marshall, the would-be mediator, "the greatest obstacle to peace has been the complete, almost overwhelming suspicion with which the Chinese Communist Party and the Kuomintang regard each other. Sincere efforts to achieve settlement have been frustrated time and again by extremist elements of both sides." Blaming reactionary, "irreconcilable groups within the Kuomintang, interested in the preservation of their own feudal control of China" and the "deliberate misrepresentation and abuse of the action, policies and purposes of our Government . . . without regard for the truth" by the Communists, General Marshall condemned such propaganda and told the President that China's best hope lay with "the assumption of leadership by the liberals in the

*Acheson, *The China White Paper*, p. 258.

Government and in the minority parties" and their "successful action" under Chiang to "unify through good government."*

After General Wedemeyer's special mission and especially during the tenure of the U.S. Ambassador to China, John Leighton Stuart, from July 11, 1946, to August 5, 1949, American policy toward China shifted away from the desire for a coalition government, in which the Communists would have a share, to a simple, stern anti-Communist line. The United States was experiencing strong anti-Communist sentiments at the time, especially through the reactionary accusations and self-serving work of Richard Nixon, then a congressman, and Senator Joseph McCarthy, whose name today stands for political defamation and character assassination of the worst degree. To recall the tensions of the United States in 1949, former State Department official Alger Hiss began his long series of trials on December 15, 1948, when he was indicted on two perjury charges concerning his alleged activities with Communists.

Meant as an objective and frank discourse, *The China White Paper* documents the Truman-Acheson understanding of U.S. relations with China from July 3, 1844, the date of the signing of the Treaty of Wanghia, the first Sino-U.S. treaty, to June 3, 1949, when Yan Xishan became the prime minister of China. Though anti-Communist in tone and written to justify U.S. actions, the *White Paper* also openly criticizes Chiang Kai-shek and the Kuomintang for causing most of their problems.

Because of the *White Paper's* anti-Communist tone, America's role in the defense of the Kuomintang, and U.S. foreign imperialism in the past, Mao Zedong hotly criticized *The China White Paper* and Acheson. In particular, Mao attacked the secretary's letter of transmittal which said that the Chinese Communists represented

*Acheson, *The China White Paper*, pp. 686–689.

the "foreign yoke" of Russia and that the United States should do all it could to "encourage all developments in China which now and in the future work toward (the) end" of reasserting "the profound civilization and the democratic individualism of China." Acheson had also written a "clear" warning that any aggression against China's neighbors would be met with confrontation from the United States and the United Nations. Mao called for a nationwide discussion of the *White Paper*, branding it a "counterrevolutionary document" and demanding exposure of American imperialistic intentions. He wrote half a dozen or more articles lambasting the work. The *White Paper* also received severe criticism from many quarters in the United States, some in defense of the Kuomintang and some questioning why we continued aid so long in spite of Acheson's assertion that "nothing that this country did or could have done within the reasonable limits of its capabilities could have changed that result; nothing that was left undone by this country has contributed to it."* People's Republic of China leaders turned the *White Paper* into its first large-scale campaign against the United States. Mass rallies were held throughout China. However, the people's knowledge of the *White Paper's* contents went no further than a translated summary, mainly emphasizing Acheson's cover letter and U.S. aid to the Nationalists.

One article Mao wrote, titled "Farewell, Leighton Stuart!", noted that Ambassador Stuart departed Nanjing on the day that *The China White Paper* was released—August 5, 1949. Mao wrote:

Let those Chinese who are shortsighted, muddle-headed liberals or democratic individualists (presumably those like Stuart who would claim love for both the U.S. and China) listen. Acheson is giving you a lesson; he is a good teacher for you. He has made a

*Acheson, *The China White Paper*, p. xvi.

clean sweep of your fancied U.S. humanity, justice
and virtue. Isn't that so? Can you find a trace of humanity, justice or virtue in the White Paper or in
Acheson's Letter of Transmittal? . . . Leighton Stuart
has departed and the White Paper has arrived. Very
good. Very good. Both events are worth celebrating. . .

As ambassador, Stuart tried continuously to convince
Generalissimo Chiang to undertake radical reforms in
the government and the military operations. On June 24,
1948, Stuart reported to the State Department that "the
crucial problem is still the personality of President
Chiang. He is fully cognizant of the current deterioration . . . listens patiently to warnings . . . seems sincerely
determined to act . . . . But there is actually very little
change in his methods." Although the ambassador had
easy access to Chiang, he reported constant frustration
in his attempts to effect changes vital to a progressive
governmental military victory. His experience with
Chiang resembled that of others before him, such as
General Stilwell during World War II and the heads of
U.S. postwar missions. Stuart would inform the State
Department in June 1948: "I feel impotent to accomplish anything that helps to reverse the downward
trend."* It is my view, however, that though Chiang
Kai-shek can be blamed for his own defeat, he was in
fact merely the tip of the iceberg. Chiang represented
the outdated traditions of old China, which operated on
feudal, corrupt principles. Perhaps incorruptible himself, he excused almost all the abuses and incompetence
of his generals and administrators. Nationalistic but
blind to a newer horizon, greatly handicapped by ex-
cessive commitment to past practices that subjected the
masses, and unable to use the good advice of others
outside of his clique, Chiang fulfilled his role exceedingly well. Old China could not have gone under with a
better representative of itself than Chiang Kai-shek.

*Acheson, *The China White Paper*, pp. 275–276.

The widespread anti-American riots and demonstrations by university students and professors that began in May of 1948 reflected the "universal dissatisfaction with the present Government and the irrational but easily understandable association of America with its existence or its failings."* Having been president of the American-sponsored Yanjing University in Beijing from 1919 to the time of his appointment as ambassador, Stuart understood the mood of the Chinese intellectuals. In fact, Stuart had been born in China in 1876, and began missionary work in China in 1905. Lasting through the summer and causing the government to close down the campuses, the often-violent unrest was directed at American plans to reconstruct and strengthen Japan. The plan, which clearly implied the restoration of Japan's economic and military powers, evoked feelings of apprehension and frustrated anger in the intellectuals. They perceived a despicable trade-off—the sacrifice of China to alleviate tensions between the United States and the USSR while Japan, China's enemy of old, resumed dominance in Asia with American assistance.

Economic reforms, begun on August 19, 1948, by the generalissimo with much fanfare, tough talk concerning reform, and a crackdown on speculators and self-interested elements, had crumbled by November 1, 1948. On that day, General Jiang Jingguo the generalissimo's son, resigned his appointment as economic czar after his harsh efforts to make Shanghai a test case had failed. The economic deterioration grew worse. The defection of entire divisions of the Nationalist army became more and more commonplace. In October 1948, the Kuomintang's finest forces, 300,000 troops, were soundly defeated in a critical struggle for Manchuria. Those troops included the American-trained and equipped Eighth Army, which had distinguished itself

*Acheson, *The China White Paper,* p. 276.

against the Japanese and which was led by the highly respected general, Fan Hanjie. Huge quantities of supplies were also lost, and almost everyone began seriously to believe that the ultimate defeat of the Nationalists was inevitable. Thousands of miles to the south, everyone at Lingnan University could see the handwriting on the wall.

From 1947 to 1949, Major General David Barr, head of the U.S. Advisory Group in China, constantly urged unified and aggressive military action, which, as before, failed to move the Kuomintang. Reporting on the "stunning" loss of Manchuria, Barr said, "To me, the loss of the troops was the most serious result. It spelled the beginning of the end."* The capture of Jinzhou, the Nationalist government's supply center for Manchuria, on October 15, 1948, precipitated the debacle. Jinzhou fell largely as a result of the generalissimo's extreme ineptitude. Chiang assumed personal charge from Beijing, and the result was that the Communists captured the area commander, Wei Lihuang, as well as the Kuomintang field headquarters in Manchuria. Mukden, the headquarters of Manchuria, surrendered without a fight on November 1, 1948.

By then, the Nationalist government could no longer pretend that it would win the civil war. Xuzhou fell with only minor resistance on December 1, 1948, Tianjin on January 15, 1949, and Beijing surrendered without a fight on January 31, 1949. After these defeats, Chiang Kai-shek retired and Li Zongren became acting president. On April 20, 1949, the Communists successfully crossed the Yangtze River without much resistance from the Kuomintang armies or air force. Shanghai fell on May 25, and the port of Qingdao on June 2. On September 21, 1949, Mao Zedong endorsed the establishment of the People's Republic of China at a Chinese People's Political Consultative Conference in Beijing,

---

*Acheson, *The China White Paper*, p. 335.

which formulated provisional policies for the new nation. On October 1, 1949, the People's Republic of China was proclaimed, and Zhou Enlai became its premier and foreign minister. On December 7, 1949, the defeated Nationalist government fled to Formosa as the Communists took Kunming, the capital of Yunnan Province.

The defeat of the Kuomintang government did not surprise me. Observing the chaos of China as soon as I had arrived in 1947, I worried over the persistent rumor that passage to the United States was sold out for months ahead. I began to think of returning home in early 1948. Disenchantment with much at Lingnan and homesickness compounded with the failure of my first love promoted the desire to go home. The war took a serious turn when the Communists captured the city of Sibingjie on March 12, 1948, a strategic point on the railway line to Mukden. Harbin fell the next day. Many rumors prevailed, such as that there was heavy fighting in the Kaifeng region on the Yellow River, where the Communists appeared to have their main forces. After a number of letters back and forth, including one letter from the family doctor urging me not to be a "quitter," my family reluctantly decided that I could return home.

My father sent a welcomed cashier's check for $500 to cover my passage back home. It had taken three or four exchanges of letters and some time before the check arrived, because my family thought I was giving up too soon. I managed to convince them that the conditions in China were not conducive to study and that the war was worsening. With the check, I made arrangements to travel as quickly as possible. I obtained campus clearance, purchased steamer fare from Guangzhou to Hong Kong and hired porter service in Guangzhou to transport my heavy baggage from Lingnan to the dock for the British steamer. I insisted that the stevedore contractor send enough help, which he did with three muscular men to whom my crates, steamer trunk, and bags seemed like trifles. They packed them with light humor on to and then off of a truck. I wanted to avoid the pathetic experience of the struggling woman who helped carry my baggage when I arrived in China. Everything went according to plan, including farewells, and I was on my way to Hong Kong without any problems other than the usual moving pains.

On the river steamer, I roamed about in the warm evening air and happened to look into the engine room entrance. Standing there with an empty pipe between my lips, I listened to the steady rhythm of the steam engines turning the twin paddle wheels. Easing up at last after an active week, as travellers typically do in the period following departure, I savored my good fortune at handling my travel and transition with little difficulty. Whether you are a jet-setter or ordinary person, that moment of pause must be a human characteristic whether the details worked out perfectly or not. After reaching the airliner, ship, bus, or train and entrusting one's transport to others, one can enjoy the relief of having made it after all, with no obstacle such as a traffic jam on a freeway. On that steamer in 1948, I relaxed in the sunset glow settling on the lowlands of the Pearl River Delta and reflected on my China experiences. Jarring me from my thoughts and completely spoiling a precious moment, a gray-haired European man shrieked at me, "Don't you Chinamen know how to read?" and pointed to a sign in English and Chinese that read "Do Not Smoke. Danger." He glared at me self-righteously. Without a word, I showed him the pipe's empty bowl and turned my back on the speechless, red-faced colonial type. It is worth noting that I did not tell him that I was an American to correct his impression that I was a native Chinese. Though I felt eager to return home and escape the collapse of old China, the little incident on the steamer indicated that a significant change in my attitude had taken place. I resented the man's arrogance and presence in China and longed for the day when China would be its own master. Even then, in 1948, smuggling and piracy dominated the Pearl River, on which we sailed forty miles from Guangzhou to Hong Kong. How could waters that had borne the weight of ninetecnth-century opium smugglers, witnessed the crude and bloody adventures of desperate pirates, and trafficked so many navies, armies, and tons of arms appear so serene and picturesque? The world has no other stretch of water that bears such a tragic tale of woe. Intimately involved with East-West relations and China's weaknesses across the centuries, the Pearl River, once China's chief commercial pasageway, must possess a despicable testimony to the passage of time in the filth of its bottom mud.

Without realizing it then, I had formed a degree of attachment to my Chinese ancestry. Regardless of my negative impressions of China and my homesickness for the United States and its comforts, I could not escape the fact that my ancestral roots were Chinese and that people related to me more as a person in China as opposed to as a stereotype in the United States. In the years after my return from China in 1948, I would reflect over and over on my experiences in old China and attempt to fill in many gaping holes of ignorance. In the next chapter, I describe the experience that most favorably evoked ancient China for me during the 1947–1948 journey. Even though I have traveled extensively in China on six different trips beginning in 1972 since the 1947 field trip, there has been no experience to compare with the visit to Deng Wu. My trip into the interior to the Dcng Wu monastery presented a momentous glimpse which showed me an age-old and stable China. Deng Wu seemed more real than Guangzhou's decay and struggle in the throes of modern-day realities, not the least of which was the irreversible outcome of the Chinese Civil War. However, the truth, which I would realize in time, was that the existence of Deng Wu would be swept away in the revolutionary changes of post-1949 China. Still, my memory of those experiences in 1947 remains. Deng Wu symbolizes a traditional China that will continue to exist in Chinese civilization and culture. How fortunate for my growing identity and awareness that it was possible to journey to China and Deng Wu.

Field Trip into the Past

The terraced chamber is so high there
Up in the mountains
I can pluck the stars.
I dare not lift my voice there
Lest I disturb
Heaven's denizens.
LI PO *(701–762), Chamber in Mountain Shrine*

At dock or under tow, the great barges in the waters of Guangzhou commanded attention. Loading or unloading the barges, coolies hauled heavy loads that seemed too much for such slight men to bear, picking up chits for figuring their wages as they passed a foreman single file up the gangplank. Great piles of grain, vegetables, and pigs individually woven into basket-like nets crowded the dockyards and the wooden barges that stretched 150 to 200 feet long. When the daily flow of the river shifted with the ocean's tides, a great cymbal and horn commanded the simultaneous turning of all vessels docked along Guangzhou's bund—a very colorful sight indeed. Rusty but ominous-looking, ball cannons from another era stood guard at the four corners of the ancient-style ships. Pirates and bandits were a dangerous reality in pre-1949 China; their exploits seemed straight out of the comic strip "Terry and the Pirates." I recall reading of one attempt in 1948 by the Hong Kong government to put down the great bands by sending out a force of several army battalions, a destroyer, and

Spitfire fighter planes. The Chinese navy, which was as ineffective as it was corruptible, had stopped patrolling the Pearl River area by March 1948, thus increasing the trafficking of illegal contraband and pirating. High above the colorful bustle of a barge flew banners and a great neon light with the craft's name in Chinese characters. At its bow, two painted eyes saw the way and nothing. At night, such craft moved along quite gloriously—cabin lights of the several-storied stern shining brightly from within, neon lights above, occasional strings of trailing lights and banners, and sparks flying from the churning tow boat ahead, equipped with modern engine, 20 mm cannon and machine guns.

During a trip into the interior of Guangdong Province with a group of American students in December 1947, we travelled 200 miles from Guangzhou on one of these barges toward our destination, the monastery of Deng Wu, on the Xi Jiang or West River. Deng Wu's history is related to the famous monastery of Nanhua near Zhujiang on the Bei Jiang River. Nanhua is known as the first Buddhist monastery in the region and is unequalled in the history of Buddhist life in South China. An Indian monk named Tamo arrived in Guangzhou during the reign of King Wu of Liang (502–549 A.D.), and on his way north to Nanjing founded the monastery. The building we visited in 1947 may have been built during the Tang or Song dynasties.

The barge's first-class cabin area was an open room without much individual privacy. It had comfortable bunks for each person, perpendicular to the vessel's sides, and each bunk area had a thermos of hot tea and a cup attached to a wall holder. Long dining tables stretched down the middle of the fluorescent-lighted cabin. After dinner, we students huddled at the bow and sang American school and folk songs, with sparks from the tow boat spraying us and the barge. Small villages with flickering lights and pagoda silhouettes broke the dark, lowlands scenery. Caught up in the lovely atmosphere it seemed as if we were singing around a campfire at home rather than riding an ancient-style craft to an ancient monastery on a historic river in China. "Home on the Range" and "I've Been Working on the Railroad" could not have been more out of place but youthful camaraderie has a way of making young Americans loosen up and feel snug wherever they may be together.

We should have sensed our incongruence with the age-old environment as we sang "Old MacDonald Had a Farm." Staring into the calm, dark waters just ahead of the foaming impact of the *Marine Adder*'s steel crossing the Pacific, I had had strong, almost hypnotic compulsions to leap overboard and join the moonlit, phosphorescent waves. Looking out from the deck of the barge at pastoral China, I felt like a giant who could see all but was compelled to do nothing lest anything be changed or spoiled. China seemed more than changeless; its unity of being caused you to accept it whole and timeless, whether you liked what you saw or not. For Americans, change stood as a basic rule and alternative—interchangeable parts made up the plastic whole. Though I both cherished and abhorred much that flowed about me in China, I could not shake a sense of benign passivity and impotence. If I were to become a doer, I could feel at home in the United States, but not in China where my role became more of an observer and sojourner.

After two days on the great river barge without any sign of pirates, at which I was naively disappointed, we landed at a town of perhaps 3,000 people, named Xiu Hing. The stone and brick buildings huddled closely together in a uniform, grayish mass unbroken by any commercial or decorative color and flair. The tile-roofed houses opened abruptly onto the alleyways separating the rows of houses. Wooden doors amidst solid walls indicated individual dwellings, some of which sported semicircular capstones above the doors. A series of broad, terraced steps of flat stones led from the water to the street level where a crowd of people had gathered to stare at the debarking Americans.

Chinese peasants typically stare at strangers. When blond and red-haired people chanced by, as happened at Xiu Hing when we landed, curiosity got the better of the local people, and they actually went up to the white coeds and ran their fingers through their curls to test their reality. The gals had endured such behavior in Guangzhou, so they were not very surprised here and politely guided the hands away. The locals wore slight variations of the pajama-like blouse-and-pant suit with cloth buttons, which appeared clean but were as dull-colored and drab as the buildings. Small children wore little at all, and if they wore bottoms, large, circular openings in the rear took the place of diapers. Cut closely, the children's hair looked as if bowls placed upside down on their heads had formed the hairstyle, making them look quite cute. As we waited for our host to arrive, the crowd stared at us quietly without speaking or moving. As the boats departed with farewell hoots, dusk fell quickly and kerosene lights in the houses shown brightly, casting long shadows and little reflection on the gray walls as night took hold upon the narrowing scene. I felt far back in time, as if out of my world, except for the small kids who seemed the most common bond between this world and mine.

During the trip into the interior, people would assume that I served as official guide for the group and would speak to me as such. Wearing a surplus GI cap and field jacket, which I had purchased at a Guangzhou street stand, I must have looked the part. I felt ambivalent about the mistaken impression, sometimes explaining that I was a *wa-kew* or overseas Chinese, and at other times trying to act the role of the responsible leader. My Cantonese had improved in the several months since I had come to China, but lacked depth. Thus I committed some faux pas, such as when I pompously asked a persistent young man who came up to me on the boat where his mother lived and used a term for mother that is roughly translatable as "old woman," but is cruder in Chinese. Without flinching, the scrubby-haired fellow actually answered politely. Perhaps the usage suited my supposed position. Learning the meaning of the expression after the excursion, I hardly recalled the incident without embarrassment and regret over what was, though unknowingly, an elitist and arrogant act. Other terms I knew from home went over badly at Lingnan. My family being from the *Sze Yup* as discussed earlier, I spoke a Cantonese dialect that was essentially backcountry, rural talk. A Lingnan coed that I grew very fond of put me straight once when I referred to whites as *fon gway*. She said, "If you talk like that, people will think you are from the village (back country)." Amazed, I asked what was wrong, and she said *fon gway* literally meant "foreign devil," which I had not realized. She said the proper term was *sai yun* or "Westerner." Thus, I began to learn to speak the more urban Cantonese or the *Som Yup* dialect. However, when I returned to Califoirnia all of my *Som Yup* had to be abandoned, as the men teased me for taking on pretentious airs or speaking like a female—the Chinese ladies of my parents' generation in the United States spoke *Som Yup* in social circles as a sign of cultured training. The elders had sent me to China to learn the Chinese language and culture; my speaking to them in *Som Yup* provoked their unexpected laughter. As the saying goes, "Sometimes you can't win at losing."

After a long wait at Xiu Hing, a matronly, white-haired English lady, about sixty years old, came to receive us. Her voice and movements were so active and well-directed, I would not have known at first that this missionary was totally blind, except for her guide dogs. Several big German shepherd police dogs darted in and out through the crowd, and I noticed several hours later how she depended ever so slightly on her dogs and her cane. It astonished me that she could be so effective in assisting the villagers and that she had stayed there long after her husband died. She had been there for about twenty years, if I remember correctly.

The lady gave especially warm greetings to the leader of our party, Mrs. Frank, whose husband had served Lingnan University for about twenty years as a professor of chemistry and as provost. He left China in 1951, after the Communists tried him publicly for being a spy and rudely evicted him. Earning his Ph.D. in chemistry at the age of twenty-one or so, the youngest to do so in the history of the University of California, Berkeley, Henry S. Frank, following his fine sense of Christian values, developed a reputation as scholar, teacher, and academic leader in China. Dr. Frank sent his wife and family to safety in the United States during the Sino-Japanese War which began in 1937 and continued at Lingnan into World War II. The Frank's eldest, Austin, and I became friends at Lingnan and have been in touch since. As do the other children, Austin speaks perfect Cantonese, and his command of the language used to astound people in Guangzhou, who never thought a red-haired, freckled man of only nineteen or twenty could become so acculturated. Once at a restaurant in Guangzhou, Austin and I paid no heed during the meal to the prejudiced comments of the waiters about foreigners, obviously directed at Austin. When we paid the bill and got up to depart, Austin made elaborate farewells to all and sent compliments to the chef in exuberant Cantonese. The waiters' mouths and eyes opened wide in utter surprise and embarrassment; they seemed frozen in their natty white jackets and black, pantaloon-like trousers fastened tightly at the ankles. Austin and I held in our guffaws until we got out into the hotel lobby.

During my first year at the University of California,

Berkeley in 1950 to 1951, I saw from my apartment window someone who looked like Austin running by Edwards Field down Bancroft Way. Shouting his name, I saw him stop and turn inquisitively. I rushed out for my first Lingnan reunion since leaving in 1948. Over the years, in our own way and time, the two of us became educational psychologists and have had the pleasure of meeting now and then. His father capped a dedicated career in China by teaching and research at the University of Pittsburgh from where he finally retired in 1974. I recall how kindly Mrs. Frank treated me at Lingnan, even responding warmly to her son's request that I come into their home to play the piano and inviting me to dine at times. As we gathered at the Frank's residence for the monastery venture during Christmas break, 1947, Austin saw how skimpy my bedroll looked and informed his mother, who smilingly clucked at me once and quickly fetched a blanket from her home. Far from being affluent, Dr. Frank's income was much lower than what he would have earned at a stateside university. As I played "Sentimental Journey," "June Is Busting Out All Over," or some other pop piece on the piano in his living room, he read the newspaper and appeared tolerant and friendly toward my intrusions into his parlor. Remembering that today, I see that his parental sense of patience surpassed my own with my children's friends and the stray pet animals they found. I photographed the Franks' family home when I revisited the Lingnan campus in 1972 and 1980. I took about twenty pictures of the campus in 1972, and Dr. Frank eagerly requested through Austin that I have fourteen sets made for the Lingnan Board of Trustees. Austin said his mother and sister cried when they saw the picture of their former home. Besides the typical human attachment to a place that had played such an important role in their lives, the home had been given to them for life according to the Chinese custom and was one of the better fringe benefits of being a scholar in old China. It was good to learn that Zhongshan (new name replacing Lingnan) had invited Professor Frank to visit in 1981, but I was sorry that Mrs. Frank was unable to go because of ill health.

At the village in 1947, Mrs. Frank greeted her missionary counterpart enthusiastically. The two ladies exchanged great bundles of sentiment and news in animated conversation. Recalling that precious reunion of the two ladies, I must say that good and decent people such as they and the Frank family contributed much to pre-1949 China and deserve greater credit than the People's Republic of China has granted. Mrs. Frank's parents had been missionaries in Beijing and had helped to establish modern medical education. However, no matter their efforts, China needed more than the devotion and contributions of so few to throw off the yoke of the past.

We spent the evening in the mission compound and had a light supper, mainly from the simple supplies we had brought. Mrs. Frank had brought the mission some medical and miscellaneous supplies, such as soap and cloth, and all of us tried our best not to tax the little mission's budget. With only a cup of tea for breakfast, we were eager to put aside our hunger pangs through activity. Beginning the climb up the mountain to our destination pleased everyone, though the hour was only about six A.M. As we formed a line of march and bid farewell to the blind missionary, she conveyed remarkable warmth and had the uncanny ability to find each person's eyes as she spoke to us. As we trudged up the steep slope away from the little town, I noted two frail-looking militiamen wearing faded, worn-out uniforms accompanying us. Each carried a long-barreled, rusty rifle that appeared to be useless as a weapon. We learned from them that the lady missionary had asked them to escort us to the monastery. Instead of protecting us from bandits through possible force of arms, the militiamen provided more than adequate security simply through their presence. Apparently, their town had worked out a mutually beneficial accommodation with the local bandits in an understanding that whenever the militiamen guided a group, the bandits would stay away.

Moving up the gently rising trail, we found rectangular blocks of granite embedded parallel lengthwise with the path. Each approximately 1½ by 4 feet, I lost count of the blocks and marveled at the laborious work they represented. As large granite deposits were not indigenous to the region, they must have been transported from some distance and at great expense long ago. Bamboo thickets and trees, mostly willows and Chinese elm, lined the trail. Quite unexpectedly, three pairs of young boys, perhaps no more than fourteen years old each, came running past us carrying large sacks of rice, each of which was strapped onto the middle of a long bamboo pole. As the boys swung past us, one on each end of a pole, the large sacks of rice bounced up and down with the rhythm of the fast pace that the boys maintained. After twenty minutes or so, we came across the boys again quietly resting by the trail and seeming quite exhausted. In another fifteen or twenty minutes, the boys trudged past us again, swinging their loads of rice up the path. This intermittent running and resting by the boys made me curious enough to ask them why they rushed so, and they said they worked in such a fashion so as to carry their heavy cargo as little as possible. However, we could not convince them that by running, they were actually being less efficient and were liable to exhaust themselves sooner. Running a locomotive or truck extra fast to minimize the carrying time would be as childish, but the lads were really only children. They turned out to be orphans whom the monastery had adopted; they were doing odd jobs before they began their training as Buddhist monks several years hence.

The trail followed the banks of a small stream and at times the granite blocks served as narrow bridges across a rivulet or branch of the brook. The ground gradually sloped upward and away on one side of the trail to hilltops and ridges where grass grew, since it was not feasible to cultivate such places. Terraces for rice had been built where the land could be cultivated, much the same as I would see in Korea during the war. As we moved along, I got the feeling that the terrain had been unchanged for ages. Each rock, small or large, seemed to have been picked up a hundred times and placed down by human hands. Nothing seemed randomly placed on that trail or, for that matter, anywhere in China. Acquainted with the forests of California, especially the virgin redwood groves, I thought about the tremendous contrast between the terrain of the United States and that of China and I wondered if California would look like this and remain as picturesque in three or four thousand years.

After two to three hours of hiking up the lovely trail and being refreshed by occasional sprinkles, a tremendous gong resounded unexpectedly ahead and its sound reverberated through the hillsides every fifteen seconds. I have not heard a greater percussion sound since. Learning that it was coming from the Deng Wu monastery, I determined to search for the instrument, for it must have been quite huge and beautifully crafted. The interval between each sounding of the gong gradually lengthened until the ringing finally ceased. Fifteen minutes before we reached the monastery, we began to encounter more and more evergreen trees. Stone steps took the place of the path, and gradually lengthened in expanse so that the last 200 yards led to the main gate of the monastery. A gradual elbow bend at about the middle of the stepway broke the sharpness of the climb.

As we rounded the turn, Deng Wu stood before us. Beyond the front gate, I could see an establishment more magnificent than I had expected. The monastery seemed to be an entire village of its own with many tiled structures extending up a hillside behind the tall stone walls. As we walked through the open gate, a monk came forward to greet us. Without any words or fanfare, he smiled genuinely and guided us into a room near the entrance. Dressed in a saffron-colored robe, the man of peace wore metal-rimmed eyeglasses and his head was cleanly shaven. As is characteristic of all Buddhist monks I have met, he seemed completely at ease and content. He seemed to be beyond the frailties of human emotion.

After the several days on the boat and the long hike up the mountain to reach the ancient monastery, I hardly expected to find a framed sign, to which the monk gestured, giving a general orientation to the monastery in English, French, German, and Chinese. We told him that we had complied with the monastery's rule that visitors must bathe and don fresh underclothes before entering. This pleased him and he told us in Chinese that we were welcome and could stay a few nights as we wished. He led us to our quarters which were quite high up in the left-hand corner of the monastery compound, so we passed through several spacious courtyards and climbed long stairways to reach our very attractive suite of rooms and our rooftop courtyard. Mrs. Frank and the other leaders of our group went to discuss meals with the monks and worked out an agreeable arrangement for evening meals . Dedicated Buddhists never eat the flesh of animals, but I hardly missed meat those three days. With many varieties of dried and fresh vegetables, peanuts, dried bean curd, other soybean products and an abundance of rice, we ate royally at night and I still savor the excellent meatless dishes furnished by the monastery kitchen. The monks apologized jokingly that Deng Wu had no running water or electricity, for they had not recovered from the drastic decline in their income during the Japanese occupation. Not only did the monastery's population of monks and staff decline sharply because of the severe poverty during the war, but the monastery had to sell off its plumbing and other goods in order to survive at all. They said good-humoredly that during the war they had "eaten" their water pipes. During the day, the lighting through windows and the open courts and corridors was more than adequate; but at night, without moonlight, the place became pitch black, which made it difficult to wander about. Day or night, however, I explored and searched in vain for the great gong that we had heard on the trail.

Hearing music the second evening, I went down the many stairs to locate its source with one student who seemed equally curious. Stumbling about and often falling in passages and on stairs so easily traversed in the daylight, we struck innumerable matches, pursuing the music through the darkened maze until at length we discovered what we sought at the monastery gateway. By the light of a small kerosene lantern, one monk, dressed in a white mourning gown, sat on a small table about four feet high with his legs folded in front of him. He wore a white, rectangular hat with a string that tied under his chin. A huge book containing script and illustrations was propped before him, and he sang in a high-pitched tone. His back to the monastery proper, he sat cross-legged facing the front gate. In front of and below the singer were three or four other monks who played the accompaniment instruments, a *sona*, drum and cymbals.

A small wooden oboe, a *sona* has a conical bore and flared metal bell. Akin to the Persian *zurna* and Indian *shahnai*, it is much more piercing and shrill than the relatively mellow tones of the modern Western oboe. The *sona* is a common instrument in Chinese opera, especially for military and tragic performances. We learned that the performance had ben commissioned by a wealthy family far off, perhaps in Guangzhou, to obtain the mercy of Buddha and the compassionate goddess Guanyin for a departed one's acceptance into

Jingtu, the Pure Land, equivalent to the Western concept of heaven. Following an eclectic life philosophy of Confucian, Taoist, and Buddhist beliefs, all blending into a realistic, live-and-let-live world, a benevolent, hierarchical family structure, balance between man and nature, and *yin-yang* complementarity throughout the universe, the Chinese sought eternal happiness through Buddhism.

There was once a nobleman in northeast India who realized that life was ephemeral and often mean and that the people needed guidance to right living and eternal salvation. Siddhartha Gautama (ca. 563–483 B.C.) became a Buddha or Enlightened One after many years of study, meditations, and travel initiated on the advice of the gods under the pipal tree in Bodh Gaya (ca. 525 B.C.). Thus Gautama Buddha did not originate as a god but achieved godly qualities through self-study, sacrifice, and love for others. Gautama's disciples taught from noble truths that earthly suffering is inherent, that life's misery comes from the craving for pleasure and from not following the right path, that human cravings can be overcome, and that eternal salvation can be obtained through a methodical path beginning with faith and self-purification during life. Over the centuries since Gautama, many Buddhist sects have developed and been shaped to satisfy varied cultural needs. The Pure Land school of Buddhism became the most popular throughout Asia, especially in China. Expressing the greatest love for all creatures and achieving the greatest good from helping others, the Pure Land school recognizes Buddhas-to-be or bodhisattvas—those who refrain from entering nirvana, the final beatitude for Buddhists, in order to compassionately save others. Thus, bodhisattvas are worshipped as deities and the Buddha becomes manifested in multiple Buddhas and Buddhas-to-be.

The Pure Land, or Jing tu, can be reached after death if one calls the Chinese name of Buddha, O-mi-tuo

(Amitabha in Sanskrit), the Buddha of Unlimited Light. Salvation to the Pure Land school of Buddhists does not come from individual effort or the merits one has achieved but from faith in Buddha's grace, especially the pietistic, repetitious invocation of the name of O-mi-tuo. The Pure Land possessed no evil and its inhabitants would be long-lived and without want of any kind. Those passing into the Pure Land would also have the opportunity to enter nirvana, the godly state of the Buddha.

Touring Mount Fuji in 1972 while my family and I were in Japan, we found ourselves on a crowded bus. The overloaded bus was going too fast on the crude road, and everyone grew alarmed. As we rounded a sharp turn, the bus bounced and lurched so to the side that I could see far down the mountain. At that terrifying moment for all on the bus, several people cried out "Amida!" (the name for Buddha in Japan). As the bus righted itself and continued on, many chuckled at their fright.

Underlying the Pure Land school of Buddhism, the most popular in Chinese history, is the *Sukhavativyuha*, a text written in India in the first century A.D. The text or *sutra* concerns a Buddhist monk named Dharmakara who was said to have studied for millions of years and then promised to fulfill many vows if he became a Buddha. Eighteen vows are revealed, emphasizing various approaches to salvation such as reflection and good deeds, but the eighteenth involved the calling of the name of the Buddha at death. Achieving Buddhahood some time after he made his vows, Dharmakara resides in the Pure Land, helping others without discrimination to reach salvation too. As the Buddha of Infinite Light, Dharmakara is flanked by his bodhisattvas, Aralokitesvara, the Goddess of Mercy (Guanyin in Chinese) to his left and Mahasthamaprapta on the right, who helps to bring the pietist into the Pure Land. The monk conducting the funeral services at Deng Wu may have been reciting from the *Sukhavativyuha* or the *sajya-guru-vai-durya-prabhasa*, a text that elaborates the twelve vows made by Buddha in his previous lives to assist unfortunate creatures who suffer.

About 650 A.D., after its introduction to China from India in the third century, Amitabha, the Pure Land school of Buddhism, in contrast to other Buddhist sects in India, which emphasize mysticism, captured the pragmatic, down-to-earth people of China, who have never taken well to supernatural beliefs and life-long concern for the afterlife. Amitabha spread to Japan in the twelfth and thirteenth centuries, where Buddha is called Amida. The much-photographed great bronze Buddha sitting in restful contemplation at Kamakura, Japan (1252), is Amida. A monk named Yin-guang (1861–1940), working mainly in the provinces of Jiangsu and Zhejiang, helped to revive the concept of the Pure Land, in which faith in Amitabha Buddha and realizing the Buddha-nature within oneself brought salvation. Thus everyone, rich and poor alike, could enter the Pure Land by practicing *nian-ruo*, invoking the Buddha's grace by uttering O-mi-tuo over and over again. By doing so with a faithful mind, all sins and evil would be overcome and one could be reborn in the Western Paradise or Jing tu. Using rosaries to count the repetitions of *nian-ruo*, reciting scriptures, and celebrating the new year and other sacred days with *zhai* or meatless meals, the Chinese are fairly ritualistic in expressing their faith in Buddhism but become quite serious at the supreme event of death.

Chinese Buddhism became a far cry from the mysticism, literate exercises, and contemplation found in its Indian roots. Besides the Pure Land school, the Chinese developed a Zhan school of Buddhism which was iconoclastic. Advocating intuitive insight, sudden enlightenment, mental agility, keen wit, and the universality of Buddha in all things, the Zhan found the spiritual essence in bamboo, flowers, plants, mountains, streams, animals, and so forth. "The voice of Buddha may speak in the songs of birds, the silence of the mountains, the crashing of waterfalls, or the whisper of trees in the wind."* Thus, the landscape artists of the Song encapsulated the Zhan spirit in magnificent scenes such as the one by the master Ma Yuan, with mountains that seem to float in the distance and a solitary fisherman, sitting in his boat with rod in hand. The fisherman's boat is suspended with no real existence, it seems, lost on the waters with no banks visible and only several smooth waves near the boat to indicate water.

The ceremony we observed at the monastery gate in December 1947 was also being conducted in the monks' dining area, probably in respect of Mi-luo-ruo, the popular image of Buddha as a jolly, fat man with protruding tummy, heavy jowls, and a happy, laughing look. About 1,200 years ago during the Song dynasty, the image of the Buddha-to-be Maitreya, formerly a huge, heroic figure, evolved into a jovial, fat figure which embodied significant life-ideals of the Chinese—wealth and plenty of good food, leisure and contentment, good humor, friendship, and, shown often with a number of male children, a large family. Standing with his hands raised high, Maitreya invites all to obtain good fortune by rubbing his fat tummy.

At sunrise and dusk, the monastery's regular services took place in the shrine hall where great images of Buddha resided. Three of those figures were over ten feet tall. The room contained a central altar where the great Buddha, in an attitude of meditation, resided above a series of minor icons and incense burners. To the lower left and right of the hall were the altars of the bodhisattvas. I was astounded to see that the stone before these statues had been worn with grooves by the thousands upon thousands of kneeling and prostrating

*Kenneth Ch'en, *Buddhism in China: A Historical Survey* (Princeton, New Jersey: Princeton University Press, 1964), p. 480.

monks across the centuries. The service began with lines
of monks coming from the left and right, meeting in
front of the center icons. Incense hung heavy in the
open air, and several candles had been lit. The monks
chanted a monotone liturgy which continuously in-
voked the name of O-mi-tuo. The baritone chant began
as a murmur and became more entrancing as its volume
increased after five minutes or so, when the ringing of a
small bell, which one monk rang with a pull-string, began to punctuate the chanting. The occasional synco-
pated peals of the bell resonated above the masculine
chanting. Almost in counterpoint, the beating of a large
wooden block began and then a kettle-like drum joined
in, so that the ceremony grew into a stirring service with
the increasing intensity and interplay of the chanting
and three percussion pieces. At the climax, the great
gong for which I had searched, but could not locate,
sounded and drowned out all else. As the gong reverberated between strikings, the chanting, bell, block, and
drum could be heard in concert. The Buddhist service
was quite moving, even for an observer unfamiliar with
its details.

For varying reasons, three of us had to return to
Guangzhou ahead of the group. It was decided that we
would hurry down the mountain to the river village
before sunrise, since we would be without a militia
escort. Taking leave shortly after a downpour, we scur-
ried as quickly as we could down the dark, wet path. As
we began to pant and breathe little clouds of steam, the
great peal of the gong for the morning service reverberated through the mountains and trees. The sound
seemed to come from all directions. In awe, we looked
back up the path and saw the rays of the dawn's bright
sun shining upward in an arch directly behind the
monastery. Framed by the surrounding trees, the monastery appeared to be the source of the brilliant rays of
light and grew increasingly golden-colored as the sun
rose higher. We stood staring at the glorious spectacle as

if transfixed, oblivious of all else. Soon the clapping of the mighty gong ceased and the radiating sunbeams passed to the brightening of the entire landscape. Birds stirred on a tree nearby; we glanced at one another and continued our trek without speaking.

Reaching the river without incident, we secured the aid of the lady missionary. With her help, we hired a sampan to ferry us to a point down the river where we could catch the train to Guangzhou. Sitting in the cold air, I watched the rhythmic forward thrust of the boatwoman at the rear, propelling the small craft with the crossed double oars. After a stroke, the oars would return to a crossed position because of the motion of the boat and the ingenious design of the fixed paddles. Standing up, the woman worked at rowing without much strain and acknowledged my gaze with a golden smile and pleasantries. Most of her teeth had been capped with gold, a popular custom among the lower classes. Barefooted, she wore dark loose trousers and a tight blouse with the typical Chinese high collar and cloth buttons down the side. Her hands were dark and rough with thick callouses, and the constant exposure to the sun had burnt her face dark brown and crinkled her eyes. Her coarse, almost unkempt black hair was piled on top of her head and held with a hairpiece. With her bronze complexion, the golden smile seemed a natural color combination. We chatted and teased one another as she rowed. An example of China's millions upon millions of peasants, the woman gave little heed to religion as represented by the monastery, but was not without her superstitions. Eking out an existence that made one American dollar a worthy sum, the peasants attended to survival needs first, last, and always. To the boatwoman, religion, education, and aesthetics were just luxuries meant for those who had the means and leisure to pursue them. Safety was related closely to survival, too. As she whispered her dread of pirates and searched from side to side for any sign of them, we wondered silently if pirates would be on the prowl so early in the day.

The sampan ferries that grouped about the dock at Lingnan University utilized an additional woman to handle an oar at the bow, since the current between the university and Guangzhou could be tricky especially when the tide shifted or flowed in the opposite direction. I once made a twilight ride to Shameen when a note on my dormitory door informed me that Canadian missionary friends from the S.S. *Marine Adder* had been by and wanted to see me. Along with the young journalist Philip Foisie, Eldon and Caroline Andrews surely helped to enrich the more than two-week voyage across the Pacific with their humor, counseling, and tolerance for a Chinese American teenager who knew less Chinese than they did. I had to find a sampan so I could see the missionary teachers but the women at the dock were highly reluctant to venture out into the river at that hour. They scolded me for asking them to endanger their craft, valuables, and lives with the strong possibility of pirate attacks. Suppose I got kidnaped? What would their reputation be then? By convincing them of the emergency and sweetening the toll by paying three-fold, I found one sampan crew to accept my offer, claiming that they wanted to go to Guangzhou anyway. The other women hooted at them, and what a loud and lewd chorus it became! We went as fast as the two women could row, and if I had any doubts about the sincerity of the protests at the dock, I discarded them when I observed the unmistakable expressions of apprehension on the faces of the two boatwomen. Then I began to imagine that pirates and bandits were responsible for any and all activity on the river and its banks. Though sampans rode so low that passengers could easily trail their fingers in the water, I felt our size on the river was greatly magnified and wanted to row, too. After one attempt on another ride, I had found that rowing requires far more muscle and coordination than I had, much to the hilarious humor of the women. As we entered Guangzhou, we passed rows and rows of barges and sampans that I scanned for danger. Yet nothing happened, and I never saw happier sampan workers than those at the end of the memorable ride of fearful haste and apprehension. The Andrewses and I were reunited but for a short time. Before dawn, they boarded a truck and were on their way to teach in Kunming. That was the last time I saw the two. However, after twenty-eight years of unsuccessful attempts at locating the Andrewses, a friend of mine in the East Asia office of the National Council of Churches obtained their Toronto address for me in 1975. Though we have not met again since that evening at Shameen Island in 1947, after the tense sampan ride, we have written and look forward to a reunion.

As Deng Wu slipped further behind on that sampan ride to the train stop, the river looked much broader and more forbidding than it had during the ride on the river barge several days earlier. Small and low in the water, the sampan seemed to be more in the midst of a large, placid lake than on a river. Below the river banks, which were almost 200 to 300 yards away on either side, we could see no other craft or person. The sky became overcast, and we wondered about rain and wind. According to the boatwoman, we could save much time and be assured of getting a seat on a train if we went to a closer stop along the river. The idea raised my suspicion since she had not mentioned this stop when receiving instructions at the mission. The three of us discussed her suggestion and decided to take a risk, each of us wanting to end the sampan voyage and to return to Guangzhou as soon as possible. Turning the sampan toward the shore as soon as we had agreed, the woman landed us in less than half an hour at a very small village.

In relief, we saw a passenger train at the stop with a

few people boarding. Dismissing my suspicion of possible foul play, which on reflection seemed highly unlikely to occur with someone chosen by the mission, I realized the woman's scheme when we finalized the fare. Though she had taken us only half the distance, she wanted the fare originally agreed upon. Putting up only mild protest, which really meant, "Aha, you came out ahead this time!" we paid her the money and in return got a golden farewell. She docked near several other sampans, beginning a noisy conversation and rolling up a great smoke typical of the sampan women.

Taking a sheet of paper about five by seven inches, the women would form a cone which they would stuff with tobacco and seal with saliva. The improvised cigarettes seemed comically grotesque and primitive, especially when they got close to the end of the cigarette. They illustrate the resourcefulness of the Chinese poor. Nothing is wasted in China, as the saying goes, and I can testify to that. The compliment must be qualified by noting the desperate necessity of the masses who have learned to be resourceful and to make much that Americans would discard useful and productive. For example, writing only on one side of a sheet of paper is wasteful when the other side can be used, even for writing that has no relation to what is on the other side. The paper wasted by an ordinary elementary school in the United States would easily serve the needs of three times as many Chinese pupils. Regarding smoking, I once purchased a pack of Camel cigarettes in Guangzhou and to my great surprise found the quoted price quite low. With the peddler's reassurance on the price, I took the pack but the first puff nearly gagged me. After close inspection, I found that the wrapper was genuine but the cigarettes within had been constructed from leftover butts. The peddler probably though that I knew what I was getting. My experience was certainly in accordance with the saying, "You get what you pay for."

While the sampan lady puffed on her cone cigarette, the

three of us boarded a third-class car of the train which was empty then, but which after innumerable stops had become "standing room only" by the time we arrived in Guangzhou. The sampan lady had taken us to the right place. In China, trains were run with great bravado and daring. Throughout the runs, the whistle squealed frequently whenever the trains approached each of the many villages and warning had to be given. Alternately building up steam and slowing or stopping, the trains' frequent jerks and jolts compared poorly with the comfort of American streamliners, now also of bygone days. Although they provided strong appeal for the venturesome minority, the trains provoked the apprehension of the majority. To ride the trains was to flirt with disaster, as holdups and kidnapings could occur. With windows that were usually open to catch the air during the hot seasons, the coaches provided wooden benches except in the cushioned first-class cars. All the varied bags and baggage the passengers could carry aboard was acceptable. The four-hour trip, from Guangzhou to Hong Kong, provided an interesting panorama of scenery: ancient pagodas amidst innumerable villages; now and then an elaborate guard tower; miles and miles of colorful agricultural fields under intensive care; a child, wearing a straw hat wide enough to serve as an umbrella, herding a flock of ducks with a long pole; the brooding, mysterious rivers and deltas; and the broad hills so prominent in the landscape and shaded in various degrees of blue, gray, and black.

Trains have appealed to me since my youth. There are those of us who share a common nostalgia for the siren-like sound and sight of the steam locomotive, especially the far-off peal of the train's whistle. My fascination originated and was fixed by night walks in Santa Barbara and Merced to see the trains come and go. Also, I recall that while visiting my maternal grandmother I would watch the trains that ran down the middle of the street, setting off swinging bell signals at street corners in the old Chinatown of Los Angeles. That Chinatown is gone now. A monument of the past glorious days of the rails, Union Station in Los Angeles was built in the late 1930s for streamliners such as those of the Union Pacific with domed seating to Chicago, and the Southern Pacific's Daylight and Lark. As a sixth grader in a small town, I went regularly to the train station after school to watch the 3:45 P.M. passenger train come in and leave. The switch engines about the yard and the incoming steam locomotive with its clanging bell and hissing steam gripped me, perhaps because of my desire to travel and find adventure. After breaking one lens of my glasses at the station when it slipped out of its adhesive-taped, broken frame, my parents forbade my tarrying at the railroad station after school. Thus China's trains had a special appeal to me, even though they were far from being as sleek, swift, and smart-looking as Southern Pacific's Daylight. Though crowded, noisy and jerky, they seemed exotic and challenged the senses. The Chinese name for trains is literally "fire vehicle" which reflects in a small but telling way the disparity between centuries-old China before 1949 and the modern world outside. One would hope that Deng Wu still continues today in the new China, that one could retrace the steps of hundreds of years ago and 1947 to find the peace and serenity of such monasteries.

Great changes, as in transportation and surely in socio-political revolution, lead one to ask, "What value and role can remain for the old in the face of new ways? Can it be that either/or choices, as in the critical life-and-death dimensions of medicine, arise?" The next chapter tackles such questions and finds some answers which help to address other concerns regarding ethnic identity and self-concept.

Medicine:
Cross-Cultural Clues
to Understanding*

[*The natural*] *laws are not forces external to things, but represent the harmony of movement immanent in them.*

I CHING *(antiquity)*

There are no elements so diverse that they cannot be joined in the heart of a man.

JEAN GIRAUDOUX, *Siegfried (1928)*

During President Nixon's historic visit to the People's Republic of China in 1972, the American columnist James Reston fell victim to appendicitis and received prompt treatment at Beijing's Anti-Imperialist Hospital. Fascinating the American public, Reston's accounts of his experience with acupuncture anesthesia and modern, skillful surgery in the Chinese hospital highlighted the bits of information obtained about life in China during those early days of U.S.-P.R.C. relations. American newswriters quickly focused on the popular interest in the medical practices of China. Acupuncture soon became a common topic throughout the United States, and most discussions of the People's Republic referred

*A list of the names and titles in this chapter, and Lao Tzu's quotation is provided at the end of the chapter.

to acupuncture, its miraculous health benefits, and its unknown qualities.

Reston's experience with acupuncture was not exactly simple: thirty-six hours after his emergency operation he was "in considerable discomfort if not pain" from gas in his stomach and intestines. With Reston's approval, the Chinese medics inserted three needles in his right elbow and below a knee and twisted them "to stimulate the intestine." According to the columnist, "That sent ripples of pain racing through my limbs and at best had the effect of diverting my attention from the distress in my stomach." However, relief was achieved when the Chinese doctor used moxibustion, another treatment of old consisting of two pieces of an herb which Americans know as wormwood (*Artemisia vulgaris*) that were lit and held smoldering near the abdomen. Western physicians have no more understanding of why the moxibustion treatment works than they do of acupuncture. Dr. Li Pang-chi, the Chinese physician who supervised Reston's care, indicated that he had once had doubts about acupuncture but changed his mind after he saw its positive results and began to believe that it "can help to restore (organ) balance by removing the cause of congestion or antagonism." Flex Mann, an English physician who specializes in acupuncture and has written many books on the subject, feels that acupuncture works by stimulating the nerves. Yet he admits that his theory is highly speculative and that little is known beyond that. Reston had been told the same in Beijing by the modern Chinese doctors.

Visitors to the People's Republic of China since 1972 have given repeated reports of observing major surgery in which the patient had no other anesthesia than several needles inserted at unlikely locations and activated with light electric charges. Patients undergoing hernia and more serious operations under acupuncture anesthesia appeared perfectly conscious and in no discomfort, even sipping juice and eating fruit. Traumatic aftereffects seemed to have been avoided, as patients often walked away from the operating room. Another theory of the effectiveness of acupuncture is that it has a psychosomatic basis, but little is known of this and other possibilities. In 1972, the psychologists at Beijing University told me that they planned to research the psychological effects of acupuncture to ascertain how the method affected pain and behavior. However, I learned during visits in 1980 and 1981 with the same psychologists that no follow through had materialized. During a 1972 visit to China, I was invited to visit hospitals and observe the use of acupuncture anesthesia in surgery. A bit squeamish at the sight of blood, I said that I had heard and read of the acupuncture "miracles" and believed that they worked.

The Chinese make no bones about the fact that they do not have a scientific explanation for acupuncture and other age-old treatments that cannot be explained through Western theories and methods. For the Chinese, the important thing to note is that Mao Zedong's instruction in the early 1950s to combine the old and new medical practices helps to overcome the nation's shortage of trained physicians. The masses are encouraged to be self-reliant with folk practices they can use and understand culturally. In sharp contrast to the United States, health care in China relies far less on highly trained practitioners and specialists and makes use of family care and so-called barefoot doctors, similar to the nurse-practitioners of the West. I assume that there is much variation in the competence and experience of the barefoot doctors in China, for a young teacher informed me in 1972 that his secondary students, who were studying acupuncture as we spoke, would accompany him into the country during the summer, where they would serve as barefoot doctors.

As a youngster, I would watch my grandfather (Yee Kee-chong), a part-time Chinese herbalist, carefully feel the pulse of his patients and then prescribe herbs he handed them in neat paper packets. My grandfather's ancient practices seemed mystifying to observe and to compare with those of Western doctors. Grandfather's business—half grocery store, half herb shop—had an entire wall covered with at least 100 dark-colored, lacquered drawers containing different dried herbs, some containing reptiles, leaf and seed of all kinds, and small, ocean animals.* Indeed, the herb shop in Santa Barbara, California, represented a strange contrast to the offices and clinics of the M.D.'s downtown. Grandfather expressed disdain for Western medical practices. He said that to compare their methods with those of the Chinese would be like comparing his butcher shop to the rest of the grocery store. He gently asserted the superiority of Chinese medicine by arguing that Western methods required all sorts of machines and instruments in order to make a diagnosis and used knives to cut the flesh and to make one lose blood and become anemic. The Chinese, on the other hand, diagnosed with their fingers upon the pulse and could cure with powerful medicines. He supported his case by pointing out that the Chinese knew about smallpox inoculation 2,000 years before the West. It seemed contradictory to me, however, that my family did not hesitate to take me

---

*About thirty-five miles east of Sacramento, California, is a small hamlet called Fiddletown. Over a century ago, a tiny Chinese colony of some 150 to 200 Chinese dwelt there. In its midst was a small store made of rammed earth owned by a Chinese herbalist. He maintained a well-kept herb shop catering to the needs of the Chinese, who came from far and near. The herbalist was the great-grandfather of Herbert K. Yee, D.D.S., a trustee of the University of the Pacific in Stockton, and this author's cousin. Somehow the herb shop remained intact over the years. In 1967, the Fiddletown Preservation Society, under the leadership of a Mrs. Vose, contacted the Chinese Historical Society of America in San Francisco. She asked for assistance in restoring the herb shop as a museum. The society sent Him Mark Lai and Philip P. Choy, who worked over a period of many months to help restore the shop. On February 24, 1968, dedication ceremonies were held.

to an M.D. downtown whenever my health was in question.

I began to feel that both Chinese and American medicine had their strengths and weaknesses, but doubt crept in over certain assumptions underlying Chinese medicine that did not make sense in light of my readings and scientific studies at school. A book titled *Doctors East, Doctors West** given to me by Rev. and Mrs. Gordon Foster of the hometown Congregational Church, dramatized Chinese medical philosophy and practices, especially diagnosis by pulse-taking. The author, E. H. Hume, a missionary doctor in old China, praised the Chinese medics for their uncanny skill and related stories of miraculous diagnoses and cures. Fascinated by Hume's book, I wanted to find out how traditional Chinese medicine could possibly succeed and survive through the centuries when its philosophy and practices did not agree well with the empirical principles of modern Western medicine. The question has been an interesting one to pursue since it first arose during my early observations in grandfather's herb shop. Over the years, however, I have found that the question raises a larger issue, that is, the medical thought and health care of the two societies are reflections of their own histories, their particular cultural world views, and their preparation of practitioners.

A brief overview of the development of traditional Chinese medicine will show the extent and nature of its long history. During the Han dynasty (206 B.C.–220 A.D.), the court physicians made systematic medical examinations of the palace staff and had hospitals in which to work. Selected officials studied medicine and wrote on medical topics; others became physicians. In the Tang dynasty (618–907 A.D.), government support made it possible to establish the first medical school in China.

*New York: Norton, 1946.

The government revived medical books and studies and held medical examinations for those who would be practitioners and scholars of medicine. During the Sung dynasty (960–1276), the government established a school of acupuncture. It also commissioned the casting of a life-sized bronze statue which showed all of the acupuncture points with their related channels or meridians and collaterals. During the Yuan dynasty (1280–1368), popular medical works were published. Chu Tan-hsi wrote seven medical books which became famous for giving new and definitive treatments of many diseases. Chu's books served as a model for the Chinese medics that followed him. In the Ming dynasty (1368–1644), the *Great Pharmacopoeia*, a monumental work to be discussed later, was completed by Li Shih-chen. Among the many topics covered, Li compiled the efforts of eight others before him who had identified special channels or meridians for acupuncture. To illustrate the advanced nature of Chinese medical practice during the Ming, the discovery of smallpox vaccination antedated Jenner's 1796 work by centuries. Especially during its last century of rule, the Ch'ing dynasty (1644–1911) brought a sharp decline in the development of Chinese medicine. Under the Ch'ing, suppression turned traditional Chinese medicine largely into hair-splitting studies and critiques of the classics. After the Opium War of 1839–1842, the Western powers secured an imperialistic hold on China that hastened the dissolution of its ancient social order. Western medicine advanced steadily in China, especially through its introduction by missionary services. In 1887, the College of Medicine for Chinese in Hong Kong began instruction for its first class of twelve students, one of whom, Sun Yat-sen, would later become the father of China's revolution. The college set an example for medical education in East Asia with instructors of international repute. One such was Dr. James Cantlie, who was instrumental in freeing Sun Yat-sen from his famous kidnap in London in 1896. However, it remains that the British authorities prevented Dr. Sun and his fellow graduates from practicing Western medicine by licensing them only as herbalists, a status that required no formal Western training. Undaunted by such contradictions in philanthropic aims and actual practice, Dr. Sun provided medical services in clinics located in Macao and Guangzhou through a combination of Western and Chinese methods for two years following his graduation at the top of his class in 1892. The practice did not profit because of Dr. Sun's habit of not taking payment for services and the restrictions brought upon him by Portuguese physicians who feared his intrusion into their lucrative work. In 1894, he committed himself completely to building a new China.

In 1918, the first medical school for Chinese medicine in China was established, in Shanghai. However, traditional practices had lost so much ground that by 1929 the Nanjing government went so far as to consider a plan to forbid the practice of Chinese medicine. However, the government relented after a heated controversy during which Chinese practitioners demonstrated that their methods brought about equal if not superior results to those of Western medicine. Because of the almost continual unrest and turmoil in China during the first half of the twentieth century, brought about by famine, imperialism, civil war, and Japan's invasion and occupation (1937–1945), traditional medicine suffered lost opportunities for further research, and the training of new practitioners declined greatly. What new medics there were learned their profession both intuitively and through much practice and observation as apprentices, most often with their fathers or other relatives. By 1950, however, less than one year after the victory of the Chinese Communists, there appeared signs of a systematic approach toward furthering health care for the people and promoting efforts to relate the best of Chinese and Western medicine. In that year, the first National Hygiene Conference in China formulated a new set of medical principles which included the call both to all traditional practitioners to find ways to relate their work to Western methods and to Western-trained medics to incorporate traditional practice into their work.

One of the greatest contributions by the Chinese to health care is the work of Li Shih-chen (1518–1593), who produced the *Pen-Ts'ao Kang Mu,* known as *The Great Pharmacopoeia* in the West. Colin A. Ronan, in *The Shorter Science and Civilization in China,* acclaims it as "the greatest scientific achievement of the Ming."* After spending twenty-six years compiling the illustrated *materia medica,* Li Shih-chen completed the monumental work in 1578. In it, he describes in great detail 1,000 animals and 1,000 plants and classified them into 62 divisions according to their ecological characteristics. The great work included 8,000 prescriptions for ailments and described the process and history of distillation, smallpox inoculation, and the therapeutic use of many medicines, such as chaulmoogra oil, ephedrine, iodine, and kaolin long before the West knew and made use of them. An important reference for pharmacologists around the world, *The Great Pharmacopoeia* remains in use today.

It has been said that William Harvey's (1578–1657) revolutionary discovery of the circulatory system had been anticipated in China about 2,000 years before the birth of Jesus Christ. This belief comes from some quotations from the *Nei Ching,* the oldest and what many consider the greatest Chinese medical classic. Its writing is credited to Emperor Huang Ti (ca. 2704–2598 B.C.), who is Taoism's legendary founder and is renowned for inventing money, the compass, and building blocks, for developing both the Chinese calendar still used today

*New York: Cambridge University Press, 1978, pp. 56–57.

and mathematical calculations, and for writing the *Nei Ching* or, to be complete, the *Huang Ti Nei Ching* or *The Yellow Emperor's Esoteric Classic*. Huang Ti has been called the Yellow Emperor because he was born on an "Earth Element Day" and yellow represents earth. In regards to the circulation of the blood, the Yellow Emperor wrote:

> The blood current flows continuously in a circle and never stops.
> The blood cannot but flow continuously like the currents of a river or the sun and moon in their orbits. It may be compared to a circle without beginning or end.

Typical of the Chinese preference for deductive versus inductive paths to knowledge, the *Nei Ching*'s deductive statements assumed there was no need for any experimental verification. With no clear distinctions between arteries and veins and no evidence of true anatomical knowledge, Emperor Huang deserves credit for superb speculation. In contrast to the scientific method of the West, which began to take hold in the seventeenth century, much of the traditional Chinese medicine has developed from nonscientific sources—the native philosophy of the *Tao* and historical and literary references. However, it would be a serious mistake to view traditional Chinese medicine as developing from religious and shamanistic sources, such as witch doctors. In Western medicine, anatomy is a strict requirement in medical studies, while Chinese practitioners keep surgery to a minimum. When treating patients, Western medics typically follow biomedical approaches and make great use of physical tests, such as urinalysis, x-rays, electrocardiograms, blood analyses, etc. According to the Hong Kong scholar, Lam Chin-man,*

---

*Scholar Lam Chin-man is most highly qualified for his contributions to this chapter for which I thank him very much. With a B.S. in physics from Lingnan University in Guangzhou, and an M.S.

who graciously revised and supplemented this chapter and gave freely from his knowledge of Chinese medicine,

> In ancient times, a Chinese sage with thorough knowledge and practical experience of the *Tao*, would eventually develop in his body a full power of *Chi* (vital life energy), circulating continually in his whole body, so as to maintain his health and longevity. By means of his *Chi*, he could produce a radiographic or fluoroscopic effect of any patient he treated, together with the picture of the internal organs, circulation of the blood, and the continuous flow of *Chi* in the channels or meridians, and thus the anatomy and biomedical knowledge of the patient being fully studied. He could also transmit his own *Chi* to the patient at any distance, and thus cause the patient to move his body, four limbs, head, fingers, and eyes, etc. so as to become healthy again.

Frena Bloomfield, in *The Occult World of Hong Kong** corroborates Scholar Lam's testimony when she describes a sage in Hong Kong possessed with *Chi* for healing patients. Unfortunately, the method of teaching others how to develop *Chi* has been strictly by means of discourse and example, and textbooks and other writings on the subject are nonexistent. At present, there remain only a few people in China, Taiwan, Hong Kong, and elsewhere who are qualified to practice the *Tao*. Developing the *Chi* within themselves in order to heal others without thought of enriching themselves, such

---

in radiation physics from London University, Mr. Lam served as a medical physicist in Hong Kong for twenty-one years before retiring. He has studied the *Tao* since 1936 in order to better develop the *Chi* through the whole body system, exercises for therapeutic and life-prolonging processes, and Taoist meditation. Also a student of the *I Ching* since 1965, Mr. Lam has been guided by numerology as developed by Shao Yung of the Sung dynasty. The scholar is particularly interested in human behavior as it affects health, the individual, social relationships, and so forth, in this and other ways helping himself and others to find the way to harmony with the universe.
*Hong Kong: Hong Kong Publishing Co., Ltd., 1980, pp. 68–74.

practitioners shun publicity and show no interest in forming any religious groups.

Philosophical Taoism, discussed above, should not be confused with the religious form of Taoism, which is quite different. Before the introduction of Buddhism into China in about the third or fourth century after Christ, the Chinese had the philosophies of Confucianism, Taoism, and their various schools. Chang Tao-ling later founded a cult to encourage a native religion to compete with Buddhism. His teachings differed from the original philosophy of the *Tao* in many ways, chief of which was that he felt the *Tao* should be worshiped as a personal God. Chang's religious Taoism gained further strength when it attached itself to the philosopher Lao Tzu, "The Old Master," (ca. 604–531 B.C.), whose thoughts dealt with a naturalistic cosmology, relativism, and the unity of opposites, in contrast to the ritualism and prescriptions of the Confucian classics. Religious Taoists rejected the writings of Chuang Tzu (ca. 372–289 B.C.), a philosophical Taoist, whose brilliant literary works are still read for their intelligent insightfulness. In one of his works, for example, he wrote that he dreamed he was a butterfly enjoying a beautiful day. After he woke, he was not sure if he was still himself who had dreamed that he was a butterfly, or actually a butterfly that dreamed it was the philsopher Chuang Tzu. In the fifth century, followers of Chang Tao-ling's form of Taoism reorganized themselves with other Chinese and Buddhist elements to form the religion of Taoism that continues today. Those who practice the religion are called *Tao Shih*, "Gentlemen of the Tao"; they are also known as the Taoists, which leads to confusion with the philosophical Taoists. The *Tao Shih* make their living by performing religious services and by calling upon the divine spirits to exorcise the devils believed to cause human suffering and world calamities. The religion appeals mostly to the poor, and educated Chinese consider such practitioners to be superstitious and do not accord their beliefs much credence. Unfortunately, many Westerners have assumed incorrectly that traditional Chinese medicine originates from the Taoist religion.

The *Nei Ching*, China's most celebrated medical treatise, consists of two major parts. The first, *Su wen*, meaning "general questions," covers the full range of medical knowledge of ancient times and forms the core of the *Nei Ching*. The *Ling shu* or "spiritual nucleus" supplements the *Su wen* with a thorough discussion of acupuncture. The *Su wen* exhaustively covers features of traditional Chinese medicine, such as the *Yin, Yang*, the five elements, the gross entities of the internal *Ts'ang-Fu* organs (i.e., the six *Ts'ang* organs and the six *Fu* organs), the channels, the collaterals, the *Chi* (Vital Life Energy), and the extraordinary *Fu* organs: the brain and the uterus.

Since most Westerners have heard of acupuncture, let us examine its main points and try to understand how it works. According to the book on acupuncture, the human body has twelve regular channels, eight extra channels, and fifteen collaterals. Channels and collaterals are passages through which *Chi* and blood circulate. They perform the functions of circulating *Chi* and blood, warming and nourishing the tissues, and systematically interrelating the entire body. Without the channels and the collaterals, the body system could not operate synergically and be an organic integrity. In the body's interior, they connect to the internal organs, and on its exterior they connect to the body surface, where the acupuncture points are located. According to Scholar Lam Chin-man, scientific devices, such as the Kirlian photographic method, have been devised recently to detect the acupuncture points along the channels and the collaterals.

Acupuncture points along the body, therefore, are the specific sites through which the *Chi* is transported from the internal organs and channels to the surface of the body. When the human body is infected by a disease, acupuncture treatment aims to regulate the *Chi* and blood circulating in the channels and collaterals. In practicing acupuncture, the Chinese medics puncture and penetrate the surface of the body at very definite locations. They make use of gold, silver, brass, copper, steel, or iron needles; in ancient times use of flintstone needles was common. Each metal needle has its own particular characteristics and may be either fine or coarse, short or long—from 3 cm to 24 cm—depending on the medical effect desired.

Because it is strictly a Chinese invention and practice, learning about acupuncture is thus one of the best approaches to take in attempting to understand the Chinese cosmogony, the basis of all Chinese medicine. The theory consists of the cosmic concept of the *Tao* (literally, "path" or "way"; spiritually, the absolute Way of nature) about which philosophers have said:

The Way that can be mapped is not the eternal Way
The Name that can be named is not the eternal Name.

Lao Tzu wrote in the twenty-fifth chapter of his *Tao Te Ching* a description of the *Tao* which probably mystifies most Westerners more than it helps them to understand what the *Tao* means:

Before the Heaven and Earth existed
There was something nebulous:
    Silent, isolated,
    Standing alone, changing not,
    Eternally revolving without fail,
    Worthy to be the Mother of All Things.
I do not know its name
    And address it as Tao.
If forced to give it a name,
I shall call it "Great."
Being great implies reaching out in space,

Being out in space implies far-reaching,
Far-reaching implies reversion to the original point.*

According to the cosmogony of the *Tao*, by evolving
itself, commencing at the time of the *Hun Tun* (the
Primeval Darkness or Chaos), the *Wu Chi* (the Non-Ab-
solute) formed the *Tai Chi* (the Great Absolute). In turn,
the *Tai Chi* formed the *Liang-I* (the *Yin* or *Yin-I* and the
Yang or *Yang-I* are the Vital Essence or Aspect of the
universe) which becomes manifested in the chief, dual
qualities of the Chinese cosmogony.

In the diagram, the *Tao* is represented by the *Tai Chi*
circle, where the *Yin* is the dark part and the *Yang* the
light part. Both *Yin* and *Yang* have a bit of the other as
shown by the small circles. According to the *Tao*, any
creation or destruction of anything in the universe, even
the spirits, is possible only when the two act together.
God is also the natural creation of *Yin* and *Yang*. The *Yin*
symbolizes the earth, the invisible, annihilation, night,
illness, demotion; it is female, low, weak, bad. The *Yang*
symbolizes the heaven, the visible, creation, day, life,
gain, promotion; it is male, high, strong, outer, corpo-

*Translated by Lin Yutang.

real, positive, long, hot, good, healthy, flourishing. Contradictions and struggles between the two opposites within one object, as well as harmony and equilibrium, can be portrayed by the above diagram. They are not fixed and static but stay in a state of constant change. As Heinrich Wallnofer and Anna von Rottauscher write in *Chinese Folk Medicine:*

> Before our era Chinese physicians were essentially aware of the function and significance of the nerves [which] can be traced back to their doctrine of man as an integral part of the universe. And on the ensuing concept of an eternal duality, of positive and negative, and on the recognition that they are of equal value and that one cannot exist without the other—on these were erected the very pillars of Chinese philosophy. *Yin* and *Yang* are the primordial twin potencies that regulate the universe, and they bestowed power onto all the "ten thousand things" within that universe. . . . As *Yin* and *Yang* manipulate heaven and earth in the waxing and waning of seasons and days, so they exert their power over the human being.*

While the Western approach to medicine is reductionist, the traditional Chinese posture is holistic. As elaborately stated by Fritjof Capra, a modern physicist, there is a vital need for both approaches to work in concert. Capra writes:

> In everyday life, then, both the mechanistic and the organic views of the universe are valid and useful; the one for science and technology, the other for a balanced and fulfilled spiritual life. Beyond the dimensions of our everyday environment, however, the mechanistic concepts lose their validity and have to be replaced by organic concepts which are very similar to those used by the mystics.†

*New York: New American Library, 1971, p. 17.
†*The Tao of Physics* (New York: Bantam, 1975), p. 295.

In the heady field of subatomic physics, the Newtonian emphases on physical objects and particles, mechanical predictability, time-space separation, and cause-effect relationships, while applicable to the solar system and to daily life (the "zone of middle dimensions"), cannot explain the true workings of the subatomic world. Albert Einstein's relativity theory, first published in 1905, has led to a most remarkable set of scientific discoveries. The discoveries have resulted in many new theories which physicists still grapple with and find baffling because of the very human limitations of their knowledge. In general, what is believed now about the universe is that there is a oneness of everything in it, that the things we observe in nature are not real but features of our own discriminating and classifying mind, that absolute time-space frames of reference are deceptive and false and have been replaced by relativity and uncertainty. Describing the world of subatomic particles as a network of events and emphasizing process, change, and transformation rather than basic entities, S-matrix (Space matrix) theory, a leading concept of modern physics, according to physicist Capra, closely approximates Eastern thought, especially the *I Ching*, in its ultimate conclusion and general view of matter and the universe.

Having overcome the centuries of Aristotelian deduction, Western medicine relies on inductive methods and premises rather than a philosophical universality of absolutes. In fact, the very number of subjects facing a Western medical student indicates the great difference in approach. Physiology, anatomy, histology, pharmacology, pathology, and so on, are all studies that are based on Western science and techniques. As John Hunter once said to Sir William Jenner, "But why think? Why not try the experiment?"

We can safely assume that medics of the East and West approach their patients with the same desire to cure the sick and promote health. Yet as soon as they begin to administer to the sick or hurt, there can seem to be a world of difference. In discussing his concept of "world view" in his book, *Cultural Anthropology*, Felix M. Keesing says:

> A culture is interpenetrated by knowledge in the form of explicit or implicit premises, assumptions, axioms, tenets about the 'uncertainties' of life. These latter form a bridge between scientifically verifiable knowledge, on the one hand, and philosophy and religion, man's concern with the larger views and "why" questions of life, on the other.*

Western medics and modern practitioners in the People's Republic of China have separated scientifically verifiable knowledge from culturally loaded philosophical and religious principles. Some historical background will help to show how this may have come about.

Galen, a leading Greek physician in the second century, contributed much to the knowledge of physiology. However, because he used deductive methods, Galen made many errors of fact that shaded his discoveries with an assumption that he already knew the general scheme of nature. With preconceived notions of nature's processes, Galen arrived at deduced conclusions that matched his belief that God had made all organs of the body as perfect as possible for their functions, even when he had little or no real proof. Earlier, Hippocrates (ca. 460–377 B.C.) had demonstrated the value of clear observation and accurate description, but his methods have received greater acceptance in modern times than in his day and Galen's.

In 1628, William Harvey published a monograph on the movement of the heart and blood in animals that achieved a major breakthrough for scientific medical thinking. Harvey demonstrated the experimental

*New York: Holt, Rinehart & Winston, 1960, pp. 322–328.

method by devising experiments to test and verify his hypothesis on the circulation of the blood, which he had postulated from his anatomy studies. It was not long before other scholars brought in the new sciences of mathematics, physics, and chemistry to advance physiology. The seventeenth century also brought the microscope, the formation of learned societies, the first publication of scientific journals, and new knowledge in macroscopic and microscopic anatomy.

Today, Western medics continue to solve medical problems in much the same inductive way. Profiting from the advances and failures of the past, they test hypotheses empirically and proceed from each new bit of factual knowledge to the next bit. In contrast, the Chinese doctor of the traditional school referred to ancient writings and philosophical thoughts developed hundreds of years before Christ. The question is, when compared with the scientific methods of Western medicine, why do the ancient writings underlying Chinese medicine give a satisfactory measure of success? In order to ferret out some answers, we shall examine the cultural patterns that sustain Chinese and Western medical approaches.

1. *World View.* The answer to questions regarding relative medical effectiveness lies in part in the degree of success expected from medical practitioners. The traditional Chinese view of the world and afterlife seems quite different from the view of the Westerner, especially that of the American. While Chinese medical writings refer constantly to philosophy and derive their practices directly from those tenets, the literature of Western doctors seldom refers to philosophical views. In the preface of an advanced embryology text I once studied, the author clearly stated that the scientist can describe the development of one living cell into a complex organism and can answer questions concerning what, when, and how, but questions concerning why are never considered. The author wrote, obviously with

considerable reflection, that questions such as why a particular cell could develop into a human being went beyond the purview of embryology. Scientific cause-and-effect relationships must be sought in fields of medicine such as pathology, but philosophical explanations do not appear. Westerners generally perceive no contradiction in their separation of abstraction in the philosophical sense from the sciences, art from technology, or morality from business as usual. In other words, Westerners distinguish facts from values, which was not the case in traditional China. We see this interesting contrast in the oppositions that comprise major premises for the West, particularly in America, such as Heaven versus Hell, white versus black, male versus female, rich versus poor, young versus old, and win versus lose. To the Chinese, such propositions appear contradictory and irrational.

In *Doctors East, Doctors West,* Hume writes that the "Chinese attitude toward the ordered universe has been to consider danger, disease, disaster, and death as a normal part of the universe, like health and happiness." Natural catastrophes that disturbed Hume and other Westerners were accepted stoically by the average Chinese. Suicide as revenge or as a face-saving device was a familiar event in the Chinese society that the missionary doctor knew. Before an execution of three prisoners by sword, Hume was given permission to take the pulse of each prisoner. One man had a pulse count of 72, another 74, and the other prisoner, a woman, had a count of 78. Hume reported his own pulse count as 128! A culture's responses to illness and its therapeutic practice may be indicative of the personality structure of people in that culture, acxording to John Whiting and Irvin Child, authors of *Child Training and Personality.** Analyzing the customs related to illness in order to develop a projective test for a society, Whiting

*New Haven, Connecticut: Yale University Press, 1953.

and Child concluded that "reactions to illness are probably much more importantly influenced by personality
under primitive conditions of life than in our society at
the present time." For the West, this difference comes
from the use of scientific knowledge and methods,
which restricts the possibility of variation in the inter-
pretation and treatment of sickness. Less restricted by
scientific knowledge and methods, therefore, the traditional Chinese were more likely to reflect cultural customs and personality traits in their approach to medical
practice. Whiting and Child's use of the word *primitive*
betrays their cultural bias, but it can be understood as
non-Western-oriented or less scientifically developed.

Westerners seek professional health care far more
actively than did people in old China. When ill, the traditional Chinese seeking the aid of a practitioner would
probably not assume that the healer could be instrumental against something that may have been prede-
termined. Americans can only try to imagine the Chinese attitude of submission to heavenly fate and the
forces of nature. For example, a great uncle of mine
passed away in the United States even though his doctor
said he could perform a fairly routine operation that
would cure the problem. My great uncle somehow
sensed that it was his time to die and turned down the
operation; he said that the money for the operation
would be an unnecessary waste. Few Westerners would
react as did my relative. Rather, a Westerner would
demand whatever action medical authorities said was
necessary to save a life, for the Westerner senses a great
finality in death. It would be gross stupidity to say that
the Chinese have less concern for life. The peoples of
both East and West all appreciate health and life, but
despite Christianity's promise of heaven for the worthy,
Westerners perceive an extreme significance in the opposition of life versus death. The people of old China
saw less finality in death, as can be seen in their worship
of ancestors, in which the living gathered around the

graves of their ancestors to communicate with the dead. Elders of my family still follow such customs.

The Western concept of mankind's role in the world is that the human species is the finest creation of the evolutionary process and that human intelligence and reason can fathom and rule the universe. The Hebrew psalmist asserted that humans had been created "but little lower than God, and crowned with glory and honor." This glorification of the individual has flourished in the West, in part due to the higher life expectancy rates brought about by modern medicine. In the main, growing secularism in the West has brought about the abandonment of the soul as a meaningful element and of the religious pursuit of individual immortality as a goal. "Heaven on earth" has become the unspoken slogan. The finality-of-death attitude is not a modern or new phenomenon. Can it be that supernatural beliefs in the hereafter have never been as true or as deep in the West as they have in the East? For example, Shakespeare's Macbeth laments the news of his queen's death by saying:

> Tomorrow, and tomorrow, and tomorrow
> Creeps in this petty pace from day to day,
> To the last syllable of recorded time,
> And all our yesterdays have lighted fools
> The way to dusty death. Out, out brief candle!
> Life's but a walking shadow, a poor player
> That struts and frets his hour upon the stage
> And then is heard no more. It is a tale
> Told by an idiot, full of sound and fury,
> Signifying nothing. (Act V, scene V, lines 19–28)

For the Chinese, at least before 1949, attitudes toward life on earth and a real afterlife had changed little. To them, nature's laws governed the universe and everything contained therein, and human life was hardly a dominant element. Operating in harmony and equilibrium at its best and in turmoil and chaos at its worst, nature's systems were inextricably interwoven and so complex and mysterious that the only proper human attitude toward the universe was acceptance, adaptation, and compromise. The Western attitude, embodied in a philosophy based on change and focused on individual worth, in sciences monopolized by reductionist methods and analytical inquiry, and in a stance that glorifies human will and goals over nature, typically belittles the Chinese for their passive and slow-to-change beliefs. In recent years, however, more Americans have come to the realization that the Chinese approach to nature makes good sense. This appreciation has come about through ennui brought by individual and social ills, environmental pollution and destruction, and ecological studies and theories. In short, while the Chinese have viewed the totality and deduced the relative condition of the parts, with little impulse to change what was given or to understand the whys and hows in causal terms, the Westerners have done the reverse. Western and Chinese medicine clearly reflect these dissimilarities in world view.

2. *Education.* The manner of transmitting the culture also helps to answer our basic question on relative medical effectiveness. Jules Henry's discussion of target-seeking and diffuse additive learning describes the traditional Chinese method of teaching children by the additive method, where the teacher adds one bit of information to another as the learner follows what the teacher chooses to teach. In contrast, Henry showed how the American system uses the "spiraling method," in which the children respond to the teacher's output which touches off further responses from the teacher, then the pupil, and so on. Henry says: "Here a reasonable hypothesis is that the additive type is related to cultures that emphasize stability, while the spiraling is related to cultures in a process of rapid autogenous change."* Henry uses examples from Chinese educa-

*In *Education and Anthropology*, George Spindler, ed. (Palo Alto, California: Stanford University Press, 1955).

tion to illustrate how additive learning emphasizes traditional order and a system that keeps information at the same level. Americans make use of the additive style of learning and storage, but also use the spiraling type of teaching and learning while the Chinese do not. In the interchange between teacher and pupil, similar to the Socratic method, the teacher and children "mutually stimulate each other to higher and higher levels of awareness." This style of learning encourages a sense of change and threatens traditional values that cannot stand the test of such challenge. In aesthetics, it tends to create greater freedom and more original expressions and in science, the discovery of new facts and perspectives would be stimulated.

The contrast between the Chinese and American approaches to learning is not difficult to see. In Chinese aesthetics and science, conformity in terms of past glories and knowledge has been preserved. The age-old nature of writing in China went unchanged until the development of a romanized script in the 1950s, which the People's Republic of China is bringing into use very deliberately, in addition to incorporating with greater speed the simplification of many ancient characters. When I attended Chinese language school after American public school hours, it was exactly as Henry describes. The pupils never discussed the concepts expressed in the stories or even the meanings of the characters they learned. In learning to write, we traced over model copies covered with tissue paper. Each character had to be written exactly according to a set pattern and sequence of strokes. This type of learning would offer little threat to traditional values. By observing calligraphy lessons on television, one can see this additive learning process. Visiting classrooms in China today, American educators find that lecture-recitation methods predominate, with large classes giving compliant, studious attention to the teacher. The higher social regard for the role and status of teachers in China provides another cross-cultural contrast between China and the United States.

3. *Role of the Individual.* Another striking difference between the East and West is found in their respective attitudes toward the individual. The traditional Chinese see life as part of a totality that allows little room for an entity to be out of step with natural laws. Death is but a return to the original primal stream and the workings of the universal cosmology. The individual is only a link in the entire chain of being, made up of parts that have always existed, and death is the separation of those parts, which may be united again in a somewhat similar form. Both the Buddhists and Taoists reflect this with their quietistic philosophies. The attitude of traditional Chinese toward life and death and their real belief in the hereafter contrast with the Western concept of individual worth, achievement, and self-determinism under the philosophical and religious framework of the West, especially in America.

Differences in medical thought and practice can follow from these dissimilar views toward the individual. Westerners, dreading pain and fearing death as a final conclusion, depend on their medical agents to use their skill and knowledge to preserve life and limb. If the physician and hospital fail, they stand a good chance of being questioned, as illustrated by the great number of malpractice suits in the United States and the great increases in malpractice insurance rates, which first shocked the medical community in 1977. In contrast, the Chinese accept the fate of death more stoically than the Westerner. Not held personally responsible as in the West, the Chinese practitioner felt little compunction to change what had been held to be true for centuries. Public pressure in the West for more effective medical treatment and improved educative methods encourages further challenge to established knowledge. While the group is the key element of Chinese society, the individual is emphasized in Western society. In the United States, physicians number about 400,000, which makes for a ratio of one M.D. for less than 600 people. Figures for China are not available, but we can assume that the number of fully trained physicians, with training equivalent to doctors in the United States, is less than 400,000, or one for every 2,500 persons. In Great Britain, there is one physician for less than 700 persons which is comparable to the American ratio. Both Western societies have a high level of commitment to the individual, and the resources allocated to health care match such values. The much higher level of investment by society in physicians and other medics, facilities, and equipment spells out a difference that cannot be explained entirely by national wealth. Should the data be available for China, we would no doubt find a lower level of societal investment in professional health care than in the West. Visiting psychological centers in China in 1972, 1980, and 1981, I learned that the nation with the largest population (estimated at one billion) had 500 psychologists in 1965, 1,000 in 1980, and 1,500 in 1981. The figures come from the Chinese Psychological Association (CPA), whose leaders I visited. Although we can assume that the number of psychologists in China will continue to grow, the membership of the American Psychological Association (APA) is about 65,000 in comparison. Since psychologists in the United States need not be members of the APA, the figure of 65,000 is a conservative one. The reverse would be true of the number of psychologists given for China, since only members of the Chinese Psychological Association are considered psychologists and not all CPA members have been trained to the extent deemed acceptable for APA membership. Therefore, assuming China's list of psychologists reaches 2,000, there would be one psychologist for every half million persons, while in the United States there is one psychologist for less than

4,000 persons overall. Of all the social sciences, psychology by definition most represents a commitment to the individual.

No one should assume from this discussion that people in old and new China do not cherish their loved ones as much as do Westerners. As discussed earlier, life itself was not the ethos of traditional China. Changes are coming about in the new China. National programs of health care have only begun and what has been accomplished so far in terms of available resources has been impressive. In fact, the wide use of paraprofessional health workers in the People's Republic of China might be a good lesson for the West, which is so dependent upon overly trained physicians and specialists for needs that could be handled by paraprofessionals. Time will bring more improvements; yet the social orientation toward the individual, which is a revealing cultural pattern, will not change significantly. One of the world's wealthiest nations, Japan, probably reflects the extent of its Asian perspective with its physician/population ratio of 1 to 840 compared to 1 for less than 600 in America. Perhaps Taiwan would be a better example for comparison with China; that Chinese society has one physician for every 3,030 persons.

The above discussion on the cultural patterns of world view, education, and the role of the individual in the West and the China of the past provides some insight into the relative status of medicine and expectations of its proper effectiveness. Though based largely on unscientific premises, traditional Chinese medicine must have had considerable practical value to have withstood the test of centuries. Even though the above discussion indicates significant cultural differences in medical outlook, theory, and practice, it would be a mistake to think that Chinese healers were entirely wrong and ineffective. It is unlikely that a people would allow practitioners to continue to use methods that would be little better than chance or no help at all. For example, Michael Gelfand, in *Medicine and Magic of the Mashona,** writes that medicine for the Mashona in Southern Rhodesia is directly related to the larger medico-magico-religious complex of the culture. The African healer would shake out diagnostic dice and then administer remedies that seemed to succeed more often than chance would allow. Gelfand was convinced of the great psychological benefit of the native healer, an effect that is no doubt also true for Chinese and Western practitioners. Gelfand was unable to assess the actual pharmacological worth of the herbal medicines of the Mashona, but he believed that they had healing value that the medicinemen had learned through trial and error.

Equipped with the *Pen-Ts'ao Kang Mu,* the *Huang Ti Nei Ching,* both described earlier, and a great body of literature on the *materia medica* and other aspects of medical practice, the Chinese practitioner, as did my grandfather who was a part-time herbalist, felt confident in the effectiveness of his methods. Hazel Lin, a Western-trained M.D. known for her work in uncovering new medicines for the West by digging into ancient Chinese *materia medica,* describes in her book *The Physicians*† the uncanny ability of her grandfather to make accurate diagnoses by feeling the pulse. Working with his fingers, the traditional Chinese doctor would feel the pulses of large numbers of patients in Dr. Lin's hospital and match every diagnosis that her Western methods had found earlier. The so-called pulselore theory stresses extreme sensitivity and careful attention to multiple symptoms that can be detected with nine pulse readings in each arm. Examining the card catalog files at Stanford-Lane Medical Library, I found a number of books published in the West on the pulse and its usefulness dating mostly from the early 1900s. For

---

*Capetown, South Africa: Juta & Co., 1956.
†New York: John Day, 1951.

example, James Mackenzie, in *The Study of the Pulse,* writes that the pulse is not a safe guide alone, but "with careful practice the trained finger can become a most sensitive instrument in the examination of the pulse. The recollections of the sensations are conveyed to the mind, are stored up, and are afterwards utilized for the purpose of comparison."* Chinese practitioners, particularly the most successful ones such as Dr. Hazel Lin's grandfather, no doubt developed a highly sophisticated sense of touch and the ability to recollect and organize the sensations to be compared and interpreted. Even though Chinese doctors may have thought that they relied mostly on analyses of the pulse, they could not help but learn much from observing the patient when possible (although some ladies only extended their wrists through curtains) and from hearing the patient's symptoms and history. Many Western physicians are aware of the information to be gained from the pulse but make little use of it other than as an indicator of heart rate because of the many other diagnostic techniques available to them. To draw attention to the merits of pulselore and support its greater use, Arthur Coca (*The Pulse Test,* 1956) conducted controversial experiments on the use of the pulse in controlling allergies by diet.

China's greatest contribution to modern medicine has come from her ancient *materica medica*. Western pharmacology has yet to exhaust its study of Chinese herbal writings and practices. The Chinese used digitalis as a cardiac stimulant thousands of years before the West learned of its medicinal value. It was the same with a slender twig called *ma huang,* which the Chinese used to treat asthmatics. Western pharmacologists extracted the drug ephedrine from *ma huang* and it is now a recognized asthma remedy. Chinese medics treated lepers with chaulmoogra oil as early as the fourteenth

*New York: Macmillan, 1902, pp. 3–4.

century; the West adopted this remedy 500 years later. For years, the Bristol-Myers pharmaceutical company maintained a research laboratory on the top floor of a Taiwan herb factory to extract new drugs for the West from Chinese herbs. We might wonder if Westerners will ever take to ginseng root tea for a health tonic, dried tiger penis for male hormone deficiency, New Zealand deer horn shavings for restoring energy and vigor to the dispirited, wine of tiger bone for rheumatism, and skull cap of deer for liver maladies.

Ginseng root from New England made up the first American cargo shipped to China when the *Empress of China* sailed to Guangzhou in 1784. The ginseng native to North America is *Panax quinquefolium,* while the Asian ginseng is *Panax schinseng,* native to Korea and Manchuria. Most Chinese prefer the Asian root, but there are those who swear by the American variety. Ginseng root branches in forms that resemble human figures. For males, the ginseng root should have two equally developed extremities. For females, ginseng with unequal appendages is used. Prescribed in numerous combinations with other herbs for a great variety of ailments, ginseng is primarily taken as a stimulant and to boost longevity and potency. It can be taken as a tonic, tea, or soup, or chewed as gum. Roots in the form of a man are in great demand because of the folk belief in the aphrodisiac powers of ginseng. Quite expensive, as high as $2,000 an ounce for some varieties, ginseng root is big business in the East. The Korean root is highly prized and while in Seoul in 1972 as a visiting Fulbright scholar, I purchased large roots and ginseng tea bags for relatives. American ginseng grows wild in the cool and rich-soiled hardwood forests of the East— from the Canadian provinces of Manitoba and Quebec south to the gulf coast. Ginseng takes from five to seven years to grow from seed to maturity and grows in rich, shaded soil such as forests provide. In Korea, where cultivation began at the turn of the century, shade is artificially created for the small, hard-worked ginseng gardens.

Joseph Needham, whose monumental series, *Science and Civilization in China,* five volumes of which have been published, and fifteen more of which are planned or in production, uncovered many original achievements by the Chinese in science and technology.* Attempting to learn why the Chinese did not advance in the sciences as the West did in the seventeenth century with its experimental approaches, Needham found that the Chinese knew more about the natural world and how to apply that knowledge fourteen centuries before Galileo. He discovered that there has been more exchange of ideas between East and West than was known heretofore, and that the coalescing of knowledge has benefited all sides. According to Needham, the Chinese knowledge, measured in practical therapeutic results, surpassed that of Western medicine before 1900. Significant gains, therefore, should materialize as the coalescing of knowledge from the Chinese and Western traditions of medicine continues apace. We can see this development in the People's Republic of China. As reported by *Beijing Review* of December 7, 1981, "a new medical science is emerging in China" with the founding of the Institute for Combining Traditional Chinese and Western Medicine in November 1981. Established as a specialized academic organization in Beijing, the new institute explores the theoretical basis of Chinese medicine, which views disease as a malfunction of natural balances among organs of the human body. The institute is intended to promote development of medical theories and practices in China through scientific studies and to seek scientific combinations of Chinese and Western medical systems.

In 1981, while on a tour of Chinese universities to

*New York: Cambridge University Press.

promote educational and cultural exchanges, a professor who accompanied me on the tour developed a bad cold and cough. I insisted that he consult a physician and we went to a hospital in Hangzhou. Dressed in a white gown and cap, the woman doctor competently examined my friend using a series of Western-type procedures before prescribing several antibiotics, throat salves, and some Chinese medicines. During my wait, it occurred to me that I should see if relief could be found for the painful "tennis elbow" I had been suffering from for half a year. My orthopedic specialist in the United States had treated me unsuccessfully with shots, braces, and sympathy. He said that the next step could only be surgery to soothe the sore tendons. I had acupuncture in mind, and the physician who examined me asked if I would like to see the acupuncturist. It took the acupuncture specialist less than a minute to diagnose "tennis elbow"; he asked me if I played much tennis. He offered acupuncture treatment, which I unhesitatingly accepted. Resting on a treatment bed, I could feel the slight, sharp insertion of the needles on each elbow, one toward the end of the elbow where the tendon was sore and another needle about three inches away into the arm muscle. The Chinese doctor hooked the two needles up to a box that had a bank of electrical connections and a timing mechanism. For each elbow with the hand open and relaxed, treatment lasted fifteen minutes, during which a pulsating current caused my arm muscles to flex involuntarily about every three seconds. The action caused my hand to rise rhythmically with each flex of the muscles. I felt a little discomfort, especially at the needle points, which may have come from my unfamiliarity with the treatment. After the treatment, the doctor said that if the one treatment were sufficient, the pain would gradually fade away. Since we would be leaving Hangzhou the next day and China in a week, I hoped that one treatment would do. Less than two months later, without any further professional assistance, I realized one day that the elbows had been cured. In that visit to a modern Chinese clinic, I could see both Western and Chinese methods in effective use side by side. By 1982, fourteen states were licensing acupuncturists to practice without supervision by a physician and Congress was taking action to allow Medicaid coverage for acupuncture treatment under the Social Security Act. Veterinarians have founded a society for acupuncture.

Another important benchmark in China's cooperation with world medicine came about with the publication of the first Chinese medical atlas in 1981. The *Atlas of Cancer Mortality in the People's Republic of China* provides statistics on cancer incidence and geographical distribution that will greatly benefit cancer research throughout the world. Produced by the National Cancer Control Office of the Ministry of Public Health, the *Atlas* has been well received by cancer researchers worldwide. Data that link the incidence of cancer to geographical distribution fuel the search for the causes of cancer and how best to prevent it. For example, the *Atlas* reports that stomach cancer ranks higher than all other forms of cancer in China and appears most prominently in the northwest, northeast, and southeastern coastal areas. Concentrated in Henan Province's Taihang Mountains, cancer of the esophagus ranks second. Liver cancer ranks third and the *Atlas* clearly shows that such cancer mortality is especially concentrated in Guangxi and northern Jiangsu. Researchers believe that the *Atlas* contributes significantly to the theory that local dietary habits cause many of the leading forms of cancer mortality in China. As such exchanges of research and practice increase, the coalescing of Chinese and Western medical traditions will create a new tradition of medicine beneficial to all. Medicine, therefore, illustrates the validity of blending cultures and sets a lesson for ethnic identity and self-concept.

Romanization of Chinese Names and Terms

Wade-Giles	*Pinyin*	*Chinese Characters*
Acupuncture Points (Hsueh)	Xue	穴
Chang Tao-ling	Zhang Daoling	張道陵
Channels (Ching)	Jing	緽
Chi	Qi	炁
Ching dynasty	Qing	清
Chu Tan-hsi	Zhu Danxi	朱丹溪
Chuang Tzu	Zhuangzi	莊子
Collaterals (Lo)	Luo	絡
Confucius		孔子
Emperor Huang Ti	Huangdi	黃帝
Five Elements		五行
Han dynasty	Han	漢
Huang Ti Nei Ching	Huangdi Neijing	黃帝內經
Hun Tun	Hundun	混沌
I-Ching	Yijing	易經
Lam Chin-man		林千文
Lao Tzu	Laozi	老子
Li Shih-chen	Li Shizhen	李時珍
Liang I	Liangyi	兩儀
Ling Shu	Lingshu	靈樞

Wade-Giles	Pinyin	Chinese Characters
Ming dynasty	Ming	明
Nei Ching	Neijing	內經
Pen Ts'ao Kang Mu	Bencao Gangmu	本草綱目
Su Wen	Suwen	素問
Sun Yat Sen		孫中山
Sung dynasty	Song	宋
Tai Chi	Taiji	太極
Tang dynasty	Tang	唐
Tao	Dao	道
Tao Shih	Da oshi	道士
Tao Te Ching	Daodejing	道德經
The Tao that can be told is not the Absolute Tao.		道可道非常道
The Names that can be given are not the Absolute Names.		名可名非常名
Ts'ang Fu		臟腑
Wu Chi	Wuji	無極
Yang	Yang	陽
Yee Kee Chong		余鎮中
Yin	Yin	陰
Yuan dynasty	Yuan	元

GI American, 1952–1955

So did John Adams, Jackson, Jefferson.
So did Lincoln on a cavalry horse
At the Chancellorsville review
  With platoons right, platoons left,
In a wind nearly blowing the words away
  Asking the next man on a horse:
  "What's going to become of all these
    boys when the war is over?"
                    CARL SANDBURG, *The Fireborn*
                    Are At Home In Fire (1943)

Those who are not fully aware of the dangers of
war cannot wage war profitably.
          SUN TZU, *The Art of War (500 B.C.)*

Shortly after graduating from the University of California, Berkeley, in a ceremony which my grandfather and father attended but could not find me among the thousands receiving degrees, I and a friend drove to New York. Although there was no reason to hope at all, my purpose was to find a young lady from Shanghai whom I had met at UC Berkeley and have her return to the West with me. New York, the nation's largest city, must be the loneliest place, especially for the down-hearted. Upon my arrival, the one I loved scolded me for coming and said that she had decided to marry the man her family had chosen when she was about fourteen. She told me, "We can be like brother and sister." I felt as lost as I had with my first love at Lingnan University, which had ended somewhat similarly. I searched aimlessly for a job in the hot, muggy weather before returning to California in a bizarre carpool I found through the want ads of the *New York Times.* As we crossed the great expanse of the United States, the beer-bellied man who owned the car not only stole the sheets and pillow cases from each motel at which we stayed, but also engaged in the foulest language and attitudes toward women and blacks that I have ever encountered. It was a hard and trying ride, and my emotional state could find no relief in the close quarters of the sedan. Her words rang loudly in my head, "Go home or you will be here when I marry." What was I to do?

Reaching home, I learned that my closest friend, 2d Lt. Robert Studnick, had been killed on the front line with his platoon in Korea and that another friend had committed suicide after joining the Marines. Bob Studnick and I had known each other since high school, where we became good friends on the debating team and were two of a group of fellows who took forays into San Francisco for the theater, foreign films, and cuisine. We had shared an apartment while at UC Berkeley, where his French-Canadian humor and wit always seemed to have me at a disadvantage. I seldom could beat him in games of "paper-rock-scissor" to decide who would take the garbage out. Always enthusiastic and energetic, Bob surprised his friends by deciding to pursue a military career. Bright and hardworking, he won one of the coveted Regular Army commissions granted annually to only 200 ROTC graduates in the nation. His eyes would shine brightly and a small blue vein would protrude in his forehead in spirited debate. Learning of his death, his parents became so distraught that they seemed in a stupor, enlisting the aid of spiritual mediums in an effort to understand how one with such promise could be gone. It made me think that the best of life was so intangible and so fleeting. The other friend, who drove powerful motorcycles and was ever so carefree, committed suicide with carbon monoxide while on leave. For years, he had pursued a certain girl, whom none of his pals knew, and finally persuaded her to marry him. On their wedding night, the tragedy began to unfold when she confessed to marrying him only for his money and would not let him touch her. Our friend had sought escape by joining the Marines.

With great emotion, feeling patriotism mixed with great distress at the loss of my close friends and my failed loves at Lingnan and Berkeley, I joined the army with the goal, worked out with the recruitment sergeant, of becoming an officer as Bob had been. Berkeley had expanded my intellect and tastes. However, my inner being had not synthesized the knowledge and experience accumulated over twenty-three years. Contradictions and disappointments abounded, and going to war seemed to offer a way to resolve the difficulties: I would be given a new sense of purpose or I would die, I thought. That feeling of glorious and honorable escape, it seems, came partly from growing up during the military-intensive years of World War II and my subconscious desire to become 100 percent American. No one except my mother argued against my decision. Seeking advice at the UC Berkeley counseling center, I found the director as disillusioned as I was with the McCarthy era and the Korean War. Strangely, I found myself counseling her that brief visit. Being nearsighted, I was afraid I might be rejected by the army. To make sure that I would be allowed to enlist, I obtained an examination by one of San Francisco's leading ophthamologists to support my application if necessary. As it turned out, I probably would have been accepted with less than corrected 20/20 vision. Waiting in line for the medical checkup at the army center in San Francisco, I had the 20/20 line memorized—D E F P O T E C, before my turn came. However, I told the examiner that I had to wear glasses, and they ironically took my honesty as an attempt to achieve F-1 status and treated me rather arrogantly.

Surely, I was not the first to seek escape from home and society by going to war. Except for a few provocative courses at Berkeley and my success in fencing as a member of the 1951 Pacific Coast Conference championship team, I had been quite disillusioned and confused by the cerebral gyrations expected in most classes. Competition for grades had become so tense that some students would go so far as to contaminate the chemistry samples of other students. When this happened to me, I was more distraught over the act than the loss of a good grade. To succeed, one needed excellent recall and command of the lectures and readings. In the vertebrate zoology laboratory examinations, for example, fifty microscopes would be set up, and each student would study them for a few seconds each. An "A" was awarded to those with perfect scores of 50 right out of 50, and a score of 49 right out of 50 received a "C"; there were no "B" grades. While at Berkeley, the Loyalty Oath controversy demoralized the campus and many fine professors left their positions in protest of the regents' requirement that the faculty sign oaths of loyalty to the United States. McCarthyism gripped the nation and there was little hope for change, though Adlai Stevenson's candidacy for president against Eisenhower carried hope and refreshing wit.

I had given up the idea of becoming a physician during my junior year at Berkeley and that decision upset my family terribly. I had worked one summer in a county hospital and the next in a blood bank. As an orderly, I worked throughout the hospital; my jobs included ambulance duty, helping in the emergency room, and performing odd jobs, such as transporting corpses to the morgue. In the latter job I would be greatly disturbed when I would have to put the bodies, especially children and stillborn babies, on the autopsy table and disrobe them. A pathologist heard of my medical ambition and invited me to observe an autopsy, which nearly caused me to faint and which I shuddered throughout. Severely disoriented, I did not identify with the pathologist's casualness in demonstrating the action of organs and explaining how the boy had died from a shotgun blast after he was accidentally shot by his father. To me, life seemed dangerous and transient on one hand but exhilaratingly precious and full of potential on the other.

The first patient I lost was an elderly black man who had a cardiac condition and required oxygen, which he received through a tube in his nose. We used to joke with each other a bit and had established a fairly friendly relationship. One night as I began to straighten his sheets, I noted a change in the sound of his oxygen intake, as if a leak had occurred. I called the nurse and she went to get an M.D., telling me the man had passed away and to draw the curtain (which may be where the expression "curtains" comes from). The experience sobered me. I did not realize how quickly and silently life could pass away; I felt guilty for not providing some ceremony, but I knew of none. Seeking advice from a minister that same night, I could not even obtain a standing prayer from that confused cleric who could not focus on my feelings and what I needed. His ineptness helped to lead me away from the church as an institution.

The camaraderie of the hospital staff, residents, student nurses, and aides held us all together, and we had good times, usually at mealtime when the night cook produced marvelous "Bumstead" sandwiches and desserts. However, I found it difficult to project myself into the doctor's role, especially when it became apparent that doctors were not infallible. Asking myself the question, "could I continue as a doctor if a patient died through my error of judgment or slip of the scalpel?", I finally answered "no" when an aunt died tragically mainly because of her physician's badly mistaken diagnosis. My father rushed her to a specialist when her husband said she was not improving from a skin rash. The specialist quickly found that her problem was not a rash but pneumonia and ordered hospitalization and drugs. But it was too late and Aunt Mary died the next day. Everything combined, therefore, to make me seek escape and possibly death itself.

My first week at Fort Ord made me realize that army life does much to discourage patriotism and idealism. Dry routines and meaningless duties filled the day, such as when I had four straight days of KP, ten to twelve hours each day. Washing trays and pots without wearing rubber gloves, I thought for sure the skin would fall off my hands. Marching in company or squad formation to the "hup-two-three" cadence of disinterested corporals, many of whom were unsoldierly in appearance and manner themselves, seemed a farce at the Ord reception station. Except for the three days of aptitude testing, which placed me quite high in a number of proficiencies, and the extremely careful fitting of our footwear to secure the best match of boots and feet possible, the initial entrance into the U.S. Army seemed drab, dehumanized, and purposeless. Some sergeants who exercised or marched us took such direct command of the situation and task at hand that I began to sense distinctions in the quality of leadership and authority. On close observation, military posture and uniform ceremony, such as a youth imagines in toy soldiers and war novels, were mere illusions. All those in positions of responsibility seemed to assume that we recruits had been forced into service by the draft and treated us as such. Fort Ord served also as a center to discharge soldiers, and I saw highly disillusioned and embittered veterans from Korea argue with and curse out officers. They expressed their utter contempt by failing to rise to their feet when ordered to do so.

Though in dress uniforms, the war veterans appeared terribly beaten and tired, their attitude reflecting the chaotic situation of the war at that time. Shouting matches between dischargees from Korean units and Fort Ord officers and noncoms shocked us recruits. In sharp contrast, 300 yards from our barracks basic trainees screeched away during bayonet training—the psychological effect of mass screaming on the enemy was taught deliberately, as it had been in the days of Genghis Khan. During the presidential campaign that summer, Eisenhower seemed invincible, promising that he would personally go to Korea to end the deadly fighting.

In 1953, the army sent me to Korea as a signal corps-man after training me in infantry basics, electronics communications, and leadership. If I was not ready by then, I was surely sick and tired of being trained and drilled. What a relief it was to leave the lectures, the petty inspections, the twenty- to thirty-mile marches carrying full packs and weapons, and the constant exercising and drilling. Occasionally, military pride would come forth, such as when the company commander ran our platoon through the manual of arms and complimented us for the smart job we also knew we had done. Marching back to base after a hard day's grind, in the sunset glow, the company picked up a collective pride, marching in sharp step to the sergeant's cadence and echoing in unison his crisp banter, such as "You had a girl when you *left* . . . You're *right!*" Scheduled for officers candidate school, I decided not to go even though I was elected top man of my leadership class. I did not want to prolong my service time. Disgusted with garrison superficialities, I welcomed the reality of Korea.

Another highlight of my army training was being housed during infantry training in a five-man hut with a man who would become the greatest ballad singer of the

1960s. Completely unknown then, Glenn kept to himself. After we met his attractive wife and visited her apartment in town, Glenn proved to be as bohemian as he had claimed he was. While her husband strummed a guitar and sang ballads in an almost inaudible tone, the lady quietly drove the rest of us mad by undressing to her panties and flirting with each of us. Retreating to the kitchen, I cooked a crude meal of spaghetti with canned tomato sauce for the party. Each night when the company marched in from field training, Glenn's wife would usually be standing at the head of the company area dressed in a bright red, form-fitting knit outfit. Needless to say, our particular hut carried special notoriety that went beyond the company. Somehow we made it through the compressed training, rising at 4 A.M. or earlier and double-timing about. During our stint at guard duty, our hut quietly protested the assignment of parading about weedy fields and the chapel by bringing several cases of beer into the hut, which we drank between the two-hour stints. Fortunately, our hut, which technically served as the "Guard House," was not inspected.

Like most Americans then, I did not question the appropriateness of our action in Korea and believed it befitted the spirit of the United Nations. I felt a pang of patriotism when my small group of replacements was marched to the headquarters of the Fourth Signal Battalion in Korea for orientation. Two smallish flagpoles stood in front of the tent—one flying the Stars and Stripes and the other carrying the light blue flag of the United Nations. Seeing the two flags side by side, I thought then that I knew why we had to be there.

Between that moment and the time I left Camp San Luis Obispo, where I had taken training, I had been on leave for a month and spent another month in the "pipeline." To reach Korea, one had to go through the Army replacement process or "pipeline" which involved five to six days of utter boredom waiting at Fort Lewis,

Washington; over two weeks aboard a troopship with men packed into five-high tiered hammocks with about three feet between tiers, costing the government only $65 per man to ship across; three nights at Camp Sasebo, Japan; one night at Pusan; one night at Seoul; and two nights by train and truck to the 38th Parallel where the Fourth Signal Battalion was situated. The transfer process, which hundreds of thousands of soldiers experienced, seemed callous and irrational, contradictory to good discipline and training. I could not see treating POW's that poorly. The most touching and truly American feature of the process occurred at the dock in Seattle. We had boarded the troopship before dawn with all our gear and waited for over three hours before we could move from our assigned ranks on the ship's deck to formation down on the dock. At 7 A.M., matronly ladies wearing Red Cross uniforms arrived with great quantities of hot coffee and doughnuts and fed us a most welcome breakfast. The warmth of the coffee and the smiles of those ladies made us feel almost human again. One of the few good aspects of the Vietnam War had to be the transport of troops by air rather than by ship. With our shipload of 3,000 men, the equivalent of 250 man-years were lost! Boredom and the lack of anything to do, except for watching the same film in a tiny compartment, made the days drag by ever so slowly on the ship. An officer picked twenty of us out of the mass to sweep down the port side of the ship twice a day, but after two days, the number dwindled to two of us doing the work. Then I swept alone and performed the duty only to have something useful to do. The orange peels, cigarette butts, and other debris strewn across the gray-painted deck contradicted the fetish for neatness and order in military training, which would even find fault in a matchstick found in the crack of the barracks floor. Military contradictions amused me. One humorous experience occurred in Seoul as I awaited truck transport to the north. I had seen films of and heard much about the well-trained troops of India, so I went to the barracks of the Indian soldiers to see how sharp they looked. Those I observed drilled about as poorly as recruits and used the toilets to wash their feet.

My misfortune with ships is that I become miserably seasick aboard them for the first several days. On about the third day hunger begins to fight with nausea. On the third day of that trip, I joined the evening chow line on deck as it gradually worked its way down into the increasingly steamy and smelly interior of the ship. Feeling nauseous, I almost gave up several times, but I stayed in line to get some food. The mess hall itself seemed a mad cauldron of unpleasant odors and sounds set within the rolling ship. Men stood eating at tall counters fixed to the floor in rows. Picking up a tray, I took courage. Steam clouded what was being slopped on the several segments of the GI tray, and I nearly added my own but suppressed the nausea and passed to an opening on a counter. At first sight, it seemed unbelievable, yet it was true—the *pièce de résistance* was tongue! My piece stared arrogantly at me with its taste buds sticking out. Holding my mouth with one hand, I grabbed some bread and butter with the other and ran up the gangways to the relief and cool of the ship's railing.

Great as it was to leave the troopship, Camp Sasebo, the army's huge replacement depot at Japan's southwesternmost point was as hot and humid as Guangzhou ever was. Idiocy reigned during mail call as I and my contingent stood in the rain for over two hours waiting to hear our names and the last four digits of our serial numbers. The mail call was not in alphabetical order and the noncommissioned officers (NCO's) refused to repeat any names. Mail call must be the soldier's best routine pleasure. Letters from home and friends helped add some variety to the monotony of the army. Camp Sasebo fortunately had a big lean-to affair made out to be a beer garden where we lined up for lukewarm but appealing cans of beer. It was my first experience with warm beer, which I would drink daily in Korea in place of the unreliable water supply.

Several buddies and I "worked our tails off" folding and stacking winter blankets for a supply sergeant who showed up and approved our work, but who seemed to forget for the longest time his promise of a pass. After several more hours of work beyond the original arrangement, he produced the passes and we quickly changed to dress uniforms. Out in Sasebo, we wandered about, staring at the neon lights casting colorful reflections in the rain-splattered streets. The nature of the city fascinated us and we craved a soldier's fling. We found many bars that catered to American GI's and then turned ourselves over to the clever pitch of a pimp. Petite and young, the girls seemed like princesses and their tatami rooms looked like regal settings contrasted with our group, which resembled a gang of barbarian brutes who had been confined in prison-like quarters for some time. I told mine as we lay side by side, my head on my arm to gaze at a soldier's dream, "You beauty, me beast." She replied, "What-so matto, GI, you sick?" With that question, the prostitute became my therapist. I doubt if we said much more than that except *sayonara*, but the unintended provocativeness of her query made me examine my role as a GI, and how much I would let the army change me. If the army was inhuman, petty, and sick, did I have to catch the disease too?

If Sasebo and the troopship did not sicken one, Pusan did. Before leaving Japan one night, we were hastily told to strip down and were handed a new set of battle fatigues. Why the Army had us bring our duffle bags full of stateside-issued gear to drop them in Japan is difficult to understand. Giving up everything but our personal essentials, we quickly found ourselves on a landing assault craft which arrived in Pusan after several hours. We reached the replacement depot by bus, and from what I could discern, Pusan was filthy, wet, and muddy.

I noted the many rows of barbed wire around the hilly, slimy camp and the high watchtowers spaced at intervals along the wire. The tents were moldy and repulsive. In the latrine tents, helmets imbedded in crude planks served as wash basins. It repelled us and I wondered if this was the absolute rear of the Korean peninsula, what the fighting lines would be like. No replacement could sleep that night. In addition to the incredible mess into which we had been thrust, the occasional rifle fire from the watchtowers kept everyone awake. According to the MP's, they were shooting at thieves, which made one wonder how desperate those people must have been to want to steal through such defenses. The long passage from training camp to Korea could not have ended any more confusingly. No one complained. We were only GI pawns and we knew it. Yet how far up in rank did one need to go before he felt any less of a pawn?

Responding to the invading North Korean armies, the United States acted properly and justifiably. However, General Douglas MacArthur, for reasons of his own, did not heed the warnings of China once he had the advantage over the North Koreans. He raced his troops closer and closer to the Yalu River, which separates Manchuria from Korea and where the Chinese had many hydroelectric and industrial works. On November 26, 1950, a month after American forces reached the Chinese border on October 26, Mao Zedong's Chinese People's Volunteers entered the war. Under Beng Dehuai, the Chinese armies overwhelmed the U.N. forces. Beng was a general who had been outstanding in the Chinese civil war and who had conquered Xian, a key Nationalist stronghold, in that war's final stage. Evacuating Seoul on January 4, 1951, the U.N. armies stiffened their resistance, held the Chinese forces of about 600,000 to seventy miles south of the 38th Parallel, and then by March 31 forced them back to the 30th Parallel. General MacArthur called publicly for a general war on China itself, an action which President Harry Truman viewed as a challenge to his foreign policy,. On April 11, 1951, the president relieved MacArthur of his command and replaced him with General Matthew B. Ridgeway. Until the signing of the armistice on July 27, 1953, the war remained fairly fixed around the 38th Parallel.

During my time in Korea, China seemed very remote and alien. From Pusan, we replacements rode the train to Seoul and then the Seoul-Chunchon train that earlier in the week had carried Chinese prisoners of war. Its windows were still covered with barbed wire. I felt little connection to the earlier passengers, but felt a tinge of wonderment over the relativity of time, place, and person. Was it comedy or tragedy that I was not one of the POW's but instead a "Chinese-American GI"? Beyond that, however, my thinking had no appreciation for the People's Republic of China, and everything I heard and had read reinforced that narrow view.

From Chunchon, trucks transported us about fifty miles to the Fourth Signal Battalion over hard terrain, often following the creek beds through steep passes. The carrier-repeater platoon received only one replacement from our small contingent of newcomers, and that was me. The men of the platoon, mostly from New Mexico and Oklahoma greeted me warmly, even though I probably looked more "beat-up" and weary than they. Those waiting for replacement, which seemed to be almost everyone, had a special reason to welcome me into the close-knit group. No replacements had been received for months, because the Army produced few carrier-repeatermen, supposedly the best trained personnel in the Signal Corps. Although the carrier platoon was manned almost entirely by draftees or "short-timers," only a handful ranked less than staff sergeant. By the books, carrier-repeatermen had senior rank for their MOS (military occupational specialty). However, a moratorium in promotions had been established for Korea, and making private first class became a harder one-step promotion than to first lieutenant.

Our main duties were operating electronic communication facilities and managing Tenth Corps' long-line
telephone and telegraph systems for half of our front.

An army corps is a large tactical unit composed of
several infantry divisions and front-line supporting
arms and services; the Tenth Corps covered much of the
eastern front in the Taeback Mountains facing the
Communists. Our command terminal's task was to
control the "long-distance" telephone-telegraph systems; whether master sergeant or private, the carrier-
repeatermen on duty managed the long-line communications systems. Very simply, communication lines
consist of either radio or wire. Open radio is obviously
more appropriate under battle conditions, especially for
tactical operations. However, such equipment is tricky
over long distances and is hard to operate well. Large
command units, such as corps, require reliable and
multi-channel communications. Walkie-talkie communications, which we see used in war movies, are very
short-ranged and are geared for portable combat situations, not for long distance. Reliable, long-line communications, especially for printed teletype transmission like that found in newsrooms, was best achieved,
before the advent of microwave facilities, by laying
ground cable and battlefield wire over the terrain
between units. A weaker but workable second-best system was VHF radio transmission, which is what we are
familiar with in FM radio and television. When our field
lines went out or no wire had been laid to a new location,
such as a swiftly moving front, we would make use of
VHF equipment which we carrier-repeatermen also ran.
The trouble with VHF is that it must have a straight
line-of-sight connection to its next station in order to be
able to communicate. Given points A and B which are
fifty miles apart and blocked by a mountain or two, at
least one relay station must be installed between them
which is in the line of sight of both A and B. Having a
mountainous terrain, Korea presented particularly

difficult challenges for carrier-repeatermen as well as all
soldiers. Undaunted, we carrier-repeatermen pushed
the army three-quarter-ton truck (we disliked the jeep
because of its tendency to flip over) to its extreme limits
by driving up to the tops of the highest mountains to set
up relay stations. Signaling with the headlights, we
quickly learned whether we had a line of sight, but we
also risked revealing our presence to the enemy. Not
knowing if the enemy had spotted them or not, a VHF
relay crew of from two to five fellows up on a peak got
lonely and skittish. Korean terrain in the region of Tenth
Corps required a number of relay stations for radio
communications over distance.

Because transmissions lose volume over long distances, we used repeater equipment to boost the signal
so as to facilitate reception and telegraph signaling. The
carrier operation is essential for maximizing the use of
precious lines of communications. Without carrier facilities, only one channel can be provided, that is, there
can be only one conversation on each line. With frequency modulaton and demodulation, we could turn
one line into several channels. Given a VHF and at least
one wire hookup between terminals A and B, we had a
maximum of eight channels that could operate simul-
taneously and independently of each other. Because he
needed to originate, organize, and manage the whole
communications system, the carrier-repeaterman would
oversee the work of others involved, especially the
wire crews who laid and tested the ground lines. In
an elaborate terminal, such as at Tenth Corps, the
thousands of cables that fed into and out of the terminal
had to be carefully and neatly banked for proper identification and usage. A properly established terminal
was a work of skillful craftsmanship. Our six-wheeled
vans carried carrier-repeater equipment as well as VHF
relay gear. They served as our rolling sub-terminals and
could be operated if absolutely necessary by only one
man. Hooking up was always a scramble and until we

actually got communications going, everyone held their breath about the guys on the other end. The work provided a great appreciation of organizational design and communication networks, and offered many opportunities for thought based on know-how and creative improvisation. Elaborately laid out in an underground installation, Tenth Corps terminal in Kwan-da-ree Valley controlled a number of relay and subsidiary stations, used by infantry and artillery units, that the platoon served mainly with mobile vans. Those who worked the vans bemoaned the denial of combat pay to signalmen and related tales of hearing the enemy charging so mightily as to cause a retreat. Receiving long-awaited orders to move out, more than once the vans retreated with ripped-off cable and field wire flying behind.

In time, I became the senior NCO member of the platoon and I tried to maintain the high sense of comradeship developed before. Because our military occupational specialty (MOS) meant faster promotions, the other signal platoons carried easily understandable resentment toward us. It just made us work and live together as closely as any group of soldiers could. Under trying conditions, soldiers of all times and nations have developed primary-group relations that seem difficult to duplicate in other social settings. In sociological terms, primary groups are face-to-face, informal social settings that give each member a "we-feeling" of belongingness and interpersonal significance. *American Soldier,* the great World War II study by Stouffer,* et al., attempted to answer questions, such as why soldiers continued to fight against tremendous odds, and found that soldiers did their best not for patriotism, not out of fear or hatred of the enemy, not out of discipline and duty, nor even out of desire to win the war. According to the study, soldiers fought their best so as not to let their buddies down. In other words, the success of an army arises

*Princeton, New Jersey: Princeton University Press, 1949.

from its units' primary-group relationships. My experiences agree completely with the findings of *American Soldier*. I still remember with warmth and gratitude the familial concern for one and all and the close familiarity of the brawny, crude society of that army platoon. Sharing joys and pain together, we men felt as a superb football team must feel after victory. Woe be to any foe who would challenge or harm even one of us. Army camaraderie, however, is situation-directed, as the old army adage about leaving a unit makes clear: "All debts and friendships are forgotten." I found that to be true as well.

Well-accepted in the platoon, everyone received me as an individual and I responded in kind to the other men. Outside the unit, almost everyone unacquainted with me assumed that I was a Korean soldier or, in disparaging terms, a "gook". The United States and Republic of Korea (R.O.K.) uniforms were not that similar but upon my promotion to private first class, I thought no one could possibly mistake me again for an R.O.K. soldier because the chevrons of the two armies were quite dissimilar. However, despite the chevrons and later even the stripes of a staff sergeant, people still viewed me as a stranger. I later met a Chinese American who had been drafted into the U.S. Army and served in Korea as a translator. He had been drafted shortly following his return to the United States after living most of his life in China and Hong Kong. Naturally, his work with prisoners aggravated his confused situation. I suffered recurring nightmares myself, of being captured not by the enemy but by fellow GI's who would not believe that I, too, was a GI and fellow American. No matter what my actual identity might have been, Americans who did not know me intimately, at college and in the army, regarded me as an Asian in America, a foreigner in my own country. Ironically, I found my greatest sense of belongingness with an army unit of diverse Americans in a war against China. We were a mixed group with black, Chicano, Japanese, Chinese, and white fellows. The Korean War involved units from many different nations and I saw troops from Australia, Great Britain, New Zealand, India, Turkey, and Canada. Once, while some of us rested by the road after finishing some difficult work, one of the non-U.S. units passed us and saw the mixed ethnic makeup of our platoon. One of the soldiers asked what nation we represented and I said, "Haven't you ever seen an American outfit before?"

America's armed services, as did most of the governmental system, segregated its people by race until President Harry Truman boldly ordered an end to discrimination. Although his action provoked heated controversy, he persisted and brought about a host of civil rights changes. Clearly emphasizing the color-conscious nature of the United States, even after World War II, Congress failed to comply with President Truman's request that the Selective Service Act of 1948 abolish the traditional practice of segregation and unequal treatment by race. Publication in 1950 of the report *Freedom to Serve* by the Presidential Committee on Equality of Treatment and Opportunity in the Armed Services, began the process of eliminating discrimination and segregation in the army and other military forces. During World War II, the U.S. Armed Forces largely grouped its men by race, and the outstanding achievements of segregated units stand today as a record to prove that a man's race and color make him no less able, loyal, and brave than any other man. President Truman's wisdom and courage in abolishing inequality in the armed forces have improved the efficiency of America's defense system and removed another barrier to equality. I had six uncles who served in World War II. Four from my mother's family went to India and Burma with Chinese-American Air Corps units whose men served on planes flying the Burma hump. Making it sound more fun that I am sure it was, my uncles told my brothers and me about the dangers of handling and pushing parachute drops over the jungles and China. Uncle Charlie Lee contracted a type of malaria that the medics said had no cure and he was put aside to await his fate. One corpsman, who would not accept the doctors' conclusion, went to comfort my uncle and pray with him each day. In time, Uncle Charlie showed improvement and then recovered completely to the great surprise of the M.D.'s. Because he believed that the prayers of the Catholic corpsman brought the miracle about, Uncle Charlie converted to Catholicism and so did his family. As an ironic note to this discussion of discrimination in the armed services, the medic who cared for and saved my uncle was white.

Two uncles from my father's side served in non-segregated units in World War II. The youngest of the six uncles, Bill Yee, went to the navy and became an "Amphib," one of those brave sailors who sailed the amphibious landing crafts. Uncle Bill spent many of his summers with my brothers and me, and he came to be our leader and role model during his high school years when he won an ROTC saber and commendation at graduation. Wearing his cap at a cocky angle, which he said suited "Amphibs" ("We don't let anyone get in our way"), and his uniform proudly carrying the insignia of his specialty, Uncle Bill walked with two of his nephews while on leave before being shipped into the Pacific. An SP (shore patrol) spotted Uncle Bill and ordered him to "Square that cap!" (straighten out the cap). Because he had spoken so proudly, almost arrogantly, about the toughness of "Amphibs" beforehand, I though there would be a scene. However, Uncle Bill instilled in us another lesson when he kept his gait, squared the white cap, and said, "He's just doing his job, and he carries a big stick besides." About the same age as Uncle Bill, Uncle Harry Yee seemed older. We youngsters treated him more as an adult. Perhaps it was becaused he had started working before finishing high school in order to support his family. Uncle Harry served in the army as an ambulance driver and medic. In France, serving with General Patton's quickly advancing Third Army, Uncle Harry won the honored Silver Star medal for bravely saving wounded men trapped in an open field under heavy bombardment by German shellfire. Without fear for his own life, Uncle Harry repeatedly drove his ambulance far into the field to rescue the wounded GI's. Upon his discharge, Uncle Harry thought that it might be possible to begin a new life away from Chinatown, where work and living conditions were poor. He said that World War II should have lessened racial prejudice against Chinese Americans who wanted to do as he did. My father helped him to find a little corner grocery store and begin negotiations for it. The neighborhood could not have been said to be exclusive and wealthy, but the store owners finally declined to sell the business and property to Uncle Harry—"The people tell us they don't want to have a Chinaman here." My uncle, who won a Silver Star, returned to Chinatown and remains there today.

Japanese-American GI's set new and perhaps unbeatable records of military achievement during World War II with their segregated units' action in the fiercely fought Italian campaign. The famed Nisei regiment, the 442nd, became the most decorated unit in the history of the U.S. Army. All of this despite the fact that most of their stateside families suffered internment in relocation camps throughout most of the war. How sad and angry one gets to see photos of those loyal and brave GI's while on leave with their relatives, having to visit them in the concentration camps. Although the Supreme Court has ruled that the internment of the Japanese Americans was unconstitutional and some financial redress has been proposed by a commission, prejudice against the Japanese and other Asians remains strong in the American populace. This was dramatized during the Watergate hearings when President

Nixon's attorney heatedly called Senator Daniel Inouye, who lost his arm with the brave 442nd, "that little Jap." Japan's attack on Pearl Harbor on December 7, 1941, shocked America. Californians feared an invasion of their shores and leaders tried to prepare for the worst. Soon, alarmist and prejudicial statements and proclamations from Earl Warren, California's attorney general, news columnist Walter Lippmann, the American Legion, Native Sons of the Golden West, State Grange of California, and many newspapers created an atmosphere of strong suspicion against all Japanese Americans. Francis Biddle, the U.S. attorney general, established security areas on January 29, 1942, along the Pacific shores of the United States and required that "enemy" aliens be removed from those areas. On February 13, 1942, a congressional delegation from the western states urged President Roosevelt to remove all Japanese, aliens and U.S. citizens alike, from the West Coast states. Agreeing, the president signed Executive Order No. 9066 on February 19, 1942, which authorized the removal of persons who military commanders felt should be evacuated from military zones to "relocation" camps. On March 2, 1942, General John L. De Witt, western defense commandant, ordered about 110,000 Japanese (defined as having one-eighth Japanese blood or more) to relocate from their homes and businesses in California, Oregon, Washington, and Arizona to ten relocation camps in seven states by March 29, 1942. Illustrating the racial arbitrariness of the official action against the Japanese in America, Attorney General Biddle declared on October 12, 1942, (Columbus Day) that the 600,000 Italian aliens in the United States would no longer be considered as enemy aliens. Absolutely no evidence of treason or sabotage by any Japanese alien or citizen has ever been found at Pearl Harbor or on the mainland. "Tokyo Rose," Iva Toguri, one of a number of Japanese radio announcers forced into their work during World War II, was found to have been unjustly tried and sentenced for treason. Although President Ford pardoned her in person after new trials in the late 1970s established her innocence, I feel certain that many people still regard Mrs. Toguri stereotypically, as an unmitigated traitor responsible for coyly serenading and propagandizing the Allied armed forces in the Pacific by radio.

After General De Witt ordered the Japanese to relocation camps, I remember our Japanese neighbors trying to sell what they could for almost nothing and their hasty packing and departure with the few possessions they were allowed to take with them. After they went, we strolled through the empty places where we had played so often with the Japanese children and had watched their parents work at their trades. Their sudden evacuation, the fact that something so unexpected could happen to good people, added to the bewilderment and fear created by the war hysteria. Not long after the relocation, an Army infantry regiment came to my northern California town and was quartered at the county race track. Going home from school, a group of boys and I came across the companies of soldiers marching from the train station to the race track on the other side of town. With their khaki uniforms, rifles, and packs, they seemed to be the real-life embodiment of heroic soldiers in war movies. My buddies and I followed them to the race track, and we eagerly watched their every move. The men noticed us and their unheroic cursing and catcalls amused and puzzled us at first. Later, we talked to a number of the soldiers and the vulgarity of their language and interests shocked us. "Hey kids, where's the whorehouse?" "Got a big sister who's got a night free?" Not all of the infantrymen presented themselves so boorishly. Perhaps the GI's we met were merely acting out the cheap role civilians expected of soldiers, as I sometimes saw as a GI myself ten years later. Some of the officers and noncoms became good customers at my father's restaurant, and my parents entertained several in our home. After several months, the regiment shipped out to the Aleutian Islands where most of the soldiers were killed or wounded in the fierce fighting there. It seemed that the servicemen in uniform before Pearl Harbor had to be sacrificed in order to gain some time to build modern armies and fleets. Almost everyone in the town's National Guard company was killed early in the war. After weekly Scout meetings, I enjoyed going to the National Guard Armory to watch the men march around the large hall and stand at attention for inspection. Though they seemed formidable then, as a GI years later I realized how very handicapped those guardsmen must have been in actual combat with Springfield rifles and equipment from World War I and little training beyond manual arms drilling and marching.

One night several years after the end of World War II, before I graduated from high school in 1947, I experienced a pathetic moment which sums up much of the pathos inevitable in relations between GI's and civilians. Studying late for an exam the next day, I heard the doorbell and went to answer. I found two soldiers in uniform. They wore master sergeants' chevrons and rows of ribbons. Seeing me, both shined with the great joy of coming home at long last. Identifying themselves, I remembered them immediately as friends of my parents from the infantry regiment that had stayed in our town in 1942. I invited them inside and called my father who had gone to bed. It was obvious that they had traveled many miles and done many things in the last five or so years. From what they said, they had never forgotten us and the good food and times at the restaurant. Caught up in the enthusiasm of returning, the two sergeants had driven many miles to see us. Before they and I even sat down, I could hear my father getting up and coming out of the bedroom. The men's eagerness rose again in anticipation of seeing him, but my father could not remember them and did not waste much time in trying to distinguish them from the many other soldiers. Father asked them to leave, which they did without any complaint. Later, I received several scoldings for letting some soldiers into the house.

In charge of the carrier-repeater platoon, I had my own jeep and could travel extensively, thus becoming completely involved in the entire communications system of Tenth Corps. My buddies and I had many memorable experiences. For example, driving a 2½ ton truck across a mountain pass during a storm, we were near the crest when the one-way road (all passes seemed to be one-way; MP's with field telephones at each end controlled the line of passage) began to collapse before our eyes. Eroded by the heavy rainfall, the road quickly splintered into layers that slid downward. We could see and hear the rocks and gravel split and crash far down the sheer cliffside. R.O.K. soldiers frantically raced on foot down the road, waving for us to do the same. Afraid of being trapped, my black buddy and I tried to turn the big truck around as quickly as possible instead of abandoning it. Inching back and forth between the road bank and the cliff edge with only a few more feet of space than the distance between the front and rear tires, going close to the edge as my buddy signaled from the ground, I turned the vehicle in an interminable quarter hour after which we hurried downhill in a great sweat. Back in camp after a long but relieved return by way of indirect routes, we learned that the pass had indeed collapsed and could no longer be used. We had been the last to make it out. Hearing the news, my buddy and I bought a bottle of whiskey from an officer and put it away as purposefully as we could.

The company commander asked the platoon to set up and run a public-address system for announcements, such as mail call, and emergencies. We not only set it up with a microphone in my tent but worked out a phonograph hookup so we could broadcast music. To announce worship services in the chapel, we would turn up the volume and put on a stomping piano piece as might be heard at a fundamentalist revival, given to us by a chaplain for the purpose. With playing that ran up and down the keyboard, the record knocked the fellows out of their sleeping bags and prompted them to call upon the Lord and Savior, but hardly in the way the chaplain would have liked. We added a switch so we could play our meager supply of three records on a small speaker without broadcasting it over the public address system. Out of sheer repetition, Tex Ritter's "Strawberry Roan" became my favorite song in those days, and we played the records each evening while we drank our tent-temperature beer or whiskey.

For each of my thirty-six months in the Army, my father sent me a mouthwash bottle full of good whiskey. In basic training, I displayed the mouthwash bottle, while its supply lasted, with the other toilet goods, and one company commander commented favorably on my use of mouthwash—"Helps to prevent colds, good!" My buddies always helped me finish the monthly ration, often in less than a day, especially when we could get a big can of pineapple juice from the mess hall for mix. One December night, fortified with the latest supply of "mouthwash," we were playing "Strawberry Roan," the church piano piece, and our third and last record, Bing Crosby's "White Christmas," one after the other for quite some time. Eventually an irate officer phoned and said, "If that goddamned cowboy groans again about that two-bit horse, or I hear those piano gyrations once more tonight, I'll have your platoon out digging holes all over God's green acres. But play 'White Christmas' again and look outside the tent." After a moment of chagrin about neglecting to cut off the PA system, and wondering why no one had complained before that, we went out and found snow lightly falling.

The mountainous topography of the Taeback-San-mack mountain range, the north-south backbone of South Korea from which lesser ranges run northeast and southwest, and from which the chief rivers, the Han, Kum, and Naktong flow, appeared to be of late geological formation. As straight as can be, the hills and mountains seemed to go from bottom to sharp top with hardly a curve. Such topography poses great challenges for men and war machines and explains why the helicopter became such an indispensable tool in Korea. None of the mountains, however, had peaks over 7,000 feet. The highest point in South Korea is ironically on the small island of Chejudo, south of the Korean peninsula. On the mountainsides that I could see in the area of Tenth Corps, evergreens grew in grotesque shapes because of the strict prohibition in Korea against killing trees but not against cutting branches for firewood. The first snow sprinkled gently upon narrow Kwan-da-ree Valley in a most picturesque manner. In the moonlight of a clear night, I could see the reflecting waters of the Soyang River flowing below the camp. As the snow covered the debris and rubble of the war, the countryside became a magnificent sight. The snowy scene was awesomely beautiful to us, but most of us had never experienced frigid winters before.

Despite more than a year of mostly raw training and brutal field experiences, I succumbed childlike to the aesthetic splendor of the first snow. One surprise for me was that snow fell without a sound. After two days of playful wonderment at the novelty of the snow and its cosmetic effect upon the battlefield, I began to curse the constant, bitter cold and its accompanying troubles. It became extremely perilous to drive or ride. Simple things, such as getting water and using the latrine, became irritating chores. The snow underneath large shell casings stuck into the ground to serve as urinals turned yellow. Guard duty in below-zero temperatures required the men to wear two sets of long johns, wool trousers and shirts, a parka and overalls, padded battle coats, fur-lined hats with ear flaps, and rubber insulated boots so big we named them after Mickey Mouse. Our silhouettes in such garb seemed more like that of a big bear than a man. Neglecting the Mickey Mouse boots once because wearing them caused my feet to sweat so much that athlete's foot became a problem, I suffered terribly wearing mere wool leg stockings and combat boots during a long haul by truck. After that I never failed to check on whether the vehicle had a heater. Even when there was one, the gasoline-powered heaters were tricky and usually either inoperative or too hot, so characteristic of our general state—SNAFU, that is, situation normal, all fouled up. Without good humor, I do not think soldiers could ever endure the hardships and frustrations of army life.

Officers understood very little about the work of our carrier platoon, particularly that involving the electronic gear and the installations in vans or underground in Tenth Corps headquarters. They usually stayed away, leaving us carrier-repeatermen to ourselves. The army took the same amount of time to train a signal officer as it did a carrier-repeaterman, so no officer pretended to know much about our business. Still, straining to exert command and to do so by admonition, some duty officers who were new to us raised our ire by pointing to the dust on the minute wiring and tubes of the carrier-repeater bays. However, the fragile interiors of the bays could not be dusted with rags lest we break a delicate connection or part. Pressed very hard on the matter of dust when the equipment was to be transferred to the R.O.K. army, I came up with the idea of hosing the dust out with the air compressors from the braking system of the 2½ ton trucks. After carrying the coffin-like bays out of the vans and the tunneled communication center into the open, we made great clouds of dust without touching any wires and parts. It was what people call "Yankee ingenuity."

Each carrier bay had a 17-second timer to heat the

blue-colored voltage regulators before they lit up. We used that electronic circuit for one of our favorite pastimes late at night. Cutting off all the lights and then the carrier's main power for a second, we would sit in complete darkness, and count to seventeen, when a most brilliant blue light would flash around the carrier chambers. However, the inevitable complaints from the telephone operators and teletype machine operators whose transmission tapes had been cut prevented us from extensive experimentation to synchronize the flashing of the mercury tubes. Running over to find out what had happened, the operators would find us scurrying around as if troubleshooting the "problem."

Accompanied by our own brass, a general came all the way from the Far East command in Japan to inspect our communications center at Tenth Corps. Spotting a line marked "Tokyo" on a carrier bay, he picked up the phone and said, "I should get Tokyo on this, shouldn't I?" In proper army form, I said, "Yes, sir!" One never complicates such moments with ifs and buts. He listened for a while and said nothing. Replacing the phone, he gave me a wink no one else could see and announced to no one in particular that the line was working fine for he had heard a Tokyo operator. However, if he did hear a Tokyo operator, it was the first time that system had given anyone more than static, such a distance being far too great for our World War II vintage field equipment. Also, whether he knew it or not, picking up a carrier phone meant that it was a monitor used for troubleshooting and maintenance. To "ring" a switchboard, we carriermen knew how to whistle at the frequency that would trigger the ringer equipment. The older equipment took a ringer frequency (20 cps) that sounded like a sincere "raspberry" given with proper tonguing and all. The newer ringers, although much lighter in weight and smaller, took a higher frequency that was harder to duplicate. The general did not "ring" Tokyo or anyone. My guess has always been that the general showed class by "putting one on" for us, knowing full well the limitations of the equipment.

Prohibited from contact with the few Korean civilians on the 38th Parallel, and having no R.O.K. troops near us until my last several months in Korea, I did not have many contacts with Koreans, even though I was often mistaken for a Korean. At shower stations set up by army engineers, we relished the infrequent opportunity to take a hot shower-bath and change our clothes. GI's usually complained about a Korean "invading" their tent bath when they saw me, and my buddies would tell them to "stuff it." In 1954, higher command disbanded the Fourth Signal Battalion and ordered a few of us, including me, to stay on to teach the R.O.K. soldiers how to operate the signal equipment. I regret that it was not possible to get better acquainted with the Korean people, but the handful that I encountered were some of the most practical and hard-working people I have known. Seeing me, Koreans invariably found it hard to accept me as an American. Even the orphaned boys we "adopted," who made themselves useful by taking care of our water and tents, never accepted Americans as a pluralistic people. One would like to think they would understand the multi-ethnic nature of Americans after having lived with us for months on end. However, with only pidgin English in common and little opportunity to relate cross-culturally, it was natural that the boys were confused. Black GI's were a puzzle, but they were positive that I was from China. They just could not understand how a Chinese could speak English and be a platoon sergeant in the U.S. Army. Many Koreans could not conceive of an Asian American and I resented their bringing people over to see me, as if I were a freak. However, my attitude was foolish, since Americans also mistook me for something other than an American.

On the road one very rainy and cold day, our jeep gave out and I went to get a tow and help from a camp up ahead. It would have been better if I had sent my

buddy and stayed with the vehicle myself. Walking several miles to the outpost and finding no help, I moved
on and wondered why no one stopped to honor my
hitchhiking thumb. U.S. Army trucks passed frequently
enough. Thoroughly wet and shivering, I began to wave
for a ride without any better success. As it grew darker
and the rain fell so hard that it obscured my vision, I
finally jumped out into the road in front of a heavily
loaded truck. The mud oozed over the tops of my boots,
but I stood my ground. Coming to an abrupt halt after a
split-second's indecision, the driver looked down at me
from the cab and cursed me out in crude broken
phrases that GI's used with the Koreans. I realized what
was wrong immediately: everyone had mistaken me for
a Korean and did not feel obligated to pick up R.O.K.
troops. On another occasion, while stranded alone, one
truck finally gave me a lift. I felt very grateful to the
black GI, who invited me in broken Korean to ride on
the truck's tailbed. That GI, therefore, did not stop and
pick me up because he had spotted another GI in need;
he did so to help a person when he did not have to do so,
which is more important than identifying me correctly.

Being mistaken for a Korean, however, became an
unexpected advantage once when Korean prostitutes
enticed several of us out through the barbed wire to go
swimming with them at a very lovely pool sunk in a
steep canyon. We were having a splendid bacchanal in
the nude by the pool's waterfall when American military
police appeared from several sides and arrested my
white buddies. MP's seemed to take pleasure in upsetting GI fun and finding fault, even dogging a jeep or
truck for miles to see if the driver would go over the 15
mph speed limit. We often felt that the common GI's
first enemy was the MP, not the Communist. Yet I must
credit the MP's with doing their work well, especially
when the going was tough. At road junctions, even in the
worst of storms, they were there, signaling sharply the

proper direction and controlling the point. At night, we stretched our necks to find the tiny light signals pointing the way from the MP. The sharpest soldiers I have ever seen were MP's directing traffic in Seoul. Needless to say, I stayed on with the girls after the MP's took my buddies away and returned to camp that evening in amused triumph. My best buddy, Dale Adamson, wrestled me down to the ground in fun and everyone cheered. Dale had saved my life in a serious experience and I wrote his love letters for him.

As the signal battalion was being demobilized and its inventory checked, one extra power generator turned up in the platoon. In the U.S. Army at that time, having extra equipment was a crime second only to having less than the correct allotment. After a prolonged search, we found a Korean hospital that needed such a power unit and transported it there. I heard that a jeep had been buried to avoid punishment for having more than was authorized. How self-defeating that policy was! Fortunately, the army has dropped that policy, as I learned from a colonel who sat next to me on a flight back to Korea in 1972.

Periodically, one of the air force AT-6 planes would fly over our tents and trenches and spray with DDT to ward off the terrible insects and diseases they carried. We had heard so many terrible stories about the bugs and germs under the battle conditions and the generally unsanitary conditions of the land that we welcomed those planes more than the daily mail-carrying helicopters that came chugging and chigging through the narrow pass between the sharp peaks. As the plane swooped low to announce its mission, we ran about excitedly dragging out our sleeping bags and clothes. We would wave wildly at the pilot, who would return our greetings, like flyers and trench soldiers did in World War I. My glasses became so covered with the spray that I could hardly see through the yellowish-brown oil. Perhaps we waved our arms and raised such a joyous howl in part because the sprayings broke the monotony of our daily existence. We did not realize then the dangers of DDT, which would be discovered later. The propeller-driven AT-6 was a sleek sight in itself, with its agility, roaring racket, and fast speed. It was always a letdown when the flyover was through and we were left to our dark holes and our own routines again. How I envied those pilots. Common among those of us in Korea, and no doubt the same in World Wars I and II, the troops looked up at the pilots overhead with envy and fascination. I contrived a heroic image of the pilot and envied the relatively luxurious conditions of his home base. On several occasions, by going far out of our way to visit and dine at an air force station, we tested our view of the air force and found it to be partially true. To our delight, we would dine on fresh meat and we ate as many helpings as we could get.

One stipulation of the armistice was that there would be no increase in troop size. As I left Korea for reassignment in Japan, military observers from neutral U.N. countries counted us as we passed through a checkpoint on a long L-shaped gangplank leading to the ferry. I have never felt so much of a pawn as I did when I passed the observer's table at the lower left corner of the L-shaped walkway. That helpless, powerless feeling of the common soldier, that makes him feel like just another number, characterizes how I feel about that war today. In the fall of 1972, I was able to revisit Seoul and Panmunjon. Instead of the gutted hulks of buildings and military convoys that I knew during the war, modern Seoul has many tall, modern buildings and traffic jams created by civilian rather than military cars and buses. I did not see one jeep in 1972 Seoul. Visiting there, I could sense Panmunjon's artificiality. The battle line's meeting point confirmed my general attitude of the futility of warfare, but incidents along the border between North and South Korea, such as the killing of two American officials on August 18, 1976, indicate how seriously tense the setting can be. Several weeks after my 1972 visit, South Korean President Park declared martial law and proposed a new constitution that would be even more autocratic than before. I told my teasing friends that I really was not that much of a terror during my latest visit.

Did the Korean War make any sense at all? Did it serve a higher cause than military gallantry and soldierly accomplishments? What about my buddies who died there and the total price paid by all combatant nations in human and economic terms? Some have said that the Korean War saved Japan from Communism. The war spurred Japan's postwar economic recovery to where it now surpasses its World War II foes in Europe and its World War II ally, Germany. The Korean War, as well as the Vietnam War, was a crude game of chance played by rash and narrow-sighted individuals at the highest levels on both sides. Justifications for the wars are given and more can be found. Historians, in the West that is, say that President Harry Truman had good reasons for his decisions. Yet the destruction of human life and the burned-out villages cannot be measured and added into the cruel calculations of political-military strategists. How far below the brassy weight and supreme echelons of command did the common soldier stand? Reading books on the strategy of the European campaigns in World War II or even on the battles of the American Civil War, one gets the definite impression that one-starred brigadier generals are a dime a dozen and that two- or three-starred generals are just higher-ranked pawns of command. Where in the scheme, then, does that place a common soldier twelve or more ranks down the line? The parameters were the same: follow orders. The chief differences concerned the scope of command from general to the lowest noncommissioned officer. I ranked low enough to know what my duties were and could carry them out myself, earning four military medals and a commendation from my battalion commandant, Lt. Colonel Stephen E. Morris, which reads:

> It is a pleasure to extend to you my sincere appreciation for the effective contribution you have made to the communications mission of both Tenth Corps and the 4th Signal Battalion.
>
> Your work as carrier repeaterman and also supply sergeant has been superior and you are to be commended highly. Your devotion to duty and untiring effort have helped insure the success of the missions of both the 4th Signal Battalion and Tenth Corps.

I visited Japan with one week's "rest and recreation" leave in Kyushu the winter of 1953. After a hard day's truck ride to Kimpo Airbase near Seoul in freezing weather, we flew to Japan in a DC-3 bucket-seated plane that seemed to want to eject us. The plane's cargo doors sprang open in flight, and we had to land for repairs before continuing our wind-tossed, nauseating journey. I held my breath, afraid something would alter the R and R privilege. Yet Japan showed up on the horizon with a sprinkling of small lights and the glistening of neat rice paddies and houses amongst the lowish gray and dark hills, a study in color perspective. In the dusk, a runway's row of blue lights lined up, and we were soon at the reception center in Kokura where a banquet was served on spotless white tablecloths. Unmindful of others, we wolfed down the steak feast without pause. Some of us remarked upon the contrast between our crude behavior and the commonplace elements of American life that now seemed so luxurious, such as cloth napkins, window curtains, flooring, central heating, plumbing, fresh food, and table manners.

Returning from R and R, I decided to seek reassignment in Japan, but then I learned how difficult it would be to obtain. My first sergeant laughed at the idea and informed me that everyone wanted the same and that any request would prove futile. Persistent and patient, I finally got him to tell me how to put through the request. To everyone's amazement, in several months I was on my way through the "pipeline" to Seoul again. Apparently, carrier-repeatermen were as scarce in Japan as in Korea and my transfer was approved. Instead of flying out, we had to leave by way of Pusan and traveled there by train. Like the welcome we received at the Kokura R and R reception center, the pullman train was completely unexpected. Air-conditioned, bright and shining aluminum, and fitted with fresh, white sheets and pillows, the pullman seemed the most glamorous experience of my Army stint. As the train pulled smoothly out of battle-torn Seoul, I rejoiced in the departure, especially in such unexpected style. However, the relative plushness of the train contrasted sharply with the condition of the people and the nation of Korea, so evident through the window. Leaving Korea made me regretful that so much harm had befallen such intelligent, proud, and hard-working people. To save their country, we had done much to destroy it. Before reaching the Pusan station, we passed the U.S. cemetery with rows upon rows of white markers in neat formation under the dark, rain-laden clouds moving swiftly in the opposite direction. I thought of my slain buddies whose graves might be within sight and wondered which of the markers were theirs. If I left Korea with any determination at all, it was that my life help overcome the waste of their lives, if only to a small degree.

A drunken brawl had commemorated my departure from the small Korean unit. Several weeks earlier, one of the men had departed with a special farewell, even though a prostitute, a Korean girl who loved him very much, squatted by the side of the rough road fifty yards from the camp entrance, her head bent over between her knees. Several nights earlier, we had forced a bayonet from her hands when she tried to kill our buddy and herself. The truck paused by the pathetic figure and her lover tried to say something. But she never raised her tearful eyes and remained squatted there for perhaps an hour after the truck's cloud of dust had swirled up the steep hillside from the dusty ruts of that stretch of road running above the Soyang River. I doubt very much if that buddy ever returned to Korea to find his sweetheart, though I know that some former GI's have done so. However, I am fairly certain that in his inner consciousness he remembers that girl and feels pangs of guilt and longing.

By 1954, Japan had regained much control of its own affairs and, with typical Japanese ingenuity, was building and organizing itself into today's great economic power. The Japanese people and the GI's tolerated each other so well that World War II seemed far in the past. The Korean War somehow forced us to work together, though it was our war and the Japanese worked for us. Japanese technicians manned some of our signal operations and many supplies such as food and clothing were purchased in Japan and sent to GI's in Korea. Wearing civilian clothing in Japan, I would go into off-limit areas without much concern. Many of the most interesting areas of Osaka, my duty station after Kokura and Kure, had been placed off-limits to GI's by the Japanese authorities. Thus, the centers of Japanese night life were kept separate from those areas of the cities open to GI's, which consisted of typical honky-tonks catering to American soldiers, sailors, and marines. GI manners and low-life cravings revolted me, and I made regular use of my few civilian togs to escape the routine GI experience by going into town.

As a staff sergeant, I could come and go fairly easily after work. With the pay of about $185 per month, I saw as much as possible and enjoyed many weekend excursions. For example, the island of Miyajima, on the Inland Sea of Japan, seemed to be one of the most beautiful places in the world when I visited it in 1954. Visiting the sacred, orange-colored Shinto temple and the *torii* of Itsukushima in October, I found the ancient scene at perhaps its most magnificent, for the vari-colored maple trees which abound throughout the island appeared at their peak of color. My Japanese friend and I were entranced by the extensive grounds and the many stone lanterns, and especially by the stream which gently flowed over rocks and around ferns and other low foliage that the Japanese take infinite care to make appear natural and pristine. Above the stream, brilliant orange, reddish, and yellow-colored maples excited the eye both directly and by their reflection in the water. Climbing to a high point, we looked out over the sixth-century temple and could see the famous *torii* or Shinto gate awash in the tide. Up to 1968, births and deaths had been forbidden on Miyajima because of its special religious shrine which the emperor attends once a year. The classical architecture of the Miyajima shrine has attracted many moviemakers, and can be seen in many films depicting Japan's past.

In early 1955, I responded immediately to an ad in the *Stars and Stripes* for servicemen who had experience as fencers. My company commander was never more amazed by a teletype order than he was by the one from Far East Command Headquarters to send Staff Sergeant Yee to Yokosuka Naval Base in Yokahama. There I joined a young officer at the massive U.S. Navy base at Yokosuka who headed a Far East Command fencing team with a date to fence the Japanese Olympic team. The other members of the team were embassy or service officers and they took me in and addressed me as "Mr.," using the navy form of address for officers. Housed at first in the enlisted men's barracks with three-tiered bunks, I moved into the attractive bachelor officers' quarters when the team captain devised the ruse that I would pretend to be an officer. As a whole, the experience was thrilling, even though we lost the tournament as badly as we had expected. However, it was disconcerting to have to accept the suggestion that I "pass" as an officer just to mix socially. To me, rank should have neither relevance nor significance in off-duty relations, such as the sport of fencing. For once, I experienced a taste of needless discrimination and prejudice in the service arising purely from social status and rank. It tasted no better than racism. From the first days of army life, I had no doubts as to the importance of discipline and the differences in rank, especially between enlisted men and commissioned officers. As a platoon sergeant, I knew my role and place in respect to other men and my record indicates a job well done. However, we were in Tokyo fencing together as a team with Americans and Europeans from all backgrounds and jobs; I appreciated their gesture of having me "pass" but resented the necessity of having to do so. Visiting a good friend from my days as a student at Berkeley who was stationed at the U.S. Air Force Base at Fukuoka, I found the VIP bungalow reserved for my use. However, as at Yokosuka, it also involved the ruse of "passing." Equality in the United States carries certain qualifications, the delineation of which I would come to learn in time.

As my date of discharge grew closer in 1955, I seriously considered reenlisting and making the service a career. The army surely had its faults and disadvantages, yet I had learned to accept them and had become proficient at the duties and privileges of rank and military life. The idea of reenlisting for a tour of three years in Japan intoxicated my thinking, so I began to write home about the possibility and advantages of reenlisting. For one thing, my frame of mind and habits seemed so set in army ways that I worried about the difficulties of becoming a civilian again. I had developed a sergeant's tongue, to which uttering profanities seemed as natural as drinking a can of beer. I feared that my way of thinking, as well as my vocabulary, had radically changed from intellectual to vulgar. Before becoming a soldier, I had used strong language at times, but had done so consciously for effect and emotion. As a non-commissioned officer in Korea, however, I learned to use vulgarity without thinking, and had to consciously use straight prose when it was needed.

My main work had become the extensive coordination of the signal supplies and equipment, and the supervision of repairs or new lines throughout southern Japan. My signal company handled the telephone-telegraph lines between Japan and South Korea through Tsushima Island. For its operations, my company supplemented cable leased from the Japanese with a number of VHF relay stations on the sides and tops of mountains up and down Kyushu, Japan's southern island, and Honshu, the next island to the north and the major island of Japan, where Osaka and Tokyo are situated. Such lines scattered the company's men and facilities over quite a large area. We worked constantly to improve and extend our lines, but maintenance seemed to be almost all we could do. However, I learned the power of persistent prodding and exhortation. For several months when I was stationed in Kure, the battalion commander in Camp Zama near Tokyo mandated that a daily teletype report be sent him on each of our stations, which numbered about twenty. My captain gave me the job of sending the teletype transmissions to fit in with my other assignments, which I welcomed both to keep busy and for the opportunity to learn to use the teletype system.

For the colonel's reports, I called each station daily and used all of the carrier tricks I knew to get through. A typical conversation, of which there were between twenty and forty each day, would run as follows:

"Okayama Station, sir."

"Yee here. What's the f—— problem with your G.D. gain, sounds like a screaming cage of castrated canaries. Say, got that SOB power unit hooked in yet?"

"Sarge, we're still working on it."

"G.D. don't give me that B.S. crap. Your station reported two f—ing days ago that job would be done yesterday. G.D. it to hell! What do you want Okie's report to headquarters to look like, anyhow to hell!"

"We had troubles, sarge. Take it easy. First we couldn't get the crate up the last 200 yards because the deuce and a half couldn't handle the bitching trailer. So we unloaded the crate and started to drag it up the slope, but it was too heavy."

"Holy Christ, I think I see the f—ing picture and I don't believe it! Oh, my God, how did you ever get to be a crew chief?!"

"Take it easy, Sgt. Yee, G.D. it, we've hired a block and tackle and a crew from the town. They'll be here in an hour or two and they'll help us get the new power unit in and take out the old bastard for 3,000 yen, our money."

"Jesus Christ, it better be your own money! I never heard of a more screwed-up job [an expression used at least ten times each day]. Now, G.D. it, get off your asses and shake up these no-good lines. Sounds like you haven't checked them out for a week."

"OK, sarge, over and out."

Field lines as long as those we were operating were supposedly impossible with the World War II-model equipment we had. Often, the lines were so weak that we had to shout at the top of our voices to be heard. Imagine the above conversation at top volume, and imagine officers and GI's up and down Japan and Korea shouting into their phones to get across at all. If blowing off steam helps to soothe the nerves, I have such work-a-day experiences to perhaps explain my wonderful time in Japan.

Captain Earle was not the "leave-it-alone, don't-make-waves" type. Having worked his way up from the ranks, the captain would always go one better than ordered. Cutting all deadlines in half, he tried to live by his favorite expression, "Nothing is impossible, G.D. it!" I must say that even before meeting the captain, I had little patience with nay-sayers and defeatists, but he greatly extended my faith in and basic attitude toward solving problems. Putting in some new lines, for example, at a typically tough site, the peak being steep and hard to reach, the captain himself went to supervise the installation of the antennas and their tower. After he arrived, he called in and ordered the following materials delivered within twenty-four hours: 200-foot lengths of two different types and sizes of rope, a cylinder of oxygen, another cylinder of acetylene, welding torches, porcelain insulators, and other antenna tower parts.

The captain never tolerated hesitation or equivocation in his men; it proved better to try as hard as one could and to allow other forces, if any, to countermand or delay his wishes. An old army man from South Carolina and a former master sergeant himself, his vituperation was sharp, hard, and overwhelming. We surely saw the limitations of his bravado, such as his off-duty proclivity for the fairer sex and booze, and his meek subservience to the colonel. Our "bird" colonel, a huge figure of a man, spent much time at the relay sites during his inspections, throughout which the captain seemed in a trance-like, at-attention posture. At those times, his trousers slacked so that the cuffs reached the heel bottoms. To superiors outside our command, he reacted normally. Those of us who worked closest to the captain respected and feared him in equal proportions and did our best to satisfy his demands. Of all my army leaders, he was the most capable and complete personality, as opposed to the plastic, orange-scarfed officers on the lookout for dust who accomplished little beyond ritual and superficialities. Justifiably, the captain despised junior and senior officers who could not perform, particularly those who would not strive to build and improve, and overcome the insurmountable. He sent the lieutenant in my section to command one of the branch stations, none of which required a commissioned officer, so as to have me directly responsive to his wishes.

I received the captain's orders for those special materials needed for the antenna tower at midafternoon, already set for a soldier's night in town. In the extremely humid climate of Japan's summer, our fatigue (work) uniforms clung to us, wet and sticky from a mixture of sweat and starch. Coming to work in the morning, we would perform our duties standing up as long as possible; sitting down, one would feel all slimy and wet from his bottom down to the thighs. Military creases, of course, would be lost. My men and I studied the list demanded by the captain's phone call. We tried to see how we could accomplish the impossible once again. After hours of phone calls to other units, most of them blind calls to strangers, we were finally able to locate a sympathetic sergeant major in an engineering command at Kobe who would supply the material we needed. Half bluffing and half alluding to future help with radio parts, and so forth, we secured the supplies from the engineers by 10 P.M. that night. Returning to our post several hours later, we learned from the Japanese workers to whom I had assigned the job of ascertaining the best route to reach the captain, that truck transport required more than one day's time. However, they had studied the train schedule very carefully, and we could just make the captain's twenty-four-hour deadline with two train transfers, the second one being very tricky to maneuver.

Japan's train system should be the envy of all countries, especially the United States. Efficient and clean, the trains of the Japan National Railway (JNR) run exactly according to the printed schedules. I travelled about 300 miles once to visit a girlfriend and took the cheapest and thus the slowest train, which stopped at all stations. With a schedule in hand, I found that the train arrived at and departed from each of the innumerable stops on the dot. On the other hand, motor vehicles negotiated very narrow, often one-way, and curvy roads between towns and cities. At that time, Japan's Highway 1 along the beautiful Inland Sea compared well with an enlarged cow path, and the rule prevailed that the larger vehicle had the right-of-way. The roads being out of the question, therefore, we opted for the Japan National Railroad system.

At 6:05 A.M., three of us left Osaka on the first leg of the journey in an electric train, with the heavy acetylene cylinders, heavy cable, and other material piled up on the car floor, much to the silent bewilderment of the other passengers. The first transfer, about one hour later, went well because the train we wanted came some minutes after we had unloaded from the first. Studying the schedules, we realized why the second transfer was going to be difficult. The train we were on would come in on one track and our transfer would come in on the opposite track, taking off in the opposite direction. It seemed bad enough that the three of us would have to lug the very heavy supplies up, over, and down the steep overpass walkway. Arrival-departure times for the third train, however, presented the greatest challenge, since it came in within three minutes of the second train and stayed only two minutes at most. We obviously did not have time to cross the tracks by way of the overpass, and the reliability of the JNR made us leery of chancing a delay. Thus, to make the transfer in time, we decided that our only course of action would be to commit the crime of crossing the tracks directly.

Preparatory to our skirmish, we lugged everything to the rear car so we could scoot across the tracks without delay and detection. As soon as the train doors opened, we quickly carried the supplies out onto the platform. Two of us jumped down onto the evenly graveled rail bed, where we gingerly avoided the feared third rail while the third handed the material to us before jumping down too. Without pause, we manhandled the gear to the other track and climbed up the opposite wall with about a minute to spare before the third train pulled in. In that minute's pause, we stared at the short corridor we had crossed and the two third rails running along the two pairs of gleaming track. A touch of either third rail would have meant instant death. The entire operation, with its physical exertion as well as its dangers of electrocution and arrest, left us semi-paralyzed and dumb, oblivious to the shock of the Japanese at the scene. As in battle, this life-and-death sensation has its worst moment not so much in the all-consuming struggle of action, but when one has time to reflect ahead or to go back over the event. The incoming train broke our momentary spell, and we piled the gear into the car for the final leg of the mission.

A week or so later, the captain ordered a similar delivery to the same site, but we could go no further than the Osaka station by train the second time. A Japanese policeman came forward and ordered both the GI's and the material off the train, after spotting labels on the cylinders clearly warning that the contents were inflammable and under high pressure. The Japanese scrutinize role and status more precisely than we do in the United States because clothing, behavior, and situation are used more as a means of identifying and judging. As a Fulbright professor in Japan in 1972, I noted that the people responded much less respectfully to me when I wore a gray-colored shirt with my suit than a white one. While in uniform in Japan, I was seldom taken for anything other than a GI. This contrasted with my experiences in Korea, where the people responded to the person. The policeman who caused us to abort our second assault on the JNR treated me exactly as he did my white buddies—"Get outta here—now!" "Take stuff out! What-so matto, GI, you craz?" Without arguing, we obeyed the policeman, for we knew he was right. We welcomed his rational upholding of standards and the end to our test of limits.

During the summer of 1955, the captain received a

massive delivery of brand-new microwave equipment with hardly any warning at all. Six million dollars worth of equipment, it filled the five railroad box- and flatcars that appeared one day on our train siding. Our first problem concerned the immediate storage of the equipment; the only available warehouse we could locate was a Japanese air force hangar that had remained unused because its roof and sides had been shot through with innumerable bullets and bomb fragments in American air raids during World War II. A party of American pilots I encountered on a train to Tokyo told me that they had participated in World War II raids over Japan. They emphasized the fact that months before the atom bombs were dropped on Hiroshima and Nagasaki, the Air Corps had begun to repeat the bombing of targets already believed demolished. Viable targets being mostly exhausted, the bombers just kept the bombs falling as an added measure. My Japanese friends told me the Americans usually flew over a day ahead of a raid to drop leaflets warning that the B-29s were coming soon to bomb, and sure enough, the planes did as had been announced. The psychological effect must have been devastating in that the enemy forewarned that they were coming and did so with impunity, time after time. My friends said the populace truly feared the American "B-'9s" and their "fire" or incendiary bombings. Our bullet-ridden and burnt-out hangar warehouse should have been torn down long ago. However, there was no other choice, and so there we piled our mysterious crates of microwave equipment and the parabolas, finishing after many hours of sweaty labor and covering it all with as much tarpaulin as we could find.

The company's second problem concerned our accountability for the signal equipment. According to army policies, the unit commander was responsible for the equipment assigned his unit. If anything could not be accounted for, the unit commander supposedly paid for it out of his salary. No army supply catalogs for the new equipment could be found, even in headquarters, and no one even seemed to know how the microwave systems worked. With increasingly impatient requests from the colonel to sign off for the shipment, the captain felt more and more trapped in a situation in which all he could do was hope to lose as little as possible. I undertook a laborious inventory, crawling over the crates and parabolas to find each stenciled list of contents and their stock numbers. Using the manufacturers' ID numbers, I typed up an inventory for the captain's signature. The captain had me hand-carry the inventory to Camp Zama near Tokyo to make his deadline. I recommended that he not sign and that he continue to protest his unfamiliarity with the radically new equipment, the nature of its delivery and storage, and the lack of military catalog specifications as to the equipment's ID numbers, value, and use. His signature automatically made the captain accountable. How many years of a captain's salary would it take to pay back six million dollars? At $7,200 a year, it would take over 833 years.

I personally delivered the signed list for the captain to the colonel's office at Camp Zama. I handed the papers to the adjutant and said, "Sir, I am pleased to present Captain Earle's compliments and his signed acquisition of microwave property recently delivered to Company B." Across the hall, over a telephone line as weak as any could get and still be usable, I had to shout as loud as possible to give my report of delivery as ordered. The captain wanted more information about the receipt than I had, and I had to field his questions carefully, knowing everyone could hear me. To better answer his questions, I searched out a more secluded phone and found one in the mess hall kitchen. The work at headquarters took no more than ten minutes and I was on the overnight train back to Osaka later that day.

Two or three days later, the captain received another

list of equipment with orders from the colonel to sign it immediately and return it with the courier. Hardly resembling our original inventory, the new listing included far more equipment and used a different system of supply numbers. However, the captain said he had no choice but to sign in the face of a direct order, though he was as red-faced and agitated as we had ever seen him. Our next task then became finding a way around the issue of the responsible officer's accountability for property under his command. Reading the regulations carefully, we found a solution to the captain's dilemma. It was a beautiful plan, and we put it into effect in the next several days.

A phone call from the captain's hometown in the states came through that informed the captain that his elderly mother had fallen ill and was expected to pass away soon. The captain requested and received approval to fly home on emergency leave. We did not see the captain for about four weeks, and upon his return he could not be held accountable for the property, having been separated from his responsibility to it for over a month's time. His mother recovered and the doctors credited her son's presence and assistance as an important factor. Thus we saved the captain's hide by beating the army with its own rules. I have always wondered if the colonel respected the way we returned the problem to him.

There is a corny line in a World War II movie starring Jeff Chandler, who plays Colonel Merrill during his command of an American elite force in Burma. At a crucial point of the exhausting campaign, the colonel replies to one of his adulatory men that should they meet on an American street someday, he would want the enlisted man to forgive the colonel's transgressions, if any, and treat him well. In other words, the colonel was saying, "I am the colonel here and as such, I make you and the men do what is impossible, because that is

what General Stilwell wants me to do. Perhaps you will
die in a stinking swamp and never be found or remembered. Back home, where we might meet as civilians on
the street, all of this will seem unworldly and I shall have
no claim on you. If that should happen, be kind and do
not take out your revenge, for I shall be myself then and
not the colonel." A good soldier could appreciate what
the colonel meant; it takes a professional warrior to
understand another. The army taught me some important facets of the American way of life and one is that
facts and values may be and often are separate and
distinct. What one knows to be true, good, and beautiful
may not be the best action to take in a given situation.
The principle of survival makes one opt for alternatives
that allow one to live to fight another day and survive. In
battle, the saying is that one must kill or be killed, which
is contradictory to the teachings of Jesus Christ and the
basic values of the United States. World War II General
George S. Patton told his men that the way to victory
was not to die for one's country but to make the enemy
die for his. The supreme test of a society's morals and
values, war and the tremendous mindset underlying its
preparation and practice, produce a domino effect
throughout the society. Americans sincerely speak of
ethical ideals and say that they believe in pursuing certain values, but actions that speak more loudly than
words often indicate that the realities of life contradict
those ideals and values. Vietnam, Watergate and Nixon,
wrongdoings by the CIA and FBI, business payoffs to
obtain secrets and sales, and so on created a strong
sense of cynicism in the United States during the 1970s.
However, the radical clamor over civil rights and Vietnam in the 1960s and early 1970s, which made morality a
national issue, caused Americans, even though be-
grudgingly, to examine the contradiction between their
values and the facts. The cynicism of the 1970s grew out
of a rapidly expanding awareness of what the realities of
life and the world really were and how they affect one

and all. Americans suffered chronic indigestion in the 1970s as they were forced to swallow catastrophes such as the oil embargo, Watergate, and the Iranian and Falkland crises.

Another facet of the American system that I learned more clearly in the army was that the role or job can make the person. Role behavior influenced the movie character of the colonel to do what he did not really want to do. The colonel in the movie in effect asked one of his men to "pity me in this job of playing colonel— perhaps you would like my real self." In a way, this is somewhat like the conflict felt by billions of people around the world who must fulfill roles they really do not want to have but which they perform anyway. However, that conflict is not the main problem. The crucial problem is the lack of self-realization, not knowing that there is this conflict of role and person. There are hopeful signs today that more people are seeking a closer relationship between what they do and what they want to be and have. In the poem, "Two Tramps at Wood-chopping Time," Robert Frost says that when a person cannot differentiate between his vocation and avocation he must be happy indeed. Learning as much as they did during the 1970s about energy concerns, the world's undeveloped nations, world economics, presidential powers and government abuses, and other issues, Americans are more knowledgeable and sensitive to what happens in the world and their country. One can only hope that this educative process continues and matures, not just in the present generation but in future generations.

In the army, discipline was the first and most vital principle. With discipline, the role always superseded the person, and rank stabilized control and order. Perhaps more so than in any other army of the world, the American soldier could shade his military conformities so that his personality was still viable and instrumental to good results. The GI also demanded to know as much as possible about a given situation in which he might be involved and his life endangered. This is reflected in the positive characteristic of American soldiers—that they can easily assume the roles of their superiors when called upon to do so. In other words, they are able to take over and take charge. Although I did not have the experience of a counterpart promoted over me, I did observe the changes in men who received promotions. Except for promotion to private first class, which carried no authority, men who were advanced assumed the authority and privileges of rank as if they had always had them. Happy-go-lucky fellows whom few thought would ever change took charge and laid the law down as soon as they became a corporal or sergeant. Role thus maketh the man in the Army.

Captain Earle denied my reenlistment on the humane basis that he thought that my potential would be wasted in the army, and I had about a month to say goodbye to my Japanese friends and cast my thoughts toward civilian life. *Sayonara* or farewell parties with my friends made it harder to think well of going home. After Korea, Japan seemed to be a paradise and the people I had become friends with proved to be more generous and hospitable than any I had known up to then. Showing that they liked me for myself, they did not notice the added stripes on my shoulders for some time after I made staff sergeant. The exception that proves the rule: One friend whom I knew because I frequented his sake bar, a tiny place at the end of a lamp-lighted walkway, turned from sumo wrestling to American-style wrestling. When I accepted my friend's invitation to watch his first wrestling match, the manager suggested that I wear my U.S. Army uniform. Even though I seldom went into the city in uniform, I complied with the manager's wish and found myself sitting beside him at ringside and being introduced to the audience as one of the wrestler's GI fans! Testing my suspicions, I did not wear the uniform to the next match and found myself seated not even in the arena but shunted to a window high up by the ceiling. Unfortunately, my wrestler friend did not win his matches and began to drink too much of his sake. There seemed to be nothing any of his friends could do to help his depression over losing another opportunity, perhaps his final chance, at fame and fortune. However, he did rise to the occasion as the host of a *sayonara* party for me. Gripping my shoulders with his huge hands, he wished me well and I felt very bad about leaving friends and familiar haunts in my GI Japan.

My experiences in Japan as a Senior Fulbright Lecturer in 1972, seven years after I left there as a soldier, were at a higher intellectual level. I tried a bit of slumming one night as in my GI days and after spending an hour at a ginza dive in Tokyo I realized that my tastes and interests had changed. During our several months in the Land of the Rising Sun, my family and I found many interesting references to the cultural ties of the Japanese to Chinese civilization. The Japanese debt to American influence is on the surface more prominent than that to the Chinese, but the roots of China's influence on Japan are deeper and subtler than those of any other foreign source. As a small example, there are three names used for what I would say is the world's most majestic and awe-inspiring mountain—Mt. Fuji (English), Fujiyama (Japanese), and Fuji-san (Chinese), with the latter being the one most often used. The Japanese did not have a written language until they adopted Chinese writing, beginning probably in the year A.D. 57, when records show that Japanese visitors were officially received at the Han court. General use of Chinese characters *(Kanji)* and literature in Japan did not occur until the fourth century and grew during the Tang Dynasty (618–907). By the ninth century, the Japanese had developed a new system of syllabic characters called *hiragana* or "common kana," which originated from simplified characters first used by women who wrote novels, poetry, and diaries. About the same time that *hiragana* was developing, another system of syllabic writing was developed called *katakana*, which was greatly perfected in the tenth century and is still used today for telegrams, typing, and office printing, and transcribing European and American loanwords and onomatopoetic words. *Kanji* (officially 1,850 characters but many more for literate persons) and *hiragana* form today's Japanese orthography in general.

I found it most interesting that the Japanese pronounced *Kanji* much as the Cantonese do and I made a self-discovery when we brought a postcard of the famous red bridge at Nikko which had the parenthesis "hungh ku" for the *Kanji* pronounciation. It was the exact Cantonese pronunciation, and I tested my hunch with a China scholar friend who said, "Of course, the Japanese got their Chinese *(Kanji)* from the great Tang Dynasty and the Cantonese preserve the Tang Dynasty dialect." I recalled too that the Cantonese, at least in the ancestral area of my people, called themselves "Tong yun," or people of the Tang, in honor of the dynasty that integrated the southern Chinese into the greater affairs of the nation and increased the migration of northerners into the virgin lands of the South. Discovering new aspects of our Chinese roots during the stay in Japan seemed ironic as well as appropriate.

During the Nara period (710–784), Japan sent four official missions to the Tang court at Changan, as well as many students who stayed to study in China. Under the great Tang emperor, Xian Zong (712–756), China of that era extended as far west as Turkistan, to Mongolia and Siberia to the north, and into Jiangxi and Hunan, south of the Yangtze. It was the beginning of two centuries of Chinese prosperity, wealth, and international exchange. As Japanese visitors to China increased during the eighth and ninth centuries, Japan's literate culture became basically Chinese. At that time there was a great cultural flowering, much nation-building, and the operation of an efficient socio-political-economic system, including the construction of great canals, the proliferation of trade centers, and the abundance of grain and food brought by advances in agriculture. By the eighteenth century, however, China clearly presented a negative example. Unlike Japan, the persistent learner, China, the teacher who cradled the East, could not adapt herself to ward off the ambitions of the Western powers by learning the ways of the West.

En route through the "pipeline" to my discharge, I worried more and more about my transition to civilian life and felt lost without my buddies. In the army, the uniform represents one well; its insignias and ribbons indicate where one has been and what one has done. Strange to say, I never felt more "American" than when I wore the uniform. What I appeared to be was what I was, without anything to prove. Returning on the troop ship, I shared a crowded cabin and enjoyed the porthole's fresh air and the extra space because of my rank, in contrast to the steamy and crowded stacks of hammocks below deck. When I was sitting by the railing one day, an officer mistook me for a private, and asked me to do a chore. Seeing the chevrons, however, he apologized. The army was hardly democratic and perfect, but after three years I fitted in all right and I felt certain that I could not adjust to civilian life, where I could see no tangible, comprehensive identity for myself. What kind of work could I do? Could I resume my objective of becoming a high school teacher? What about being Chinese in civilian life? In the army, the sergeant's uniform indicated a status that I did not have to explain, even though it was relatively insignificant in the greater society. Yet as a civilian, I would not have a readymade identity to assume.

Years later, as a 1972 Senior Fulbright Lecturer at Tokyo University and Tamagawa University, I found calling cards to be essential for polite and proper identification. Proper estimation and judgment of the strangers one met became possible through careful study of the information on the calling cards. In civilian clothes, I could pass as Japanese in the crowds, but those who attended to my American gait, tailoring, and speech spotted me immediately. In 1948, 1954 (when out of uniform), and 1972 Japan, I enjoyed the novelty of being lost in the Asian crowds and feeling strangely incognito. Face validity has always seemed greater for me in alien Japan than in the United States, my homeland. Even though many people say they can tell a Chinese from a Japanese, I am hesitant when I hear such a claim. I made the mistake of thinking a fellow passenger on the S.S. *Marine Adder*, en route to Shanghai, must be Japanese because he fitted the World War II-era stereotype of a Japanese. He turned out to be Chinese, and the director of the Shanghai YMCA. Japanese people would often ask me in Japanese for directions at stations, even though the Japanese are traditionally hesitant to ask questions of strangers. I always felt regretful when I had to indicate that they had approached someone who could hardly speak Japanese and was not a native of Japan at all. Their surprise seemed as though I had removed a mask and exposed a frightening face. My Japanese professor friends politely explained the behavior by saying I looked like a gentlemen.

Superficial acceptance as in a crowd carries no substance, especially when the Japanese discover you are a *gai-jin*, or outsider. A homogenous and insular people, the Japanese assume, even more than do the Chinese, that *gai-jins* cannot possibly understand their way of thinking and customs. However, it is this sense of cultural isolationism that makes the Japanese characterize themselves as inscrutable. I understand that sense, from my naive transition from military to civilian life when I began to grapple with the problem, unbeknownst to me then, of finding a compromise between self and role.

As a Fulbrighter, I visited only two Japanese homes. One was on the occasion of a party at the residence of a

Japanese American and the other visit was to the home of a Japanese teacher whom we had hosted when he studied at the University of Texas. My wife and children were fortunate to visit several other homes, and all visits, mine included, were most cordial and pleasant. Neither my university students nor the professors with whom I worked entertained me at their homes, but they did at formal, public settings, such as a hotel restaurant or the university center. As a GI, I had visited the apartments of friends, and there was no qualm or hesitation in receiving me. My role as an American professor made similar informalities difficult in 1972. Social status and relationships in Japan form arrangements that are more complex than those in the United States, and that make it hard to fit in a *gai-jin*, even when an American marries a Japanese. A soldier seemed closer to the people, but to the "wrong" kind of people. On the other hand, a visiting professor might be eligible to meet the "right" kind of people, but mutually satisfying role behavior and expectations may be difficult to develop. As in Chinese culture, the individual is not the unit of focus in Japanese society. The group is of first concern, and one finds that the Japanese have developed a national group sense that is unique among the so-called industrial powers of the world. In business and other institutionalized systems, a Japanese typically becomes a member of a group, a paternalistic family superior to the individual and benevolent to all. One is expected to remain compliant and loyal to the company, and the company will in turn attempt to take care of him or her, even to the extent of going under before firing its employees. Japanese corporations have strikingly low levels of employee turnover. American businessmen are not as amazed at the many group sessions that transpire before a decision is made as they are at the high productivity of Japanese workers. Companies such as Hitachi, Mitsubishi, and Sony are giant corporate families that seem motivated more to maintain group morale, stability, and productivity than to achieve the American principle of economic profitability. The Japanese say that the greatest difference between American and Japanese industries is that they plan and work for the long-term while their American competitors are only concerned with short-term returns. Japanese workers, for instance, take matter-of-factly semiannual bonuses, company resorts, marriage assistance, after-hours socials, health care for the entire family, and so forth. In return for such benevolence, Japanese workers respond with a high degree of loyalty and productivity. I heard a story of one Honda worker who fixed obvious problems, such as windshield wipers, on Honda autos as he walked home from work each day.

Similarly, once a scholar in Japan receives an academic appointment, he has lifelong tenure at that university. In recent years, inflation and the conservative budgets of the government have made it necessary for professors to take part-time teaching jobs at other universities so as to make ends meet. In fact, most of the college instructors are lecturers rather than professors, since the former are temporary adjuncts and not regular members of the collegial family. I observed tremendous bother and behind-the-scenes lobbying when an opening for an assistant professor came up, for the one chosen would be accepted into a lifelong position.

In the United States, junior faculty members are usually given an appointment for three years and if they show promise, they receive another three-year contract or possibly promotion and tenure. The American professor feels he or she earns status through proven achievement as a scholar and teacher. In Japan, promise is painstakingly determined, but before the appointment is granted in the first place. Similarly, gaining entrance into a university is the hardest step of academic learning in Japan, and students cram for months and months to do well on the entrance exams.

In fact, they do the same for admission to the best
secondary schools, which of course are determined by
the number of graduates admitted from a given school
to Tokyo University or Todai and other prestigious universities. Todai is the equivalent of Harvard, Yale,
Stanford, Berkeley, and so on all rolled up into one
institution. In order to be accepted by Todai or a top
second choice, aspirants cram exhaustingly for the examination and take extra preparatory training, often
begun as youths. It is not uncommon to find examinees
who have memorized whole encyclopedias, page for
page, in order to pass the examination "hells."

Once accepted, however, the student has passed the
major hurdle. Short of financial disaster and sickness,
he will graduate and move into a governmental or business career within a bureaucratic-paternalistic system
dominated by school-tie relations. During my tours of
American cultural centers in Japan's major cities, the
Japanese seemed most interested in my Fulbright lectures on American higher education. I found many Japanese impressed and amused at how much harder in
comparison American professors work students under
the credit system in the United States. They expressed
some pleasant astonishment in learning about the
academic grind to achieve tenure at prestigious American universities. Acceptance into an institution and
conformance to its objectives and procedures make for
success in Japan. Individual achievement and continued merit in terms of an institution's criteria help an
American to keep his or her job and be successful. As an
American soldier in 1954–1955 Japan, my work and life
ironically resembled the Japanese way of life more
closely than in the years following. It was not the military aspects so much as the submersion of the individual to group expectations and scrutiny, the steady, equal
welfare and security for all, and the opportunity to
find self-satisfaction and approval through specialized

capabilities and expertise upon which others relied in a network of interrelationship. As they said in the army, "You've found a home in the army, soldier."

As my tour of duty came to an end, I initiated a reenlistment but my captain turned me down. His response was surprising, since he had wanted me to go on to officer's candidate school. However, my letters home suggesting possible reenlistment created much consternation, and my mother wrote a long letter to the captain pleading that he reject my application and send me home. Perhaps my letters overstated my friendships among the Japanese, and my family consequently feared a GI marriage. Also, mother argued that I would waste my educational attainment. A soldier's career, the lowest form of livelihood in traditional China, would not fit in the family structure. To my amazement, the captain concurred with my mother, agreeing to send me home. According to the captain, I had a promising future in the army, but could do far better and be more helpful to the nation outside the service. My respect for the captain and his advice made me resist all inclinations to appeal his decision. In several weeks, I found myself in the transit pipeline back to the states, an American soldier who felt more at home as a soldier in Japan than he did with the idea of being a civilian in California. As in 1948, I returned home from Asia feeling changed and unprepared for life in the United States, even though the underlying circumstances differed very much. Thus ended the part of my life when I felt most American and secure. Later, I would look back on those feelings of my young adulthood and understand why I felt that way. It was a natural and healthy outcome from the schizophrenic nature of my youth and the experiences of old China and university life.

Boarding the gray-painted troopship headed back to the states, I followed one of the many long, ant-like lines of GI's hefting their bags and stringing slowly into the bowels of the steel, nondescript hulk of the troopship.

Reaching a point below where there were unclaimed
spaces, I selected an upper hammock in one of the
many tightly packed compartments. Coming down so
far, we had to be beneath the water line. Stacked four
men high with barely three feet for the aisles and with
less space vertically, the layers of bunks created a
prison-like atmosphere. The men secured their heavy
duffle bags by looping the carrying strap to one of the
many metal bars and poles about and padlocking the
hook. Stretched out on my hammock, I surveyed what
appeared to be my living space for at least two weeks.
Networks of large- and medium-diameter pipes, painted
various colors for identification purposes and wrapped
with varying layers of insulation, coursed menacingly
above and about the space, carrying unknown fluids
from unknown sources to unknown connections and
purposes. An aisle light with a metal web cover blazed
about three feet away. Claustrophobia had never before
been a problem for me, for which I felt grateful. Yet I
wondered if my selection of the top space to secure
maximum privacy seemed wise given other factors.
With the men below beginning to smoke and jaw, the
growing heaviness of the air and anticipated roll of the
ship reminded me of my proclivity for seasickness. Attempting to change my mood, I focused upon nearby
rivets and reflected upon the construction of the massive craft. After an hour or two, when we had left the
dock, a nearby loudspeaker little noticed in the shadow
cast by the pipes blared out, "Sergeant Yee, Albert Yee,
report to the troop commander!" After listening to its
repetition, I hurried up to the top decks not knowing
what to expect. An officer met me and said, "As a top-
three grader, you can move into one of the cabins up
here if you want. It'll be less crowded and there'll be a
porthole for air. What do you say?" I accepted without
hesitation and then the officer threw in the kicker. He
said, "You don't have to, but we need a good noncom to
supervise the platoon of men helping the cooks at night.

Will you do it? It'll be a snap and give you something to
do with the time."

It has been and still continues to be my habit to accept
positive challenges presented me by my superiors, so I
took the job without further ado. Where does that behavior come from—my Cantonese heritage, which hon-
ors loyalty and dependability, or from my youthful stir
to the stories of "Letter to Garcia," "Livingston and
Smith," "Sergeant York," and "Colin Kelly"? Needless
to say, the work involved far more than met the eye. My
laconic acceptance seemed a bit like taking the "Letter to
Garcia." Reporting to the galley at midnight, I found
only one cook and ten GI's and it gradually sank in that
the twelve of us were to prepare the breakfast for over
3,000 men! The galley had many ranges, ovens, and
steam-heated pots big enough to serve as Japanese
ofuros or baths. There was a potato-peeling machine
and great stainless steel sinks piled high with huge pots
and pans. The scene was hardly aesthetic or suggestive
of any gourmet possibilities. All of which made me
wonder why I left the hold for a cabin berth I had not
had the pleasure of enjoying yet. The cook, dressed in
white hat and clothing, and the ten GI's stared at me for
a long moment as I surveyed the situation. I took the
civilian cook (troop ships were manned by civilians)
aside and asked him the whereabouts of the other
cooks. Annoyed, he said there were no others and that
he was supposed to have the help of many more GI's to
get the job done.

I went off to the troop commander's station and had a
difficult time finding the officer who had spoken with
me. The young lieutenant agreed with me that the work
detail should have more men but said nothing could be
done until the next day. He suggested that I come back
after breakfast. After cursing him and myself all the way
back down, I huddled with the cook and told him he
would have to make do with those of us that were there.
Unsmiling and tight-lipped, as if he despised his trade

and job, he told us breakfast was to include canned grapefruit, which we could provide by opening the No. 10-sized cans, at least 100, and having them ready for the serving line at breakfast at 0600. Also, gallons of coffee had to be brewed. Before the grapefruit and coffee, however, we had to peel hundreds of pounds of potatoes, scramble enormous numbers of eggs, and toast countless slices of bread.

In perhaps my best rallying charge to a work detail, I approached the listless, half-asleep contingent of men. Flopped down or sitting about dejectedly, bemoaning the fact that they had been singled out for KP out of more than 3,000, they could not be blamed. However, through leadership training or whatever experiences, military or not, I had accumulated, I knew that their attitude and attention had to be conformed to the task. I began by saying, "God damn it to hell, what a screwed-up mess!" While they thought my sympathies were with theirs, I took them by surprise. Commanding them to their feet and gathering them about with a stern sergeant's tongue to establish a sense of authority, I gave a brief but down-to-earth speech, which began:

"Well, we're stuck with a real chicken-shit job this time. The men in this galley have the Goddamned duty of preparing the morning chow for all of the bastards sleeping on this f—— ship. As usual, things are SNAFU. Look around. Take a look at each other, you SOB's. There's only us to get the job done. We can't get any more help tonight. I've been up to try. None of us want to be here but we're on our way home and the SOB's sleeping up there are counting on us, so what do you say? Can we do it? What do you say we give it a go and show them and ourselves what we're made of. All right, men!?"

People will rally and perform if an appropriate appeal is made that presents the options open to them, especially in terms of polar opposites. Individuals like to have a self-satisfying, personal choice, if only for the sake of their self-respect and pride, and a collective, superordinate goal. Human beings can be driven, coerced, and frightened to work, but they perform far better in a climate of self-chosen, collective purpose and motivation. Pervaded by a common "we-feeling" sense of purpose, such groups bring out the best in people and become self-sustaining. I have seen it occur in groups of young and old, pupils and professors, and soldiers both foreign and American.

Lethargic and sullen before my speech, the GI's looked about and one of the bigger fellows said, "You just tells us what to do, sarge!" The men began to raise themselves as if to sharpen up and approach the vital duty that stood before them. In answer to my charge to them that several thousand hungry "SOB" buddies of ours would be getting up at 6 A.M. for breakfast, the quality and quantity of which we were solely responsible for, the ten men showed the unmistakable sign that they wanted to get at it right away. Getting the disbelieving cook front and center, I asked him to tell us what had to be done. As he outlined the various jobs, I assigned men to them—the most involved seemed to be the potatoes and eggs.

The fried potatoes would normally take about twenty 100-pound sacks of potatoes for the 3,000 men. The mechanical potato peeler, however, was not cooperative. To get the skin entirely off, it reduced the finished potato to half its original size no matter what we did. So we decided to run the potatoes through only once and very lightly, using hand peelers and knives to finish off the work, especially to remove the rotten parts. We greased many large pans with butter and put the sliced potatoes in them, stacking them ready for the ovens. As might have been expected, some of the men got a bit silly and slaphappy and began to throw potatoes at each other until I uttered a few choice phrases. I knew the spirit of work and mission would not last long, but hoped we could make it a one-time success without my becoming too much of a martinet.

The scrambled eggs became the greatest challenge. For so many coming to breakfast, we needed about 500 dozen eggs. As we brought out the egg crates, we verified the cook's prediction that many of the eggs would be rotten since they had been in cold storage for more than two weeks. We devised a method of cracking the eggs into soup bowls before dumping them into pots. The man holding the bowl was to judge if any eggs were rotten before he dumped them into the pot. We assigned four men to hold the weighty bowls while sitting astraddle one of the two big pots while the other men cracked the eggs open and emptied the contents into the bowls. The system went speedily and smoothly enough, though we became rather overwhelmed by the enormous numbers of eggs to be handled. As was to be expected, the men got bits of egg shells into the pot and occasionally an overly ripe egg fell into the pot. Perhaps we went too fast, for we were not always sure if all of an offending egg had been retrieved and discarded down the drain. The scene bordered on chaos, and the air became somewhat foul and heavy with the sulfurous stench of rotten eggs; the men became coated with a sticky slime, especially their hands and arms; and the deck grew slippery and dangerous with egg shells and sloppings about.

Everyone began to realize that the men holding the bowls and examining their contents had the easiest task of all. Sitting stationary and merely dumping the bowls full of eggs into the pots if judged satisfactory, the bowl inspectors were vulnerable targets for the aim of the men who had to slop about on their feet, bringing up the wooden crates and cracking open the eggs. In time, the bowl inspectors were covered with eggs and shells from head to foot and urgently sought relief. Rotating assignments, the entire crew of men soon became one sticky, bawling mass of humanity which anyone from the outside, especially an officer, would have regarded as a riot. Nevertheless, the job we set out to accomplish for the egg dish got done. What had seemed to be an endless process proved finite after all. With some similarity to the water torture technique and its effectiveness due to maddening repetition, eggs became to us the heaviest and hardest objects to lift and crack open as we finished the last hundred dozen. Surely, other ways to handle our situation could have been devised, but time to plan, decide, and act was short. In general, sergeants had to respond to situations with dispatch and settle on a decisive course of action.

Discipline in the army I knew developed from and was maintained by the noncommissioned officers; whatever his competence, intelligence, and outlook, the NCO got things done. The men could suggest alternatives and voice mild objections, but in the end the NCO had the responsibility for the decision. Should any GI seriously resist an order or speak out in excess, I had learned from other sergeants to say these cautionary words: "I am a sergeant of the U.S. Army. Now, . . ." The approach never failed to modify a recalcitrant mood, at least for the moment. I used it only twice and both were incidents with drunken subordinates who were raising hell and would not listen to reason from others.

I had one problem with a subordinate in Korea who challenged me to "take my stripes off and fight man-to-man." Although I ignored his racist taunts as stupidity and waited for reason to rule, I could not overlook his conduct when he attacked me from behind and injured my back. We were in a combat zone and there had to be discipline. I turned about and found the man with fists up ready to go. Without any ado, I stepped in and caught him full in the left eye, knocking him across the tent. The man came again with a fierce look on his face and jaw set savagely. I hit his other eye with a harder blow than the other, and he fell over and lay crying and moaning on the tent floor. It upset everyone, and I did not like maintaining discipline by brute force. However, the men could see that I had restrained myself as long as I could. In the days to come, the man would boast of his NCO, who had blackened not one but both of his eyes.

In the short lull after the egg-cracking stint, I feared the men would "get lost" or slacken off. They surely had good reason to do so and gave signs of wanting to escape, but sergeants had to anticipate times such as that. I gathered them around and teased them about their appearance, with indirect compliments on what they had accomplished so far. Their reactions indicated that the honeymoon was nearly over. I asked them to hand over their dog tags so they could take turns leaving to go shower and change if they wanted or at least go get some fresh air above. Giving half of the men an hour away at a time, those remaining worked with the cook to pour the pots full of eggs into big steam kettles shaped like upside-down rockets. Big enough to hold a man, the kettles had steam valves and gauges to set temperatures desired. Wooden steps were mounted to the kettles so that one could see over and work the pots. After we dumped in the right quantity of egg, the cook beat the goo with a large mechanized beater and probably added some milk to thin the mixture. Setting the steam temperature, he handed out large wooden paddles to the men to stir the eggs and keep the mix from sticking and caking around the sides of the kettle. The paddle-stirring was easy at first, but became more difficult as the egg mix stiffened. One could not avoid sweating profusely while working the paddles over the steaming kettles. I did not see if the cook salted the eggs, but none seemed needed with the perspiration flowing freely from the entire upper portion of our bodies into the yellow, steamy mass. It was difficult to see through the foggy air and with the sweat burning our eyes, the conditions reminded me of taking a steambath. With that thought, I quickly backed away and removed my glasses, as one does before entering the steamroom to prevent the lenses from falling out of the eyeglass frames. Somewhat relieved at having prevented possible delay and embarrassment, I was amused to think of the hassle that would have ensued if a lens did fall into the mass of eggs.

Breakfast came and went without fanfare. It seemed so simple to load the cans and trays of food onto the dumb waiters. As the large number of workers on the serving crew took over, my gang perceptibly slackened in effort and quietly collapsed out of exhaustion. The sergeant for the serving crew looked us over and sniffed in disapproval of our appearance and lack of military bearing. Yet I was too weary to say more than good morning to my properly uniformed counterpart. I went up to look over the serving line and it looked normal and proper, just as if we were in barracks duty. Only the cook and my group of ten GI's knew the conditions under which the meal had been prepared. I wondered if the expression, "What they don't know can't hurt them," really applied.

The chance to sleep up in my cabin quarters almost made the evening's work worthwhile. However, I should have anticipated a problem when the shower would not work and I had to take a cold sponge bath. After only three minutes in my bunk, when I had fallen into the deep sleep of one who is physically exhausted, I was awakened and ordered out of bed and the cabin by an officer and some NCO's. They would not listen to my explanation and said the orders were that everyone had to go out on deck. Troop carriers had the rule that the men had to spend the day on deck and that the sleeping quarters were off-limits. It took me several days before I could get permission to have my men and myself exempted, but with less than complete success. The teams clearing out the quarters never failed to disrupt my sleeping. It was a glorious victory on those mornings when I was allowed to have the day to sleep. Somehow most of those days coincided with bad weather days and my cabin mates had to be tolerated. Their loud singing, joking, and laughter made the relative quiet of the deck, bad weather or not, seem desirable.

Those two weeks at sea from Yokohama to Seattle were a blur. Without sleep and with the heavy work at night, I must have functioned through instinct and habit. The men used all of their tricks to avoid the breakfast duty. Without an alarm system and the troop commander's inexplicable refusal to regroup my men into one compartment, I had to resort to telling the men to tie a white towel or T-shirt by the rail of their bunk so I could go through the many compartments around 10 P.M. to locate and rouse my crew. There was little that could be done even if I had wanted to punish ma-lingerers. Could I blame them for shirking the breakfast duties when thousands of other GI's aboard had no duties at all? However, we maintained a kind of group camaraderie and commitment, a fatalistic sense of "Well, we have to do it so let's get the Goddamned job done." Loyalty and effort then became relative to the behavior and attitude operating among us, and the sev-eral out-and-out malingerers were disciplined by their peers. One wonders how many people in the world work at jobs that exact such a toll on their mentality and time. We did the job with the knowledge we were headed home to the states, but what about all of those who make their living like that and might consider them-selves lucky to be employed? There are those, of course, who somehow find satisfaction and strength in routine, mindless work that is physical or just minimally chal-lenging to the human mind. For myself, I still believe in doing a good job no matter the job, that things could be worse, and that things will get better in time through good effort and results. At least, do a good job of trying to make something work right.

Landfall came in the early hours of the morning, and the ship was about to dock before many of us knew we

were at Seattle. The day before we had been told to
pack up and to wear dress uniforms the next morning.
The summer dress uniform was khaki pants, shirt, tie,
peaked hat, and low quarter shoes. It felt good to put on
clean clothes even though they were wrinkled. Some of
the men took their first shower baths since they came
aboard. The troops had the appearance of being soldiers
again. They had gotten so lazy, downcast, and unruly
that another week at sea might have brought about gang
fights and daredeviltry, if only to have something to do.
A highlight of the day, for example, was waiting in line
for hours to buy a can of Planter's salted peanuts at the
tiny PX with the Dutch half door. I could have put more
men to work in the galley at night, but certainly not 3,000
additional men. Although there were other work details,
such as KP for the noon and evening meals, and deck
sweeping, most of the men had absolutely nothing to do
except wait. It seemed a waste of human capability and
potential. What best symbolized the nature of the two-
week bondage were the grimy trousers of the men's
fatigues (work uniforms), especially the seats, which
came from squatting and sitting on the deck. For some
reason, the black seat bottoms of the green uniforms
made me think of the type of monkeys at zoos with
bright red bottoms. Infantrymen, artillerymen, engineers, medics, clerks, MP's, tankers, and even carrier-
repeatermen carried the identical badge of boredom on
their bottoms.

I do not remember much about the landing. Perhaps a
band played as we filed down the long gangplanks onto
the dock, and maybe Red Cross ladies were serving
coffee and doughnuts as they had when I shipped out
about two years before. Processing was efficient and
took very little time. Overnight, Nevadans and northern
Californians, who were to go back to Fort Ord for discharge, were boarding a surprisingly attractive train
with modern sleepers and domed viewing seats on a top
deck. As a staff sergeant, I was put in a compartment

with another sergeant and a corporal. The three of us were asked to help two young lieutenants, who were also being mustered out, to watch over the men. The two officers had a trainload of GI's who were within two days of being civilians, and they were responsible for the soldiers' behavior and their delivery to Ord. From their nervous behavior, I got the impression that the officers had never had a more trying duty, but we tried to reassure them that no one would jeopardize his discharge by doing something foolish now, which was slightly wishful thinking. The overnight train trip from Seattle to Oakland traversed magnificent country, from the Northwest timber region, past Mount Shasta and many lakes and rivers, and into the bountiful Central Valley the second day. Sturdy oaks graced the golden hills of northern California that my forefathers had known in the nineteenth century. We had a long stop at Redding and most of the men got out to feel the solid earth and have most of a smoke before one of the lieutenants came puffing up excitedly ordering everyone to get aboard and stay put. We noncoms never thought one of the men would run out here, and no one did, but we got a vivid impression of the officers' worried state of mind.

It would be uncharacteristic of noncoms to feel sympathy for officers—maybe pity, but hardly sympathy. The army caste system separating enlisted men from officers was so fixed and rigid that friendship was unthinkable, no matter how unmilitarylike a commissioned officer was. In Korea, we had a tall, gangly platoon officer who might have resembled Ichabod Crane. He had taken his ROTC commission from a midwestern cow college when he faced the draft and knew next to nothing about long-line telephone-telegraph communications. His greatest sport was speeding up and down the roads in Korea leaving a trail of dust six stories high. Riding with him was like going on a school prank. His sophomoric self assigned one of us to sit in the back seat of the jeep looking backwards to spot any MP's who might catch us for breaking the 15 mph speed limit. The greatest speed we could reach over the best stretches of the battle-worn trails was about 25 to 30 mph, and it was like going 100 because of the bouncing, bucking, and noise. The lieutenant would whoop it up like a cowboy. Six months or so after the armistice, families and then the prostitutes had moved into the villages on the 38th Parallel. The officer would go out into the villages with the men, taking off his second lieutenant bar. Yet we never accepted him as one of us. We knew he wanted to be one of the fellows, but it just seemed improper. After all, he still had his authority and duty over us though he, as with our other platoon leaders, knew very little about our elaborate equipment and communication systems. Therefore, we tolerated him at arm's length and with as much aplomb as we did the two officers on the train. I suppose it might have been different in the infantry with varying types of relations possible, especially when sergeants did move up through battlefield commissions. In the Signal Corps of that time, the "second john" seemed necessary only for assuming legal responsibility for the carrier-repeater equipment and for performing the perfunctory duties of leadership. The officers knew that as well as we did and we left each other alone.

Because of my lifelong attachment to trains, the overnight ride on the domed streamliner was an ideal way to reenter California. The countryside of the broad Sacramento Valley gave way to increasingly familiar terrain as we rolled closer to the San Francisco Bay Area at dusk. Berkeley and the streets and hills I knew so well from my University of California days passed by fleetingly. For a glorious moment, I caught sight of University Avenue leading up to the Berkeley campus and an old favorite, Spenger's Seafood Restaurant, near the tracks. It was too dark to see the Campanile, the stately clock tower that symbolizes the UC Berkeley campus, which one can see from San Francisco on a clear day.

The orange-colored lights of the Golden Gate Bridge and the San Francisco–Oakland Bay Bridge provided a vague frame for the tiered shining skyline of San Francisco itself across the bay. Awed by the exhilarating panorama, we arrived at the Oakland station in a growing sense of euphoria and were put on buses to a ferry that would take us across the bay. All of these connections went smoothly enough, but the wait on the bus seemed interminable as everyone was counted several times to see that no one was lost. Those of us in place grew restless and anxious to move on to the ferry.

The large, rotary-paddled ferries, similar to those of Mississippi River folklore, have faded from the Bay Area today, but in the 1950s such ferries still remained as alternatives to the bridges for auto and passenger transport. The men gathered on the top deck to gaze at the magnificent skyline and shores of San Francisco approaching. Not a word was said. All of us stared westward. A noticeable air of anticipation grew as the lieutenants' anxiety reflected the almost uncontrollable desire of the men to embrace the setting. As we landed at San Francisco, the officers lined up and marched the men onto waiting buses for the ride to the San Francisco train station. We then marched onto a train that was unattractive and crude compared to the steamliner on which we had come down from Seattle. We found the window shades drawn down and were ordered to leave them that way. A peculiar aspect of army life then, the "pipeline" often made one think and feel like a prisoner.

The illogic of the drawn shades and of waiting such a long time to roll on to Fort Ord without knowledge of the departure time caused the men to wander off the train. Under such conditions, where mistrust and authoritarianism ruled, people naturally sought ways to subvert and get around the orders. Treated like children, the men purposely asked the officers childish questions to test the limits, such as what time it was, when they could eat, whether they could go to the bathroom, see a buddy, phone home, and so on. We had spied small bars outside the train station and a number of us took off unnoticed to have our first drinks in the states. The crowded bars represented common Americana we had missed for some time. With mirrored shelves lined with vari-labeled bottles and neon lights, and counters holding glasses and a cash register, the places seemed like long-lost oases. The aproned, smiling bartenders welcomed us, "Hi, soldier, whata-u-hav?" Our happy, free situation lasted no more than five minutes as one of the lieutenants entered quietly but with a shockingly ashen look. He hardly said anything as we gulped the last of our drinks and hurried past him wordlessly back into the train. Herding the men back into the train seats, the officers had all exits closed and patroled up and down the aisles shouting that no one was allowed to get up, even to go to the bathroom, until we left the station. Thus, we entered and passed through the city dearest to my heart like phantoms of another place.

While in Korea, the loudspeaker once interrupted a poker hand in which I held three deuces with the cry, "Yee, double-time to the chaplain!" I pretended not to notice until the PA speaker blasted, "Yee, get your ass over to the chaplain!" The game ended with my month's pay gone against three treys and I hurried out of the hole to the chaplain, wondering what he would want with me. As I rushed on, it occurred to me that the chaplain could only want to relay bad news from home, perhaps the worst kind. By the time I arrived at the chaplain's, I was rather worried for I had never seen him before. Plump but tough-looking, he immediately shouted, "Yee, we're going to pray! Get on your knees and pray!" His words confirmed my worst fears. I waited for the bad news from home. Was it my mother? How bad? The Chaplain continued: "I know all about you from your records . . . you graduated from the University of California at Berkeley and you can play the piano." At that moment, my anxiety subsided slightly.

"If you can play the piano, you can surely play the organ for us. Yee, your name is in the Bible! You have a special destiny to live up to, you hear? What do you say, play the organ during Sunday services?" Agreeing to do so with relief after my fright, I soon learned to handle the portable pump organ and enjoyed the music of the choir and the organ. At services, the colonel stayed for the last note of the organ music and was always the last one to leave. As I left the army, the greatest orchestra ever seemed to play the most beautiful music ever created as I caught the bus leaving the Fort Ord separation center for San Francisco. It seemed that I was walking on air.

Tony Bennett's hit song, "I Left My Heart in San Francisco," sums it up more than adequately: "I'm going home to my city by the bay. . . . When I come home to you, San Francisco, your golden sun will shine for me."

The First Fulbright Scholar to the People's Republic of China

The people may be made to follow a path of action, but they may not be made to understand it.
CONFUCIUS *(sixth century* B.C.*) Analects*

Something there is that doesn't love a wall
ROBERT FROST *(1876–1963) Mending Wall*

How wonderful it was to receive the first letter of invitation, sent in the winter of 1978, from the Institute of Psychology of the Chinese Academy of Sciences (Academia Sinica)! Yet, my life in the period of 1978–1979 was hectic, so I delayed accepting out of mingled desire and uncertainty. The institute mailed several follow-up invitations and finally asked a friend in Minnesota to telephone me. He explained in greater detail that I had been chosen to be the first American psychologist invited to be a distinguished lecturer ("foreign expert") at the Chinese academy and officially hosted by its Institute of Psychology and the Chinese Psychological Society. I insisted that the honor could go to any number of psychologists. Having recently moved and begun a new academic position, I felt I could not leave very soon and begged that someone else go first. In November 1979, Professor Ching Chi-Cheng (Jing Jizheng), the first psychologist from the People's Republic of China to come to the United States, and honored as such by the American Psychological Association (APA), phoned me one evening and asked why I had not accepted their invitation. After listening to my explanation, Professor Ching suggested that I consider going to China with him when he returned in May 1980. With half a year to arrange my schedule for a month's journey, I took the suggestion and Professor Ching's plan prevailed most nicely. We arrived in Beijing on May 10, 1980, and were met by a large welcoming party. A week earlier, the Asian American Psychological Association, which I served as president, had honored Professor Ching with a banquet in San Francisco attended also by P.R.C. diplomats. The 1980 tour took place eight years after my attempt to locate China's psychologists on behalf of the APA as a member of APA's International Relations Committee.* A grand dinner party at the Bei Hai Lake Restaurant on May 11, 1980, in Professor Ching's and my honor celebrated a return to U.S.–China friendship and relations.

In Tokyo with a Senior Fulbright Lectureship in 1972 while on leave from the University of Wisconsin at Madison, I received permission to visit the People's Republic of China after three applications through the P.R.C. Embassy in Ottawa, Canada. The People's Republic did not then have an office in the United States. It was only a few months after President Nixon's historic visit to China, the plans for which I had had a hand in designing through the National Security Council. Although I had concluded my lectures at Tokyo University and Tamagawa University for the semester, the Fulbright director for Japan declined permission for my departure to the People's Republic. It appeared that there was neither precedent nor policy governing Ful-

*A. H. Yee, "Psychology in China Bows to the Cultural Revolution," *APA Monitor* 4, no. 3 (1973): pp. 1,4. A. H. Yee, "Schools and Progress in the People's Republic of China," *Educational Researcher* 2, no. 7 (1973): pp. 5–15.

bright scholars' travel to the People's Republic of China. Fortunately, the dilemma of my having a very rare visa for the People's Republic and not being able to make use of it was solved by officers of the U.S. Embassy in Tokyo who overruled the director. Elated that the first American had received permission to enter the People's Republic of China from Tokyo, the embassy, however, sobered a bit when they could not answer my key question: How did one actually enter China, a nation that had been closed to Americans for twenty-three years. The visa simply said that I could enter China by way of Guangzhou or Shanghai and that the visa was good for three months. One embassy official who was particularly helpful, I believe his name was Norris Smith, formed the idea of asking Jack Reynolds of the NBC office in Tokyo for assistance. NBC television crews had accompanied President Nixon to Beijing earlier that year, and Mr. Smith thought they might be able to advise us. Inquiries to Japanese sources had provided no leads, and I wondered if NBC would be able to help. Within a week, NBC sent good news. The message said that Bob Green of the NBC office in Hong Kong had contacted the Chinese authorities there. The straightforward Chinese told him, "We know about Professor Yee's visa. Tell him to come to the China International Travel Service office in Kowloon, Hong Kong, as soon as possible. We shall take care of him."

Completing my commitment of a lecture tour in American Information Centers (USIA) throughout Japan, I hastily prepared to comply with the instructions from Hong Kong. Francis Tenney, director of the State Department's China desk and somehow related to the Fulbright Program, and Harley Preston, the APA's director of external affairs, each provided travel grants of $500 as requested to help cover expenses. Everyone seemed to share in the excitement and anticipation of the trip; such a marvelous spirit of cooperation and enthusiasm as one rarely experiences in a scholar's life and which I shall never forget. To show how very scant knowledge of the People's Republic of China was in those days, and also to reflect the unwarranted fears that prevailed among Chinese Americans, I recall that as we packed my bags for the trip there was a tinge of concern over whether the family and I would meet again, all of which seems preposterous today.

The information relayed by NBC proved to be letter-perfect. After a check of my papers and my signature (in Chinese!), the Kowloon travel office booked me on the first train to Guangzhou, which was early the next morning. After resting overnight with a faculty friend at the Chinese University of Hong Kong, I walked to the deserted train stop in the bright blaze of the December dawn over the jagged mountains across the Urinating Horse Bay. In time, the train chugged its way to the campus stop. As instructed by the travel office, I sat anxiously on a bench until a man with a big red star on his dark hat approached me. He simply asked, "Are you Professor Yee?" I said I was and he took my bags and placed them in a special car. On this return trip to China, the hour-and-a-half ride from the Hong Kong border to Guangzhou passed comfortably, without event. From 1947 to 1948, bandits would raid the trains on the same route quite frequently, which is why my relatives booked me on the British steamer on my first trip to Guangzhou in 1947. Occasionally, the train passed through villages in which there were still high watch-towers with turrets, built during the days of banditry. In 1947–1948, I read news reports of skirmishes against the bandits, by the Hong Kong-based British military, using Spitfire fighter planes, battalions of troops, and des-troyers. The bandits must have been quite formidable in their day, an age-old curse that finally ended with the advent of the People's Republic. Riding that train, I became the first Fulbright scholar and APA representa-tive to visit the People's Republic of China. For this fourth generation Chinese American, the trip to the

People's Republic carried abundant memories and special meaning, for I had been disillusioned by almost all of my experiences there in 1947–1948. Starvation, deprivation, war fever, and corruption had sobered my teenaged senses and given me a dismal impression of my ancestors' land.

In Guangzhou, the Pearl River looked relatively devoid of craft without the mass of bobbing sampans and great barges lining the bund. Now well paved instead of potholed and filthy, the streets seemed empty without the mobs of beggars, coolies, hawkers, and ricksha men milling about seeking one's attention. In 1972, twenty-four years after I left China for the United States, I could see that the general welfare of the people had advanced greatly since the old days. Food and other essentials were in good supply and at inexpensive prices too. Less than $4.00 covered a person's monthly food costs; a heavy overcoat that I purchased in Beijing for my son cost only $8.50. Though wages were low, an average of about $40 per month, the people earned enough to bank savings. However, patched clothing, common orthodontic problems, and crowded housing indicated that the Chinese standard of living compared favorably not with any Western nation but with its own past history. The quiet submissiveness of the people in 1972 versus the good-humored and often noisy, outspoken nature typical of the Cantonese in old China gave the first clue to the chilling effects of the Cultural Revolution, which had started in 1966.

Although material gains were obvious to see, those with university degrees, bourgeois backgrounds, or foreign connections, and those involved with Western and traditional Chinese arts and crafts, suffered greatly during the Cultural Revolution in 1972. With the support of the senile Mao Zedong, the radical leftist leaders (the "Gang of Four") attempted to overthrow Chinese and foreign traditions, which they thought prevented the progress of true socialism and the development of a classless society. They attacked foreign influences such as Beethoven and Western clothing, and condemned the ancient philosophers, such as Confucius, and ancient works of art. Young Red Guards, released from their studies, destroyed pianos, ancient paintings and statues, and treated as traitors intellectuals and all others targeted by the Cultural Revolution. The Chinese psychologists suffered punishment and recrimination for their "foreign orientation" and supposed lack of faith in the worth and powers of the masses.

After three frustrating weeks that frigid winter of 1972, I was able to track down only five psychologists, four in Beijing and one in Shanghai. The five conducted no teaching or research and were "undergoing transformation" to see how they could be of service to the masses. Tight-lipped about their precarious situation, I could obtain no information regarding the fate of their other colleagues, especially those who had been educated in the United States and Europe. During meetings with the psychologists, they asked very little about psychological developments in the world and seemed to know very little about current events. For example, they did not know about the campus upheavals still going on in the United States at that time over the Vietnam War, news of which they were happy to hear. The conversation livened when I suggested that I pose questions to myself for them and then answer them. We continued as proposed for hours at a time. However, each time I interjected questions about the whereabouts of their former leaders in psychology, no one would answer and silence prevailed until someone changed the subject.

In university libraries, I found psychological journals from the United States and Europe and even showed the Chinese psychologists some of my own articles in them, which seemed to please them very much. The journals showed no sign of use and the psychologists I met in 1972 exhibited little familiarity with the scientific theories and methodology of American psychologists.

As I explained the nature of the Fulbright Program, which made it possible for me to lecture in Japan and to journey to the People's Republic of China to visit them, I could see that such privileges for scholars seemed incredible to them. Invited to meet some sociology students at Beijing University, China's intellectual center, I asked the students some elementary questions about methodology when they told me that they were conducting interview surveys of peasants. The students could not answer simple technical questions, and I began to see the other side of the Cultural Revolution policy of abolishing entrance examinations and giving priority in university admissions to the political acuity of peasants, workers, and soldiers.

Following that visit and until the end of the Cultural Revolution in 1977 after the death of Mao Zedong in September 1976, I maintained correspondence with the psychologists through the Institute of Psychology and worked on their behalf through the liaison office established in Washington, D.C., in 1974 to represent the People's Republic of China. APA Executive Officer Kenneth J. Little and other APA leaders fully supported my attempts to communicate with and assist the beleaguered Chinese psychologists. Attempts to generate similar overtures of friendship from other professional bodies met with unexpected negativity based on "political problems." Such reactions, whether from an individual or a professional body, surprised and disturbed me. They clearly implied that anything done for and with scholars in China meant "political" assent, a rationale that I rejected as arrogant and short sighted. However, I always found reassurance at such times by recalling that the Fulbright Program had given assistance to my 1972 visit to the People's Republic and had therefore furthered national goals by encouraging the establishment of scholarly relations between the United States and the People's Republic of China.

The APA sent its publications to the psychologists I

had located in 1972. I sent news on psychological developments and continued to write, even though some propagandistic hate mail came to me from the People's Republic, which I interpreted as adherence to the Cultural Revolution line. The first hate letter came in 1973, supposedly from the editor of the important *Peking Review*, to say that if I ever returned to the People's Republic of China, "your dog legs will be broken!" The letter accused me of "raising the Red Flag to pull it down," which meant that my true intentions were to harm the People's Republic. The State Department and the P.R.C. Embassy in Ottawa, Canada, expressed considerable concern and asked for copies of the letter. The embassy then asked for the original copy, which I delivered. In time, I was informed that the letter was bogus and sent by persons unknown to create confusion among friends. Whether bogus or not, I shall never know for sure; either possibility is credible as I look back now. Seeing that the fragile lines of communication with the Chinese psychologists continued and grew stronger remained my key objective amidst strong distractions. Invitations from the APA to the Chinese psychologists to attend the APA's annual conventions drew repetitiously brief but polite rejections. That is why Professor Ching's appearance at the 1979 APA convention in New York signaled the beginning of a new era in U.S.–P.R.C. relations in the field of psychology. Since 1979, many more Chinese psychologists have visited and studied in the United States. Through the auspices of the Ministry of Education in May 1981 and then the Guangdong Provincial Bureau of Higher Education in October 1981, I revisited many of the psychologists who had hosted me in 1980 and met others for the first time. In 1980, I learned that there were 1,000 psychologists working in the People's Republic of China and hundreds of new psychology students. The number had increased to 1,500 psychologists in 1981, a great gain but still only one per 670,000 people!

The psychologists that I met in 1980–1981 impressed me with their enthusiasm to learn and promote psychology. The anti-intellectualism and deprivation of the Cultural Revolution remained a cloud over the psychologists even in 1981, and its effects will take a long time to overcome. However, the relative lack of negativism and remorse for their personal suffering during the Cultural Revolution drew my enduring respect. The psychologists and other intellectuals I have met express their regrets over the Cultural Revolution by saying how far behind they had fallen in research, study, and familiarity with developments abroad. Despite their past setbacks, their love of country and their devotion to psychology as a science and a means to assist societal progress made me pause and reflect on my own commitment to ideals and others. My several visits to the People's Republic often brought to mind the freedoms and privileges scholars in the United States take for granted. I wondered if Americans realized their precious advantages, such as the Fulbright Program, and were doing enough to preserve them.

Officials in the Ministries of Education and Foreign Affairs discussed with me the greater development of psychological training, the priority psychology should be given in research and social service, and government support for increased student/scholar exchanges. I also made it a point to recommend that the People's Republic accept and work with the Fulbright Program. Although the meetings with the leading officials were always warm and encouraging, it remains to be seen whether psychology in the People's Republic of China will be given greater governmental support. Resources are limited but the People's Republic has dedicated itself to modernizing its science and technology, defense, agriculture, and industry—broad, general goals that could include psychologists to a far greater extent than in the past. I gave examples of research and study in the United States that supported such objectives. At least

five departments of psychology at institutions of higher
education are training students. The Institute of Psychology resumed publication of the journal *Acta Psy-
chologica Sinica* in 1979. The Chinese Psychological Society joined the International Union of Psychological
Sciences (IUPS) at the 22nd meeting of the International Congress of Psychology in Leipzig in July 1980. I
had called for this for many years, urging IUPS
Secretary-General Wayne Holtzman (University of
Texas, Austin) as well as the Chinese psychologists to
have the People's Republic become a member of the
IUPS.

One highlight of the many experiences that came
about through my Fulbright award in 1972 involved the
Blackfeet Indians of Montana in 1980. Before the two of
us returned to the People's Republic as previously discussed, Professor Ching Chi-cheng visited the University of Montana and gave two lectures, which were well
received. He gave a provocative history of China's
psychology.* We then took Professor Ching to Brown-
ing, Montana, where the Blackfeet welcomed him
warmly. In Beijing, a model tepee and other gifts from
Blackfoot Chief Earl Old Person were formally received
as a gesture of friendship to the Chinese people. It was
quite wonderful helping Professor Ching explain to his
colleagues the friendship of Americans, such as the
Blackfeet of Montana, and the sincere sense of goodwill
the gifts represented. They have been deposited in the
Beijing University Museum. As more American scholars
visit their counterparts in the People's Republilc of
China, through programs such as the Fulbright Program, perhaps some will come across the display of
American Indian artifacts and wonder how they ever
got there.

*C. C. Ching, "Psychology in the People's Republic of China,"
American Psychologist 35(1980):pp. 1084–1089.

The Institute of Psychology sent me a commemorative scroll with the following poem writtin in classical Tang calligraphy:

> The spring flowers welcome a far-away guest
>   to be compatriots surpasses being the best guest
> Our mountains and rivers are strengthened
>   our emotions are similar to those of people of the
>   same blood
> We try to increase our mutual scholarship
>   at the same time to deepen our friendship
> We remember well your departure
>   your image lingers freshly in our minds with wishes
>   for your early return.
> Dedicated to the first American psychologist who came to China by invitation, Professor Albert H. Yee, the Summer of 1980, Beijing.

Surely the Fulbright Program can be likened to Henry Adams' famous line, "A teacher affects eternity; he can never tell where his influence stops." The above experiences, which deeply and enduringly affected so many people and institutional and international events, would not have been possible or developed in the same positive form without the Fulbright Program. As it is with other Fulbright scholars, I am sure, the opportunity to travel and work abroad provides personal perspective on critical concerns of old. Visiting China in 1972 and the 1980s, I finally realized that a search for identity and meaning, at least for myself, comes more from an inner integration rather than a process of adaptation and assimilation. There was much about China that attracted me and made me feel somehow related, yet I could see that identification with China alone was not for me. Therefore, I began the process of self-integration which will be discussed in the next chapter.

Race versus Ethnicity

What the superior man seeks is in himself. What the mean man seeks is in others.
CONFUCIUS, *(sixth century* B.C.*) Analects*

I have a dream that my four little children will one day live in a nation where they will not be judged by the color of their skin but by the content of their character.
MARTIN LUTHER KING, JR., *speech at Washington, D.C., June 15, 1963*

Breathes there the man, with soul so dead,
Who never to himself hath said,
This is my own, my native land!
SIR WALTER SCOTT, The Lay of the Last Minstrel *(1805)*

In his Invited Distinguished Address at the 1967 annual convention of the American Psychological Association, Martin Luther King described the "causative conditions" of racism and discrimination. He concluded by appealing to the psychologists, saying that "the opportunity to serve in a life-giving purpose is a humanist challenge of rare distinction." However, King's words have been forgotten. They failed to rally the thought and action of psychologists to the elimination of racism. One major reason for this is that King spoke in terms of racism, which did not fully dispute the notion of race. According to King and to social scientists in general, this concept of race, used, for example, in identifying the white and black races, is an accepted aspect of relevant experience in modern life. This writer believes that such an approach to classifying human groups and individuals must be viewed as an ingrained cultural misperception that is extremely difficult to modify. Change can come about through time once social scientists and indeed, educated people in general, realize that they are tolerating an archaic and troublesome concept, and turn instead to human classifications that relate more meaningfully to behavior and scientific study. Some examples at the start will illustrate the problem.

Moving to the South in 1964, my wife and I went to the local fire station to pay our poll taxes and register to vote. The form asked if one was "white" or "colored" and we checked "colored." The fireman quickly changed the response to "white" and said heatedly, "Y'all's not 'colored,' don't you know that? Y'all's 'white'!" Earlier, when we wrote in "Mongoloid" for the race item on the auto driving application, the clerk asked what "M-O-N-G-O-L-O-I-D" meant. I said that as Chinese, we had been classified typically as of the Mongoloid race. Without saying anything further, but gazing snappishly, she erased the word and substituted "white." It became obvious that only two groups or races of people existed officially in the South, "white" and "colored," though much dissonance existed on the subject of the social status of Spanish speakers. During World War II, several governors of southern states officially declared pilot trainees from China to be "white" in order to accommodate their social standing. The "eye of the beholder" determining racial perceptions varies with political and social exigencies.

Treated as a race, a "Yellow Peril," the Chinese have had more discriminatory laws directed at them than any other group in the United States relative to their small numbers. Their superior record as citizens contrasts sharply with the treatment they have received. In the summer of 1982, on June 19, when Asian Americans might have thought that bigoted perceptions rooted in nineteenth-century distortions were becoming less prevalent, a shocking murder and the case's subsequent handling in court became an international issue. Vincent Chin, a young Chinese American aged twenty-seven, and several friends had gone to a Detroit tavern to celebrate Chin's upcoming marriage, to be held in less than a week. Unemployed auto workers Ronald Ebens, aged forty-four, and his twenty-five-year-old stepson, Michael Nitz, harassed Chin with racial taunts and hateful obscenities. Witnesses report that Ebens and Nitz apparently assumed that Chin was Japanese and took out their frustrations at being unemployed, which they blamed on imported Japanese cars, on the young draftsman. Their verbal abuse finally caused Chin to leave the tavern, but the two were not satisfied yet. They chased Chin for several blocks and then grabbed him. While Nitz held Chin down, Ebens clubbed his head repeatedly with a baseball bat. After being in a coma for four days, Chin died from massive head injuries. It is reported that the victim's last words were, "It isn't fair."

The murder took place in Detroit where strong anti-Japanese sentiments raged because of the blame placed on Japan for the high unemployment of American auto workers. Echoing the worst smears of the 1890s, auto and political leaders mounted a campaign to discourage the purchase of foreign cars and to turn the frustrations of the populace against a scapegoat, an old tactic used before against Asian Americans. Bumper stickers, with messages such as "Toyota, Datsun, Honda—Pearl Harbor," were seen throughout Detroit. How much easier it was to condemn the Japanese and Asians than to face some facts and logic! After all, it was the American consumer who chose to pay premium prices for the high quality and value everyone agreed could be found in Japanese imports. As innumerable reports released during the recession have shown, their foreign competitors hopelessly out-classed Detroit's "gas guzzlers." During the 1970s, the American auto industry and automotive unions seemed to operate with a mutually reinforcing death wish. However, political pressure and the threat of protectionism caused the Japanese to voluntarily restrict their auto exports to the United States, which has benefited the U.S. auto companies. In the present anti-Asian atmosphere, therefore, the deeply ingrained racial fears and hatreds in America have surfaced again for ugly viewing. When German-built Volkswagens stormed the United States in the 1950s and 1960s, no racial recriminations appeared during the several recessions of those years.

Racist hysteria reached such a level that during September 1983 the President's special trade representative, William S. Brock, said that "the line has been crossed" between honest, legitimate criticism and racist demagoguery by some Americans. About that time, the highly respected Japanese-American congressman Norman Mineta found the word "Jap" spray-painted on his garage door. Then, on a radio talk show on which he urged support for reparations for Japanese Americans forced into World War II internment camps by the government, the same congressman was abused for the attack on Pearl Harbor. In the meantime, U.S. Senator Donald W. Riegle, Jr., of Michigan branded Japan's trade practices as "an economic Pearl Harbor." Congressman John D. Dingell, also of Michigan, demeaned Japanese workers as "little yellow people" during closed committee hearings and later apologized to government officials of Japan for his indiscretion. Now the executive vice president for sales and marketing at the Chrysler Corporation, Bennett E. Bidwell, while still president of the Hertz auto rental company, said that the best solution to the problem of Japanese car imports would be to charter the Enola Gay, the B-29 bomber that dropped the atomic bomb on Hiroshima. Television commercials show portrayals that ridicule the Japanese. In the lobby of the Flint, Michigan, Buick plant, the final picture in a row of hanging portraits of Buick general managers is a crudely drawn Asian face. Beside that caricature is the written statement, "Don't let your business be his business."

Japanese-American leaders and groups responded to the racial bigotry of 1983 more seriously than in the past when they believed that their superior characteristics as American citizens would speak loudly enough. As Congressman Robert T. Matsui from Sacramento, California, said in 1983, "I've never been to Japan. I can't speak Japanese. I'm American. Yet we have to bend over backwards to show our loyalty to the U.S. compared to other [non-Asian] ethnic groups." Unlike most Chinese Americans, the Japanese Americans have tried to deemphasize their ancestral ties. Surely World War II has had some influence on such an attitude. I realized its existence quite solidly when the Bureau of the Census committee I chaired was informed that many Japanese Americans refused to check the "Japanese" option (others being "White," "Black or Negro," "Chinese," etc.) on Item Four of the 1980 Census. Instead, they went to the trouble of writing "Japanese American" on the line for "Other, specify." Asian Americans are often unaware of the sensitivities within their own groups. However, I have some insight into the traumatic experiences of the Japanese Americans during World War II. After the internment of my Japanese friends, I was frightened to walk alone to elementary school and then junior high. My fright arose from occasions when grown men would confront me, even grabbing me by the collar or arm and lifting me off the ground, and demand to know if I was a "Jap" or not. Such braveness and patriotism, to treat a youngster so! My mother put a button on my coat that said that I was "Chinese American" and scolded me for taunting the white bullies by telling them that I was indeed Japanese and so what . . .

Vincent Chin's murderers thought their victim was Japanese because he looked like one. From the racist comments emanating from other depressed industries, such as steel, that are unable to compete with lower-priced goods from several Asian nations, one can be sure that there exists little differentiation, and that Asians remained lumped together into one racial mass for scapegoating. Wayne County Circuit Judge Charles Kaufman added further shock to the Chin case when he accepted a plea of guilty to a reduced charge of manslaughter and handed Ebens and Nitz the extremely light sentences of a $3,780 fine and three years probation each. Judge Kaufman did not see the report of the probation office, which said that Ebens exhibited psychological problems that made him highly dangerous, and which recommended his incarceration. The prosecution and police conducted an inept investigation, which only found the racial nature of the tragic murder after the state had allowed Ebens and Nitz to plead guilty to a charge of manslaughter. In terrible grief over the loss of her only son and the leniency accorded the murderers, Vincent's mother said, "If two Chinese had killed a white person, I believe that the two Chinese would be in jail. What kind of law is this in America? Is my son's life only worth $3,000?" When Chinese Americans packed Judge Kaufman's court on April 29, 1983, to hear arguments against the validity of the sentences, the first question Judge Kaufman asked attorney Lisa Chan of American Citizens for Justice was, "Do you speak English?" With funds solicited by ad hoc groups such as Asian Americans for Justice and Asian Citizens for Justice, and others, legal pressure was mounted for an investigation by a federal grand jury in Detroit. In November 1983, that federal body indicted Ebens and Nitz on charges that they had violated Chin's civil rights.

In l960, while still in my native state of California, all but one of the many housing developers we approached said that they would not sell a home to Asians. While a faculty member at San Francisco State College, from 1959 to 1964, I found it hard to ignore the fact that the large apartment complex across Holloway Avenue from the campus discriminated against non-whites.

Many of the pupils I taught in the college's famed laboratory school, Frederic Burk, lived in the complex. Even though it seemed to be a peculiar situation, everyone knew about the discrimination but did nothing about it. The students and professors I knew who lived in the complex did not hide their awareness of the discriminatory policy. They said they regretted the restriction very much but did not seek its repeal. It was such hypocrisy in my home area, which I cherished, that helped to lead me to decide to resettle in another state. Perhaps I expected too much of the mostly progressive people in San Francisco and California. Though they could find fault with "Jim Crow" policies in America's southland, with South Africa's apartheid policy that treated the Japanese as "white" and other Asians as "colored," they seemed blind to their own foibles and inconsistencies.

Concluding in 1850 that "race is everything: literature, science, art, in a word, civilization, depend on it" and that the "Slavonian" and "Gothic" races were superior to the "Saxon," "Celt," "Italian," and "Sarmatian" races and that the dark races were "much inferior," K. Knox, a noted scientist of his day, wrote that

> by his *nature*, the Jew or Chaldee, is a wanderer over the earth; . . . he has no settled home; the restoration of Palestine to the Jew would not in the least degree render the Jew less a wanderer. . . . The Jew has no monumental history. He never had any literature, science, or art: he has none yet."*

Based largely on China's defeat by his own nation in the Opium War, Knox observed,

Races of Men (Philadelphia: Lea & Blanchard, 1850).

Historians admit that the Chinese records furnish few materials for history. It is admitted on all hands that they are devoid of all principle, and essentially a nation of liars. How then can they progress? Without a military or naval force, they resorted to tricks more worthy of children than of grown men, in hopes of arresting the progress of the British armament.

The vast ignorance and arrogance underlying such beliefs represent nineteenth-century ethnocentrism used as a means of rationalizing imperialism which, unchecked, led to the racist madness of Hitler's *Mein Kampf* and the tragedy of World War II.

Describing his family's degradation, which as a boy he was helpless to alter, Malcolm X wrote in his autobiography that until he became an adult his view of the black people in Africa was of "naked savages, cannibals, monkeys and tigers and steaming jungles."* At age twenty-three, that self-image changed through his insatiable reading in the library at Norfolk Prison Colony. Malcolm X denounced white people as the "devil white man" and symbolized his contempt for America's history of enslavement by replacing his surname with "X". He fought racism with racism; the pathos of his life and many others is the lost potentiality.

Race as Nonscience

The preceding illustrates what Ashley Montagu, the well-known physical anthropologist and humanist who has published at least six books on race, meant when he wrote: "The idea of 'race' represents one of the most dangerous myths of our time, and one of the most tragic." Racial classification and stereotypes continue today despite the fact that they were developed during the pre-Mendelian explorations of the world, which con-

*New York: Grove Press, 1964.

fronted Europeans with great human diversity unknown to them before. The "ideology of racism," stemming from Europe's worldwide colonization between 1700 and 1900 and based on self-serving, superficial concepts that divide one group from another while mixing color, condition, nation, culture, and ethnocentrism, has changed little over the centuries. Writings by famed biologist and first director-general of UNESCO, Julian Huxley, more than a generation ago demonstrate the crisis in knowledge versus practice that affects society today. He said that because of the "interaction of constitution and environment" and the extensive "intercrossing between differentiated types," "the word 'race' as applied scientifically to human groupings has lost any sharpness of meaning" and "that the term *race* as applied to man should be dropped from our scientific and general vocabulary."* Also arguing that race is a continuing myth that must be abolished, Kluckholm's classic, *Mirror for Man*, makes the following point: "If 'bloods' mixed as alcohol and water mix, there would be many pure 'races,' and populations could be correctly described by statistical averages. But with separate and independent genes, a child is, in the genetic sense, the child of his parents but hardly of his 'race'."†

In zoology classes at UC Berkeley in the early 1950s, we learned that the inherited factors involved in the physical characteristics typically used to classify race were insignificant determinants of human differences. In other words, skin pigmentation and so on provide quantitative rather than qualitative group differences. Genetically, Africans, Asians, and Europeans do not differ in such morphological characteristics. If one should seek social differentiation on the basis of biological inheritance, which of course this writer does not advocate, blood types A, B, AB, and O could be used,

---

Man Stands Alone (Freeport, New York: Books for Libraries, 1941).
†New York: McGraw-Hill, 1949.

since they distinguish unequivocally one group from another. In other words, blood type divides people into true genetic groups that are unaffected by the environment. Since major racial groups, as traditionally classified by external morphologies, have various blood types, the genetic differences are far more significant within the races than between them. The external characteristics used to determine race have developed from natural selection, that is, through genotypic survival and adaptation to local habitat, which came during rapid evolutionary change through a small number of gene substitutions.

During the two decades since the introduction of molecular techniques, tremendous advances have come about in the study of population genetics and evolution. Analyzing genic variation using the improved concept of measuring genetic distance through the number of codon substitutions per locus that have occured after the divergence of two populations under study, geneticists such as M. Nei have concluded definitive research proving that gene differences between individuals *intra*-racially, within a given race, are far greater than the gene differences between races.

From Race to Meaningful Human Identities

In no other area of society is the disparity between knowledge and practice so great than in the issue of race, and no social issue contains more pervasive anachronisms and phobias. This situation continues despite much activity on racial concerns by scholars and political/governmental leaders for decades. In *The Columbia History of the World*, J. A. Garraty writes: "For two centuries a dreadful race prejudice has survived in the United States . . ."* which has been the

*New York: Harper & Row, 1972.

overriding issue in American history. Racial tension and
the effects of racism continue today. During the last
presidential campaign, Benjamin Hooks, NAACP's executive director, made this observation regarding the
support of the Ku Klux Klan for Reagan and Carter's tactic of accusing Reagan of indulging in racism: "This
is still a racist society, but as long as white America
doesn't like to hear that word, it can't deal with the
problem." Hooks' charge squares well with reports of
increasing bigotry in the United States and Europe.
Blacks, Hispanics, Asians, and Jews have been bombed
and murdered, and their property vandalized amidst
the growing number and strength of facist-type groups.
The Anti-Defamation League of B'nai B'rith reported
377 major incidents of anti-Semitism in the United
States in 1980, three times the number in 1979. Recent
racial conflicts in Europe reflect a rising polarization
of racial issues that goes beyond the United States.

Racism has not declined much because race as a
concept for social differentiation has not been thoroughly debunked in our culture and replaced by more
meaningful and valid concepts, even within the
intellectual community. As stated at the start, changes
in perceptions and methods of classifying human
groups must be encouraged and pursued. Psychologists
and other social scientists have argued the question of
nature versus nurture since the proposition was first
framed, but the United States witnessed a full-scale war
among social scientists on the question of racial determinants of intelligence for a decade after Arthur Jensen
wrote in the first issue in 1969 of the Harvard Educational Review:

> So all we are left with are various lines of evidence, no
> one of which is definitive alone, but which, viewed all
> together, make it a not unreasonable hypothesis that
> genetic factors are strongly implicated in the average
> Negro-white intelligence difference. The preponder-
> ance of the evidence, is, in my opinion, less consis-

tent with a strictly environmental hypothesis than with a genetic hypothesis, which, of course, does not exclude the influence of environment or its interaction with genetic factors. [p. 82]

Recalling the tensions of this historic confrontation in the social sciences, which involved many diverse individuals and groups, we can refer to the classic work on racism by Gunnar Myrdal, aptly titled *An American Dilemma*. He portrayed racism as "the split in the American soul [that] has been, and still is, reflected in scientific thought and in the literature on the Negro race and its characteristics."*

Eliminate race from intellectual discourse: A first step. Social scientists differ on how they define race and classify one race from another, as is clear from the general practice worldwide. Many studies involving race mix inherited morphologies, such as color, with cultural-social characteristics. Nevertheless, a review of the extensive literature indicates that the IQ/race debate assumed the traditional method of classifying humans into color categories, mainly white, black, and yellow, with most writings focused on the first two groups. It is indeed a curious commentary that psychologists have allowed themselves to accept such a simplex paradigm for scientific analyses and debate. Since one of W. B. Shockley's pet projects has been to correlate IQ with the degree of white "blood" in American Negroes, Shockley and other leading supporters of the "Jensen hypothesis" acknowledge, therefore, without perhaps realizing the basic genetic principle involved, that there has been a significant genetic migration that has influenced the entire population, not just blacks. All biologists of stature, as mentioned earlier, view as ridiculous and irrational the notion that the so-called races are homogeneous and separate, having passed through history in parallel evolution. The genetic combinations

*New York: Harper & Row, 1944.

possible in the human genome are many millions more than the number of humans who have ever lived.

It would be fair to say that in most educated circles, race is an ingrained concept that is extremely difficult to modify or even discuss objectively. Race has been such a significant factor in American history and is so deep-seated in American culture that Americans in general are not fully aware of its impact upon their perspectives. Comparing the interracial experience in the United States and South Africa, G. M. Fredrickson's insightful work *White Supremacy* shows that a number of rationalizations regarding race have been made to justify racial stratification. One of his key points is that the rules governing who is white or black in the United States differ from those in South Africa, and that the rule of "unilateral" race mixing (that is, any black blood meant a person was black) in the United States fostered for more than 200 years "the luxury of a kind of exclusiveness that is probably unparalleled in the annals of racial inequality."* Nevertheless, the abolition of slavery in the United States set forth a moral idealism that can still be fully actualized, while Fredrickson foresees little potential for positive change in South Africa without a great transcendental shift from the past. The myths of race can be refuted scientifically, and that is the truth that all educated people must begin to put into practice.

The biological evidence so far indicates that all human groups share all of the gene potentialities, but nothing is known about the gene frequency distribution of the potentialities in any group, nor may anything ever be known. While it is fairly safe to say that genetic differences in mental capabilities between individuals of the same and different groups exist, we have no biological evidence to support the notion of such differences between groups. Given the assumption that what we are is due to an interaction of heredity and environ-

*New York: Oxford University Press, 1981.

ment, the question arises as to how we sort out and ascertain the more significant genetic complex from the less powerful environmental effect. Race, as we have attempted to show, is not an adequate scientific approach to classifying groups genetically. Color and other morphological characteristics have nothing at all to do with intelligence, achievement, and attitude genetically, but their cultural-social correlates make an excellent hypothesis for effects. In other words, race does affect IQ and other human characteristics because people behave as though they made a significant difference. Those who discriminate and are discriminated against on the basis of whether they are black, white or yellow in a society determine and reinforce their own behavior and that of others. They make race, a cultural-social phenomenon that is of no scientific merit, a working hypothesis. It becomes extremely important to understand the relevant experience and the cultural-social conditions in which an individual or group develops. It being the business of psychology to work with individuals as well as groups, it is both possible and well-advised to understand both the life situations and the forces at work in order to be able to understand, control, and predict a group's or individual's behavior. To initiate a shift in thought and action, we must have syntactic-taxonomic frames that can bring a departure from racial schemes to more meaningful ways of classifying human groups.

The Alternative of Ethnicity

In four Statements on Race, published in 1950, 1951, 1964, and 1967, UNESCO published the conclusions arrived at by four different committees made up of highly distinguished world scholars in anatomy, anthropology, biology, economics, genetics, medicine, psychology, and sociology. All four statements condemned the tenets and results of racism and repudiated any scientific basis for racist theories. The fourth statement of 1967 differed from the first three in that it focused mainly on the consequences of racism and recommended social/political action to eradicate racism. The 1967 statement also called upon educators and social institutions to overcome discrimination and ignorance regarding race by serving as agents to broaden understanding and fulfill human potentialities. It is very interesting to note that the first statement (1950) not only declared the term *race* archaic and meaningless but also argued that the concept of "ethnic group" should be universally adopted. Serving as the *rapporteur* member of the 1950 committee, Montagu was in an excellent position to supplement the statment with a detailed exposition.* For the proposed concept of ethnic group, Montagu gave the following advantages for its adoption beyond the mere substitution of a term: (1) the education and reeducation process would be greatly enhanced with the removal of a false, emotion-laden concept and the institution of a new and more accurate idea; (2) the term "ethnic group" is non-committal, non-stereotypic, and not tainted by historic abuses; it "implies a question mark, *not* a period"; (3) ethnic group avoids the biological biases of the reductionist fallacy underlying race; and (4) emphasis shifts away from physical characteristics to social-cultural influences and potentialities and human plasticity and uniqueness. Abolishing the term "race" would parallel the elimination in the past of the terms "instinct" by psychologists, "savage" and "primitive" by anthropologists, and "phlogiston" by chemists.

Amidst the rise of Nazism, Julian Huxley and A. C. Haddon in *We Europeans* first proposed the substitution of ethnic group for race. They wrote:

*Statement on Race (New York: Oxford University Press, 1972).

The essential reality . . . is not the hypothetical sub-species or races, but the *mixed ethnic groups*, which can never be genetically purified into their original components, or purged of the variability which they owe to past crossing. Most anthropological writings . . . fail to take account of this fundamental fact.

. . . science and the scientific spirit can do something by pointing out the biological realities of the ethnic situation, and by refusing to lend her sanction to the absurdities and the horrors perpetrated in her name.*

Ethnic identity. Walt Whitman put it well: "Here is not merely a nation, but a teeming nation of nations." The land of opportunity and the free, having received tens of millions of new immigrants from Europe in the nineteenth century, began to harden its attitude toward immigration by 1890. Concern over the mixed, transitional traits of the second generation and the obvious marginality of the first generation amidst a deepening economic depression after 1893 bred a severe wave of racism. As mentioned earlier, according to G. M. Fredrickson, the mobilization against the Chinese on xenophobic, racial grounds by white workers during the latter part of the nineteenth century was "perhaps the most successful labor-based political movement in American history." The Chinese exclusion laws, fourteen passed between 1880 and 1924, represented the severest forms of racism, restrictions which I believe came through the fear of the greater productivity of the Asians and continues today such as in the hostilities refugee fishermen from Southeast Asia have faced. During the nineteenth century, Mark Twain's comments on the industriousness, sobriety, and honesty of the Chinese workers, who nevertheless suffered discriminatory taxes, robberies, and murder without the protection of the law, and Bret Harte's poems and stories

*New York: Harper & Row, 1936, pp.114, 236.

support my hypothesis. The readiness of Asians to work hard and stay productive in the face of adversity only recently has drawn praise from mainstream Americans. However, old prejudices do not die easily, as we see in "Yellow Peril"-like tirades and proposed legislation against the high-quality autos and other products from Japan. The attitude of restriction toward further immigration encompassed all "foreign" groups; it went beyond color and extended to those who were second generation, in-between, neither foreign nor American. Third generation whites did not face the same problem, since through acculturation they became indistinguishable from other Americans. The last ten years or so have witnessed a great search for heritage and self-identity. By way of print and television, *Roots* by Alex Haley affected the nation deeply, and caused millions of Americans to reflect on their own "roots."

In tandem with the heated debate over race and IQ, works on ethnicity proliferated. Ethnic identity became a socio-psychological process that led away from the negativism and frustrations of the racial polarities of the 1960s. Martin Luther King and his followers espoused the philosophies of integration, nonviolence, and Christianity as the way to overcome racial bigotry and discrimination. At the height of King's success, after winning in 1966 the drive to end de facto segregation in Chicago's housing, despite great popular and political opposition, Stokely Carmichael and others rejected King's philosophies and program with the call for black power. Advocating self-determination, black control of black organizations, and black identity, the movement for black power mobilized the socio-economic and political strength of black Americans. At all levels of education, this tremendous expression of ethnic identity and self-worth brought about the promotion of black history, black studies programs, numerous publications, and other ethnic-oriented themes which continue to some degree today. The black power movement stimulated similar action by other ethnic minorities as well as by white ethnics.

Black power drew a hostile response that is exemplified by the highly successful television comedy "All in the Family," which included jibes against Asians ("You know what Chinks are like!"). The response, primarily by lower-class whites, especially religious conservatives, who believed they adhered to the work-achievement ethic, law and order, the stability and propriety of the family, and respect for leaders and authority, attacked the black power civil rights movement of the 1960s. According to M. Novak, "The idiom of resentment in America is racism."* Ethnic whites who believed that their approach to social mobility through middle-class values, which seemed to them the "American way" to assimilation, confronted a challenge in the "social militance" of rural blacks and white intellectuals. That challenge seemed even more threatening because of the strains of unemployment, crime, political and campus unrest, and the emergence of new alliances among historic enemies.

After the assassinations of John F. Kennedy, Martin Luther King, Malcolm X, and others, the black power movement steadily declined. Ironically, as black power faded, the older ethnic concerns based on old world animosities, becoming American, racism, party politics, and so forth evolved into new ethnic identities that emphasized greater self-consciousness, awareness of cultural heritage, and a meaningful relationship with the past. What had started as a black assertion of ethnic worth and dignity, and white hostility toward that movement, became a force for a search for identity by all. Especially in metropolitan centers, the ethnic diversity of America was already in evidence. The still-growing sense of ethnicity has given pluralism a re-

* *The Rise of the Unmeltable Ethnics* (New York: Macmillan, 1972).

spectability that is new and noncontradictory to mainstream attitudes and values. Becoming American did
not have to mean casting off and being against one's
ethnic origins; rather, it could become a creative release
from negativism, from postponing gratification to the
future, and from intergroup hatreds. Ethnic belonging
provides a personal sense of reality with a clear time
continuum, including significant others in terms of the
present, and a new sense of the past.

For ethnic minorities especially, because of their being targets for racism, but also surely for all, ethnicity presents references and goals superordinate to racial polarities and outdated patterns of assimilation
and beliefs about what an American is. According to
N. Glazer and D. P. Moynihan, authors of *Beyond the
Melting Pot*, the term "ethnic group" refers not only to
subgroups and minorities but to all groups that carry a
distinct sense of difference due to descent and culture.*
This is the broader significance of ethnicity. Ethnicity
has become more than advancing special interests; it
involves socio-emotional ties that transcend the pri-
mordial, fixed groups that connote superiority and in-
feriority. We should not forget that the socio-psychological concept of attitude first became a significant
factor in psychology with the classic work by W. I.
Thomas and F. Znaniecki (1918–1920) on the Polish
immigrant and the ethnic ties and adjustments of the
Poles. Interestingly, Israel Zangwill, who wrote the play
The Melting Pot in 1909 was himself a Zionist leader and
wrote also on his people's traits and their ethnic identity. Another feature of interest regarding the origin of the
"melting pot" theme, which is overlooked by virtually
everyone who espouses it for all Americans, is that
Zangwill actually referred only to white people. In Act I
of his play, we can read: "America is God's Crucible,
the great Melting-Pot where all the races of Europe

*Cambridge, Massachusetts: Harvard University Press, 1963.

are melting and reforming! . . . God is making the American."

Learning more about ethnicity throughout the world, one gets the overwhelming impression that race is predominantly a European phenomenon and that ethnicity is the conceptual approach to identity and intergroup relations outside of Europe and America. This impression is supported by an article by L. Liebermann in *Phylon*, 1968, which says that racism is largely a Western ideology that developed to help rationalize Europe's worldwide colonization from 1700 to 1900. Canadians and Native Americans appear to identify individuals and groups more by cultural ethnicity, although the latter have responded to white racism in kind. Surely, the increasing interest in ethnicity may indicate a dramatic shift in socio-emotional attachments and introspection, which is probably related to a rising sophistication in understanding society and the world. Response to the *Harvard Encyclopedia of American Ethnic Groups* in 1980 was so great that its first printing was exhausted within a year. Written by some 120 distinguished contributors, the encyclopedia reflects the great interest of many people and scholars.

While social scientists are urged to consider ethnicity for serious study, we surely do not advise a rehash of the IQ controversy anew with ethnic groups replacing race. Ethnicity, being less a group-determined factor than it is an expression of individualistic traits, would bring about modifications and refinements in social science classification, research design, and theory. It would help to go beyond the simplistic questions of heritability in which modern biological knowledge has been neglected. The significance of ethnicity lies in the actor's own categories of identification and ascription within the boundaries of an ethnic group. Describing his identity-stricken youth and life to his biographer, Robert Coles, Erik Erickson said one's sense of identity "should be based on what one can assert as a positive core, an active mutuality, a real community." The standard Erickson would impose then upon communities would be the question: "Do they or do they not provide a positive, a nonneurotic, sense of identity?" Against such views, the Bureau of the Census has maintained the racial typology for reporting the data from the 1980 decennial census, when questionnaire Item No. 4 was changed through intense lobbying in 1978 from "What is this person's race?" to "Is this person . . ." with the choices "White," "Black or Negro," "Japanese," "Chinese," "Indian (Amer.)," etc. I have asked many, "Since you are tabulated as 'White,' what kind of identity and meaning does that provide you?" The answer has been that white carries no meaningful sense of identity, except in areas of the world and nation where differentiation between whites and blacks is socially prominent. In some pockets of the United States today, the archaic, simplex rubrics of the Census Bureau no doubt carry social meaning, as we experienced in registering to vote in 1964. Most regrettably, the entire governmental/corporate structure of the United States will be affected by racially oriented data and reports from the bureau. Whether one is white, black, yellow, or red may be information to some, yet information on ethnic identity would indicate as much and far more information. Census self-identification should and could encompass the vast pluralism of America.

Erik Erickson's approach to psychoanalysis through anthropology, history, and sociology fits the study of ethnicity extremely well. The perception of the self as an individual in society, in relationship to ethnic values, attitudes, symbols, and so forth makes for new perspectives in psychological theory and research. Examining racism and advances to a wider identity, Erickson concluded that "every person's psychosocial identity . . . contains a hierarchy of positive *and* negative elements," which are developed through childhood when "evil prototypes" as well as "ideal ones" are presented to enculturate the individual. This process of human development varies according to the life values and conditions of cultural groups, which Erickson illustrates by contrasting American Jews and ghetto blacks.

In the 1960s, Malcolm X and Governor George Wallace symbolized the "we-they" syndrome still prevalent in American society. How do such attitudes develop and how can they be modified? One vital key is to study how and when an individual adopts ethnic identity. Negative or confused identity and the lack of ethnic identity, as seen in *mischlings* (children of marriages between Gentile and Jewish parents, who are raised without ethnic references but find in later life that others regard them as Jewish), suggest ethnographic studies to ferret out the behavioral differences between *mischlings* and their counterparts, not just among Jewish groups, of course.* Another consideration for study comes from the far less static and simplex category of ethnicity as compared to race, for there is no reason why individuals cannot have several identities that could be interrelated or synthesized in general but each with sharper affinity to role, status, goal, and situation, that is, a fluid mosaic ethnicity. I am not thinking only of obvious cultural-social identities, such as Norwegian or Cantonese, that are largely determined by origin. Many interest groups across the country offer the opportunity for expansion beyond environmental, health, political, religious, or aesthetic issues to form identities and loyalties that make for rational, complex unities. One interest group that comes immediately to mind is the feminist movement, which is concerned with equality and identity,

*See L. Berman, *Jews and Intermarriage* (New York: Thomas Yoseloff, 1968); A. L. Epstein, *Ethos and Identity* (London: Tavistock, 1978).

issues that parallel those of race. Also, it is not far-fetched to consider ethnicity as an approach to industrial psychology, such as what has been described as individual corporate loyalty and work productivity in Japan. The oft-expressed ideal of "sense of community" that has been scarce for a decade may return as what has been termed the "me generation" evolves into greater shared understandings, goals, and realizations of self and others. Self-esteem could become less dependent on materialistic worth.

In 1976, Commerce Department Secretary Elliot L. Richardson chartered the first federal advisory committee for Asian and Pacific American affairs. The historic committee was formed to assist the Census Bureau in its preparations for the 1980 decennial census. With twenty-five members representing the many Asian and Pacific American groups, the body with the lengthy title of "Census Advisory Committee on the Asian and Pacific Americans Population for the 1980 Census" elected this author as its first chairperson. Active for five years, until 1981, the committee worked diligently on many issues that would improve policies and procedures to obtain the most accurate census yet of the nation's people. As committee chairperson for the three even-numbered years and as a member throughout, I had much opportunity to assess the federal bureaucracy, including the U.S. Congress. Though often no one seemed to care and all appeared intransigent, some changes and improvements came about mainly through persistence, persuasion, and perspiration. Much more than congressional redistricting rode on the ten-year count of the population, for in 1980 at least $50 billion in federal funds and unknown amounts from private and state sources were allocated according to census demographic data. It was important that the data fully represented Asian and Pacific Americans as accurately as possible, for they had been belittled as insignificant

and were largely ignored in concerns dealing with unemployment, housing, health, education, income, language usage, etc. We worked with the census bureau
and other committees on the development of the many
questionnaire forms, enumerator hiring, training, and
procedures, census funding, field organization, and the
pre-test censuses of Oakland, California, and a New
York City borough as well as the dress rehearsal in
Richmond, Virginia.

No issue concerned me more than questionnaire Item
No. 4, the traditional, so-called race item. In 1970, the
race item provided the following options for checking:
(1)"White," (2) "Negro or Black," (3) "Indian (American)," with a line given on which to write the tribe's
name, (4) "Japanese," (5) "Chinese," (6) "Filipino," (7)
"Hawaiian," (8) "Korean," and the last option, "Other,
print race." If you were an Asian or Pacific American
and not any of those listed for ready enumeration, you
would have to make use of the "Other" option. Under
the category of "Other," one is not counted until there
are at least 100,000 who have written the same "race." In
1980, out of fifteen categories for Item No. 4, we increased the Asian/Pacific options to eight from five in
1970. The 1980 categories were: "White," "Black or Negro," "Japanese," "Chinese," "Filipino," "Korean,"
"Vietnamese," "Asian Indian," "Indian (Amer.) Print
Tribe," "Hawaiian," "Guamanian," "Samoan," "Eski-
mo," "Aleut," and "Other." My attempts to abolish
Questionnaire Item No. 4 entirely received little or no
support from other committee members and gave the
Census Bureau executives little to worry about. How
ridiculous to propose such an idea— the entire federal
and state machinery has made use of race since the
Constitution in forming legislation and demographic
policies! Against such odds, I campaigned against the
use of the term race in Item No. 4 as at least a step
toward its demise in the future and development of a
more meaningful classification system. After much lob-

bying on Capitol Hill and at the commissions, the Census Bureau began to listen and then did remove the term *race* from the final 1980 questionnaires. Item No. 4 merely stated, "Is this person . . . ?" before the fifteen options listed above. Needless to say, we rejoiced over this simple but hard-won victory.

However, use of the term *race* continued in the more vital area of reporting the results of the decennial census. This action by the Census Bureau first reached my attention when a copy of the report "Race of the Population by States: 1980" reached me in 1981. Although quite disappointed over this complete reversal of the small step won on the questionnaire, I proceeded to fight back in hopes for change in the future, perhaps when the next censuses are conducted in 1990. Besides writing and speaking, I originated a resolution, which the American Psychological Association adopted as APA policy in 1982 and transmitted to appropriate officials in the Bureau of the Census, Commerce Department, Office of Management and Budget, and the Congress. The resolution reads as follows:

> The literature on "race" and the psychological effects of racism has been extensively developed by psychologists and other social scientists for some decades. Historically, "race" as a classification system, no matter how well qualified, has perpetuated racism and its dangers to human understanding and individual self-concept.
>
> Although the 1980 census questionaire Item No. 4 did not use the word, "race" as in the past censuses in asking the entire population to self-identify their groupings, the Bureau of the Census is now issuing tabulations and reports with the rubric of "race," such as "Race of the Population by States: 1980," (PC 80-S1-3).
>
> Therefore, be it resolved that the American Psychological Association strongly urge the Bureau of the Census and the Office of Management and Budget to discontinue the use of "race" for the classification

of human groups immediately and that data and reports from the 1980 census and subsequent censuses make use of terms which are appropriate, such as ethnic identity, ancestry, heritage, etc.

The abolishment of race as an acceptable concept for classifying people may take three or more generations. Progress toward more meaningful and positive ways of considering human beings will involve greater attention to what makes people what they really are and aim to become. As for this writer's thinking, I am what I am, not an Asian in America or an American in Asia. The sense of home comes more from identity and purpose rather than from place alone. Transposing from life experiences, I see that identity becomes my own and yours, without too many presumptions. We should have affection and awareness for those with whom we live and work, as well as for my being, as you are, an individual in society and culture. A search for meaning is a lifelong process. To pursue it and find fulfillment and peace of mind, one can only strive for a knowing mind, an honest heart, and a greater appreciation of one's self, the world, and potential changes for good.

In my search, the lives of two revolutionary heroes, one from the West and one from the East, have never failed to inspire me. Thomas Jefferson, who asked to be remembered as the author of the Declaration of American Independence and the Statute of Virginia for religious freedom, and as the father of the University of Virginia, died on July 4, 1826, the fiftieth anniversary of the signing of the Declaration of Independence. President John F. Kennedy, addressing the Nobel Prize laureates of the Western Hemisphere who had accepted his invitation to the White House on April 29, 1962, set aside his prepared text and said: "I think this is the most extraordinary collection of talent, of human knowledge, that has ever been gathered together at the White House, with the possible exception of when Thomas Jefferson dined alone."

Jefferson wrote:

We hold these truths to be sacred and undeniable; that all men are created equal and independent, that from that equal creation they derive rights inherent and inalienable, among which are the preservation of life, and liberty, and the pursuit of happiness. (Original draft for the Declaration of Independence, 1776)

Chinese Americans deserve a special measure of pride in knowing that without the support given Sun Yat-sen by the Chinese in America, the 1911 Revolution probably never would have occurred. Dr. Sun learned much about the West from his education at the Iolani School and Punahou School in Hawaii between 1879 and 1883; and in Hong Kong as well, where from 1887 to 1892, he completed the M.D. degree in the first graduating class of the College of Medicine for Chinese in Hong Kong. China's greatest revolutionary leader, Sun Yat-sen, blended the best of the East and the West to help elevate "China to a position of freedom and equality among the nations" and promote international peace and understanding.

Dr. Sun wrote:

[Basing] our judgement upon the intelligence and the ability of the Chinese people, we come to the conclusion that the sovereignty of the people would be far more suitable for us [than autocracy]. Confucius and Mencius two thousand years ago spoke for people's rights. Confucius said, "When the Great Doctrine prevails, all under heaven will work for the common good." He was pleading for a free and fraternal world in which the people would rule.

Index

Dr. Albert H. Yee

About the Author

Albert H. Yee was born in Santa Barbara, California and was raised in the San Francisco Bay Area. He earned a B.A. from the University of California, Berkeley in 1952, an M.A. from San Francisco State in 1959, and an Ed.D. from Stanford in 1965 after military service in Korea and Japan from 1952 to 1955. Awarded a post-doctoral fellowship at the University of Oregon (1966–1967), he completed his formal training as an educational psychologist. Dr. Yee was promoted to full professor at the University of Wisconsin, Madison in 1970, and went with his family to Japan in 1972 as a Senior Fulbright Lecturer. That same year, he became the first Fulbright scholar and one of the first official visitors from the United States to enter the People's Republic of China. Dr. Yee has served on many national advisory committees and boards and has held many national offices. He has published four books and over 100 journal articles, and has been elected a Fellow of the American Psychological Association and two other national associations. After serving as academic dean and professor in California and Montana from 1973 to 1982, Dr. Yee retired from academic work. While on leave of absence from 1982 to 1983, he studied Mandarin at the Chinese University of Hong Kong. He remains active as an author, consultant, photographer, and investor.